Sustainable Inv

CW01497967

"This book delivers on its promise of explain[
market through sustainable investing. Practica
ground information provide a good look at the current situation, and a broad
review of observations offers a view into the future. No matter whether you are
an investor or work for an investee, if you want to be among the winners of the
future, you should definitely read this excellent and highly topical book!"

—Hanna Hiidenpalo, *Chief Investment Officer, Elo Mutual Pension Insurance Company*

"The book offers an excellent perspective on seeking better returns sustainably. Its
scope is more comprehensive than that of traditional sustainability interpretations.
The modelling of sustainable strategies and return potential is particularly important, rather than focusing on the more traditional perspectives of risk management
and exclusion."

—Hanna-Maria Heikkinen, *VP, Investor Relations, Cargotec*

"I particularly like how the authors illustrate sustainable investing through practical
examples. In so doing, they provide ways of thinking that everyone can learn to
apply to their investments."

—Mika Leskinen, *Chief Investment Officer, FIM*

"The book does an excellent job of describing essential ESG values that business
executives, analysts and global investors increasingly need to understand. As shown
by the examples in the book, sustainability is a competitive advantage that requires
systematic work over the long term."

—Jyrki Mäki-Kala, *CFO, Neste Corporation*

"The significance of sustainable investing is increasing across the board, for institutional and private investors alike. This book offers excellent tools for analysing
future ESG opportunities, and it also provides a good overview of the definitions
and necessity of sustainability, as well as better portfolio returns for all investors."

—Mika Heikkilä, *Head of Equities, Taaleri*

Hanna Silvola · Tiina Landau

Sustainable Investing

Beating the Market with ESG

Hanna Silvola
Hanken School of Economics
Helsinki, Finland

Tiina Landau
Helsinki, Finland

Both authors have contributed equally.
Hanna Silvola is the corresponding author of Chapters 1-2 and 7-9.
Tiina Landau is the corresponding author of Chapters 3-6 and 10-12.

ISBN 978-3-030-71488-8   ISBN 978-3-030-71489-5   (eBook)
https://doi.org/10.1007/978-3-030-71489-5

Foreword

For a Chair of the Principles for Responsible Investment (PRI), it is perhaps natural to start an introduction to a book on responsible investment by reflecting on the meaning of "responsibility."

An important aspect of responsible investing is captured in the concept of *stewardship*. Investors are generally acting on behalf of some ultimate beneficiaries—for instance members of a pension plan—and should act in their best interests. Fiduciary duties (or equivalent obligations) exist to ensure that those who manage other people's money act in the interests of beneficiaries, rather than serving their own interests. The most important of these duties are loyalty (acting in good faith in the interests of their beneficiaries) and prudence (acting with due care, skill and diligence, investing as an 'ordinary prudent person' would do). This requires attention to sustainability as a driver of both risk and investment opportunities.

But investors should also feel responsibility in a wider sense as members of society with an obligation to act in a way that is consistent with broader societal values. In the words of the great Swedish philosopher Pippi Longstocking: 'If you are very strong you have to be very nice.' And large institutional investors are 'very strong' in the sense that they have the power to influence societal development through their investment activities and the values they promote as investors. Of course, investors—who are generally acting on behalf of some ultimate beneficiaries—are themselves dependent on legitimacy and proper social license to fulfil their role as stewards of other people's assets over time. They should therefore ensure that their investment activities properly reflect the values of their beneficiaries.

Responsible investment approaches are developing rapidly, partly as a response to growing challenges connected to our collective shortcomings in dealing with the climate crisis and a range of other environmental, social and governance issues.

Recent trends include moving from the relatively narrow objective of 'avoiding harm' to a broader assessment of impact, shifting focus from what you have *not* invested into what you *have* invested in, and understanding how these investments are aligned with broader societal objectives. Many investors find the Sustainable Development Goals (SDGs) to be a useful framework in this context. The SDGs can be seen as a list of problems to be solved, and thus help to identify investment opportunities. But it can also be a useful framework for considering risk. A business model that is only viable in a world that *doesn't* meet the SDGs is obviously a risky investment if you believe that society is serious about these objectives and that policy measures will be put in place to meet them.

This concept of 'stress testing' business models is a centrepiece of the climate reporting framework developed by the Task Force on Climate-related Financial Disclosures (TCFD). Under this framework, companies are asked to 'Describe the resilience of the organization's strategy, taking into consideration different climate-related scenarios, including a 2 °C or lower scenario.' In plain English, this simply means 'please tell me how you will make money with your strategy if climate policies are successful.' Framing the climate issue as a financially material issue connected to questions of corporate strategy, capital structure, dividend policy and investment returns has proven to be a useful platform for a constructive discussion between companies and their owners.

But as noted above, the concept of stress testing can in principle be applied to *any* of the SDGs. How will for instance the business model of a company in the agricultural supply chain be affected if we meet the goal of managing the planet's water resources sustainably? How will businesses be affected if we reach the goal that everyone should earn a living wage?

This approach reflects a more general issue in responsible investment—the need to build a bridge between the 'real world outcomes' assessment ('how does the company affects its external environment') and the 'risk' assessment ('how does the external environment affect the company'). These are clearly related issues, but we have—so far—largely treated them as separate, both in our internal management and in reporting. We need to move beyond that and identify and understand the feedback loops we create and sustain through our investment practices. The outcomes created by our investments today will shape the risks we face tomorrow.

This year has seen many positive developments in the area of corporate reporting, with a clear push towards convergence of reporting standards. This is necessary to provide investors with high-quality decision-relevant information based on common definitions. It will give investors a better basis for understanding both risk and impact, as well as a better basis for exercising ownership. But there is still a long way to go before we have a system for corporate reporting that is fit for the challenges of the twenty-first century. This is an urgent issue for investors. Without timely, comparable and relevant information, it is not possible to implement effective responsible investment strategies.

This book is a welcome addition to the growing library of literature on sustainability and investment, covering many of the issues discussed above. It is well researched and offers many practical examples of how different investment strategies have been implemented by leading investors. I hope it can serve as a guide and an inspiration for increased efforts in responsible investment. The sustainability challenges we face are unprecedented, and our efforts must be scaled up to meet them.

Oslo, Norway   Martin Skancke
January 2021   PRI Chair

Acknowledgements

When starting to write this book, we could not even imagine how many interesting people, topics and themes we would get to know during the project. It has been wonderful to notice that sustainable investing is attracting broad interest among various professional groups, and the people we asked to contribute have joined our book project with great enthusiasm. We would like to express our heartfelt thanks to everyone who has given time to our project and has shared their expertise and experiences from different perspectives.

We thank Palgrave Macmillan and Alma Talent for believing in our book and proving the opportunity to make it available for a wide audience. We also extend our warmest thanks to the Kone Foundation and the Finnish Cultural Foundation for providing funding for our project. This financial support allowed us to cooperate with the great translator Timo Luhtanen, whose support was invaluable.

Our very special thanks go to Rami Vehmas and Riku Hyppänen at Ilmarinen Mutual Pension Insurance Company, who have contributed to this book in many ways. Your expertise, encouragement and reflection at different stages of the writing process have been invaluable! Outi Helenius at Evli Bank, Mika Leskinen at FIM and Johanna Rämö at Foxa have read the manuscript as experts, as well as providing constructive suggestions for improvements and sharing their views on the world of sustainable investing.

Furthermore, we extend our greatest thanks to Martin Skancke, who wrote the foreword. We would also like to thank the following individuals who read the manuscript: Annie Bersagel, Folketrygdfondet; John Elkington, Author of *Green Swans: The Coming Boom in Regenerative Capitalism*; Carole Crozat, BlackRock; Els Knoope, APG Asset Management and Eila Kreivi, EIB. In addition, we would like to thank the following persons who read the original Finnish version: Mika Heikkilä, Taaleri Wealth Management; Hanna-Maria Heikkinen, Cargotec; Hanna Hiidenpalo, Elo Mutual Pension Insurance Company; Jyrki Mäki-Kala, Neste Corporation and Hanna Uusitalo, Kone.

We also extend our thanks to those brave representatives of companies and investment organisations who shared their experiences, as well as reading and commenting on our content, and who are now, with the release of this book, publicly discussing sustainability challenges, management practices and investment methods: Stephanie Maier, HSBC; Ulla Paajanen, Stora Enso; Marte Siri Storaker, KLP; Ole Graa Jakobsen and John Kornerup Bang, Maersk; Sustainability Unit, ABB Zurich; Piet Klop and Rogier Snijdewind, PGGM and Elina Rinta, OP Financial Group.

Numerous experts and business professionals shared their knowledge and material at different stages of writing this book. We would like to extend our thanks to Tarja Halonen, President of Finland 2000–2012; Nina Ahola and Lia Heasman, Deloitte; Jani Alenius, EY Finland; Kaj Alftan, ISS; Anne Brunila, Board professional, Shane Chaplin, Swedbank Robur; Jeff Cohen and Henrik Contran, SASB; Christina Curtin, CFA; Hugo Dubourg, J. P. Morgan; Nico Fettes, CDP; Monika Freyman, Kirsten James and Robin Miller, Ceres; Hugo Fredriksson, Kari Pietilä and Pasi Väisänen, Nordea; Pontus Grönlund, Deutsche Bank; Terhi Halme, APG; Kaisa Hietala, Board Professional and Entrepreneur, Simo Honkanen, Chrisanne Kouzas and Tarja Myllymäki, Neste; Andrew Howard, Schroders; Mikko Hyppönen, F-Secure; Niina Härkönen and Annette Fält-Vannum, Morningstar; Torstein Jakobsen, FactSet; Kirsi Keskitalo and Mikko Koskela, Keva; Reijo Knuutinen, University of Turku; Pertti Korhonen, Board Professional; Sixten Korkman, Economist; Jonas Kron, Trillium; Sari Laaksonen and Emmi Mäkäräinen, Castrén & Snellman; Matias Laine, Eija Vinnari and Markus Vinnari, University of Tampere; Daniel Landau, Gaselli Software; Anita Lindberg, Skandia Asset Management; Sari Lounasmeri, Finnish Foundation for Share Promotion; Annareetta Lumme-Timonen, Solidium; Minna Martikainen, University of Vaasa; Hiromichi Mizuno, Board professional; Clare Murray, 2° Investing Initiative; Stina Nilsson and Emma Henningsson, Sustainalytics; Jukka Oksaharju and Suvi Tuppurainen, Nordnet; Antti-Ilari Partanen, Finnish Meteorological Institute; Janne Peljo, Sitra; Sirpa Pietikäinen, European Parliament; Niina Ratsula, Code of Conduct Company; Fiona Reynolds, PRI; Ilja Ripatti, Ilmarinen; Maija

Saijonmaa, Nordic Offset; Lina Sandström and Christina Olivecrona, AP2; George Serafeim, Harvard Business School; Konstantinos Sergakis; Glasgow University; Andreas Stang, PFA Asset Management; Lauren Smart, S&P Trucost; Lauri Ström, Aalto University Endowment; Salla Sulasuo, Royal DSM; Anna Sulander and Tasmia Wafee, Bloomberg; Noora Viksten, MSCI and Piia Vuoti, Veritas. In addition, we would like to thank Jaana Reijonen, Justina Salokanto, Johanna Salomaa and Elina Vauhkonen for their research assistance.

We would also like to thank our loved ones for their encouragement and compassion during the book project.

My heartfelt thanks go to Ari, who read and commented on the manuscript in sections and as a whole, as well as having the energy and enthusiasm to discuss numerous content aspects into the small hours. Your support during the book project has been moving in many ways. I hope that sustainable investing will make the world a better place for the next generation—thank you so much, Iida, Lauri and Aino.

—Hanna Silvola

Thank you to my loved ones who have encouraged me during the writing of this book.

—Tiina Landau

Introduction

Sustainability has become a global megatrend that affects us all. Many international non-profit organisations, politicians and consumers can be regarded as advocates of responsibility and sustainable development. Companies also increasingly engage in sustainable business operations, and investors are committed to the principles of responsible investment. What is this megatrend about? Is sustainable investing profitable or must investors compromise on returns to save the world?

In this book, we explain how sustainability creates a competitive edge for companies and opportunities for investors to beat the market. We will show how sustainable investing can be used to impact companies' sustainability, analyse opportunities and risks, and outperform the market.[1]

Megatrends—such as climate change, sustainability and digitalisation—increase uncertainty and the asymmetry of information, as well as affecting the future return potential of investments. However, investors' abilities to analyse these phenomena vary greatly. *Investors with a deeper understanding of sustainable investing have more environmental, social and governance (ESG) information than others.* They analyse companies' environmental impacts, social responsibility and governance in addition to traditional financial information. They also analyse the *impacts of these aspects on the (out)performance of investments.* From a revenue and a cost structure perspective, this is largely related to how ESG factors affect the added value created by companies over the long term, as well as companies' valuation in the securities markets.

This book consists of five parts, and the first provides a comprehensive overview of sustainable investing. We have compiled the latest scientific findings of the methods and challenges of sustainable investing. The second part provides a means for active owners to promote sustainability. In the third part, we explain how to conduct sustainability analyses, and we also discuss the sustainability of various investment products. The fourth part is a summary of research-based information about the profitability and return impacts of sustainability. It also includes an overview of the current state of sustainable investing in the Nordics, which have a rather long tradition in sustainable investing. This study includes interviews with experts from 18 investment organisations. The fifth part looks into the future, discussing changes in legislation, sustainability megatrends and investment activities that are key for investors.

We will discuss sustainability from various perspectives and through illustrative cases. We will describe investors' engagement from three perspectives. The case of shareholders' resolutions at the Annual General Meetings of Shell and BP illustrates the significance of cooperation between investors. The case of the forestry products company Stora Enso illustrates how investors can support the company to promote sustainability. Finally, the case of the marine logistics company Maersk provides information about the engagement process and goals of KLP, a Norwegian institutional investor, through an example concerning the scrapping of ships. In addition, we will present an in-depth case of the preparation of a sustainability analysis concerning ABB, a technology company.

The systematisation of ESG analysis will be examined using the Finnish Evli Bank's methods, and the sustainability of funds will be examined using Finnish OP Financial Group's tools. We will also explain how Folketrygdfondet assesses the climate risks related to the investments of the Government Pension Fund Norway and how the Dutch PGGM examines water risks and sustainable development solutions. The purpose of the book is to present good practices and provide ideas for investors of various sizes and with different resources.

This book provides research-based information and practical models for assessing the sustainability of investments. It focuses on equity and fund investments made by institutional investment organisations, and is suitable for use as a handbook for everyone involved in investment decisions, from equity analysts to investment advisers. Every reader, including private investors, will benefit from an understanding of professional methods, opportunities and challenges. Based on this information, even private investors can assess the sustainability of their investments, as well as the sustainability of funds and other investment products.

This book will benefit executives, investor relations specialists, communication and sustainability professionals and other corporate experts for whom it is important to identify investors' expectations. The book illustrates what type of information is beneficial for investors. This helps companies to focus on communicating information that is essential for value creation. Universities and other higher education institutions can use the book for education on sustainable investing.

The original Finnish version of the book was shortlisted for the Investment Act of the Year in Finland in 2020. Immediately after its publication, the book was included in the requirements for the General Securities Qualification (APV1) and the Investment Adviser Qualification (APV2) in Finland. We hope that this international revised edition will promote the further development of sustainable investing.

We have interviewed a number of experts and thought leaders, whose views and experiences will help readers better understand the connections between sustainability and returns, as well as practical methods. The networks we have created as a senior responsible investment officer and an academic have naturally affected our selection of people to interview.

While sustainability offers opportunities for outperformance, this phenomenon must also be examined in a critical light. Throughout the book, we will describe risks and limitations related to sustainability and the available ESG analysis tools. It is important to understand these risks and limitations.

Sustainable investing and the related tools keep evolving, and ESG analysis is complicated. Sustainability is a rising trend, and society's expectations towards investors are increasing and changing continuously. This book is a compilation of key information about sustainable investing. The readers can use the information to improve their ESG analysis skills, identify opportunities of engagement and understand the profitability and return impacts of sustainable investing.

Note

1. The theory of efficient markets argues that the market prices for investments are always at their 'correct' levels: there are no underpriced or overpriced investments, because all new information that is public and relevant to the value of the company is immediately and fully reflected in the prices of securities. In practice, however, the market is not always very efficient, so outperformance can be achieved through active investment, superior skills or analysis, for example.

Contents

About the Authors

Tiina Landau (M.Sc.) is a sustainable investing expert and a Certified European Financial Analyst (CEFA). She has wide experience in sustainability from both the investor and company perspectives. She currently works as Sustainability Manager at Neste Corporation, leading the work to incorporate the evaluation and management of sustainability risks into new business models and supply chains. She previously served as Senior Responsible Investment Officer at Ilmarinen, one of Finland's largest pension investors (EUR 50 billion in investment assets). Her work developing sustainable investing policies, climate strategy, ESG integration and new methods of engagement have received wide international recognition: for example, in 2017, she was recognised as a top 50 contributor globally in responsible investments among asset owners in the IRRI survey, voted for by professionals in 43 countries. In addition, she has previously worked in sustainable investing at OP Financial Group (EUR 80 billion in investment assets) and in management consulting at KPMG. She has extensive experience as a speaker in the media and at seminars and also writes a column in the Finnish financial newspaper *Kauppalehti*.

Hanna Silvola (Ph.D.) is Associate Professor of Accounting at Hanken School of Economics in Finland. Her research interests are in sustainable investing and in measuring, reporting and assuring corporate sustainability information in strategic decision-making. She has international experience from the London School of Economics (UK), the University of Stanford

(USA), Monash University (Australia) and the University of New South Wales (Australia). Dr. Silvola has published on a wide range of topics in accounting in journals such as *Accounting, Organizations and Society;Accounting, Auditing & Accountability Journal*; *Management Accounting Research;Journal of Small Business Management and Journal of Management Accounting Review*. She is the principal investigator of the "How to measure and analyse ESG information to support sustainable business" research project, which received EUR 200,000 in research funding from the Foundation for Economic Education (Finland) for 2020–2022. She serves as an expert in many capacities related to sustainable finance; for example, she is a member of the jury that selects the best sustainability reports in Finland. She has comprehensive experience as a speaker in the media and executive education.

List of Figures

List of Tables

Part I

Basics of Sustainable Investing

1

Motivation for Sustainable Investing: What Is the Purpose?

Sustainable Investing is Becoming More Mainstream

Sustainable investing divides opinions. Some people see it as an ideology that means compromising on return requirements. Others see sustainability as a strategy that creates a competitive edge. However, there is a shift towards profitable sustainable investing, and sustainable investing is becoming more mainstream in light of recent statistics and studies.

Companies are by no means immune to the consequences of irresponsibility: environmental damage can become costly, operating licences acquired through bribery can be lost, and unethical and irresponsible business operations may drive consumers and investors away and thereby increase financial costs. Information travels fast on the Internet and social media. Sustainability aspects affect companies' business operations and financial figures. There are two types of companies in this respect: companies that consider sustainability aspects, even in advance, and those that will not do so until problems emerge. Similarly, there are two types of investors: those who carry out sustainability analyses to predict risks and opportunities, and those who will not generally do so until things have gone wrong.

By sustainable investing, we mean that investment decisions are based on ESG (environmental, social and governance) information that is essential for each company, in addition to traditional financial figures. Environmental impacts assessed during ESG analysis typically include energy

© The Author(s), under exclusive license to Springer Nature Switzerland AG 2021
H. Silvola and T. Landau, *Sustainable Investing*,
https://doi.org/10.1007/978-3-030-71489-5_1

efficiency, emissions, waste, climate change and various environmental programmes, for example. Social responsibility can be analysed by considering human rights, labour rights and product liability, among other aspects. Aspects related to governance can include anti-corruption and anti-bribery actions, tax payments, the actions of the CEO and the executive management group, and the selection, composition and independence of the board of directors.

The analysis of ESG aspects broadens and deepens investment analysis, because the company's value creation will be based on financial statement information to a lessening degree (Lev & Gu, 2016). Sustainability aspects provide more comprehensive information about companies than traditional financial statement analysis—particularly in terms of risks and opportunities and companies' impacts on the environment and society.

> *Taking ESG aspects into account helps investors make better investment decisions, as it provides a broader lens through which to evaluate undervalued or overvalued investments. In addition to solely looking at sustainability as a risk and return issue, investors are looking more closely at the investment impact: what is the purpose of the companies and what outcomes are you generating beyond financial returns?*
>
> *Over time, we are seeing these two elements converge as there is a heightened awareness and focus on the impact of investments. I expect to see that investors are looking more and more at these broader impacts and aligning with sustainable development goals.*
>
> Stephanie Maier, Director, Responsible Investment HSBC Global Asset Management (investment assets around EUR 434 billion[1])

Globally, an increasing amount of money is being invested sustainably. Sustainable investments by institutional investors increased globally by 34% between 2016 and 2018 (Global Sustainable Investment Alliance, 2019). There was geographical variation: 63% of investment assets in Australia and New Zealand, 51% in Canada and 49% in Europe had been invested sustainably, while the corresponding proportion was 26% for the United States and 18% for Japan.

The share of sustainably invested assets is expected to increase rapidly. Deutsche Bank (2018) estimates that the share of sustainably invested assets of all assets managed by global professional investors will increase from 25% in 2018 to more than 50% in 2020 and 95% in 2035. According to the results of a survey by the Morgan Stanley Institute (2018), 84% of asset managers are either planning to invest or are investing in companies that are sustainable in terms of the environment, social impacts and governance. In addition, sustainable companies demonstrated better resilience in the stock exchange slump caused by the Covid-19 pandemic. According to Morningstar (2020), flows into sustainable funds reached a record-high level during the pandemic.

The amount of invested assets is increasing, and the methods of sustainable investing are evolving. A recent study (Amel-Zadeh & Serafeim, 2018) examined the current and future state of sustainable investing with around 650 global institutional investors. Around 82% of the respondents used ESG information when making investment decisions. Over the next five years, investors are increasingly shifting from exclusion towards favouring more sustainable investments and towards a deeper ESG integration in share valuation.

Sustainable investing has become a mainstream phenomenon that many investment organisations seek to master. However, sustainability is voluntary, which is why the rules and methods are in their early stages of development in many respects. At the moment, numerous statutory and voluntary projects are in progress in the financial markets to create global rules and consistency between various practices. In this book, we will present good practices and illustrate the purposes, strengths and weaknesses of various methods and analysis tools so that investors with different resources can better implement sustainable investment strategies and prepare for future changes.

Better Returns Over the Long Term

Scientific research is increasingly showing that sustainable investing is profitable and investors do not need to compromise on returns to promote sustainability. Values are a primary driver for a small group of ethical investors, and these investors are also willing to compromise on their return requirements. Responsible investors take ESG aspects into consideration in their investment decisions and assess the impacts of ESG on returns. *Sustainable investing aims not only for good returns but also for a better world*. For example, the operations of a pension company cannot be financially sustainable if its invested pension contributions do not generate good returns over the long term. As research materials and metrics have evolved, an increasing number of studies are showing that investors can achieve outperformance through sustainable investment strategies by choosing the most profitable methods. According to these studies:

- A sustainable investment generates better returns over the long term, with smaller risks.

- A responsible company has better access to financing, with a smaller cost of capital.
- Customers of responsible companies are more loyal during recessions.
- Environmentally sustainable companies are valued higher during public listings.
- Investments in companies with high ESG ratings lead to outperformance.

Reports published by financial institutions are also showing that sustainable investment strategies generate good returns. For example, Nordea and Norges Bank Investment Management, which manages the Government Pension Fund Global of Norway, have reported that sustainable investments outperform general market development. According to Bloomberg (2020), nine of the largest ESG mutual funds in the United States outperformed the Standard & Poor's 500 Index in 2019, and seven of them beat their market benchmarks over the past five years. The mainstreaming of sustainable investing is also supported by financial reasons that prove its profitability.

ESG Analysis Helps Investors Find Good Investments in Inefficient Markets

Based on research results and statistics, we know that by combining systematic ESG analysis with financial analysis, investors can identify investments that outperform general market development. On the other hand, ESG analysis involves additional costs and requires investors to study more extensive sources of information than traditional financial statement analysis.

This often provokes discussion about whether the sustainability of the investee has already been included in the *prices of securities*, even if a systematic ESG analysis has not been conducted. According to financial theory, the value of a company is based on the present value of future cash flows, meaning that all factors affecting future net cash flows (income less expenses) should be included in the value of the company. In addition to cash flows, valuation is affected by return requirements and risks. In light of current research-based information, the markets are incapable of including the various aspects of ESG in the value of a company, and ESG aspects are often measured insufficiently or even undervalued.

Although ESG information is public, new information is not always immediately and fully reflected in the prices of securities. The key underlying aspects include the following: (1) *Analysts' skills and knowledge vary*. One investor may have more valuable ESG information and analysis methods than others, which enables them to achieve outperformance; (2) *The long-term nature of sustainable investing is provided as an explanation for undervaluation*,[2] meaning that the costs of sustainable investments materialise immediately but their benefits and positive cash flows will only become visible in the future. Analysts largely focus on the qualitative data in quarterly interim reports, whereas the consequences of sustainable investments are not transparent and are difficult to trace; (3) *Global megatrends concern all investments*, disrupting efficient markets, and the market prices of securities are not always at the 'correct' level.

Through ESG analysis, responsible investors seek to identify any hidden competitive advantages arising from sustainability that will generate significant positive cash flows when they materialise later.

In light of the research results mentioned above, investors can create various strategies using ESG analysis in the following ways, for example:

- *Investors who avoid risks and seek good and steady returns* select companies with an excellent ESG performance and small risks that are known to generate excellent returns. In the investment literature, such investors are often described as *dividend investors* or *quality investors* who appreciate steady returns.
- *Investors who take risks and seek high increases in value* select companies that are undervalued in terms of ESG, and they may seek to affect such companies through discussions or active ownership (this will be described in more detail later), for example. Such investors are described as *value investors* or *growth investors* in the investment literature.

Many sustainable investments, funds in particular, are marketed using the former strategy. However, under a successful active owner, the desired direct impact on sustainable development may be more significant in the latter strategy: the owner can impact how successfully the company manages sustainability. The selection of investments may come into play if a company with poor sustainability performance no longer receives funding from other investors or is offered the funding at a higher price.

Effective Risk Management

Risk management is one of the most important reasons for sustainable investing. Valuation is based on future cash flows, return requirements and risk levels. Sustainable investors seek to identify potential risks and assess their impacts up to valuation. Lenders also see the transparency of sustainability information as a factor that reduces the risk of disruptions in loan repayments. According to studies, financing is more easily available to sustainable companies and at a lower cost.[3]

Companies are also focusing on sustainability because of risk management, as **the materialisation of even a single risk related to an ESG factor may have a material impact on profitability**. When assessing risks, it is necessary to examine past liabilities, current challenges and future risk scenarios. Sustainable investing is not synonymous with risk-free investing.

According to the World Economic Forum (2018), the most impactful global risks are related to weapons of mass destruction, extreme weather events, natural disasters, failure to combat climate change, the water crisis, cyberattacks, the food crisis and the loss of biodiversity. Significant risks that are most likely to materialise include extreme weather events, natural disasters, cyberattacks, information security breaches and failure to combat climate crisis.

Generally, investors seek to manage risks by diversifying their investments to a sufficient degree. However, the discussion on risks has entered new dimensions: for example, the climate risk is quite universal and involves many risks that are considered to be material, which makes it difficult to diversify this risk.

The climate risk refers to risks arising from climate change that concern companies' business operations and society at large. The climate risk may arise from trying to create a low-carbon or carbon–neutral society in an effort to mitigate global warming. The climate risk may also arise if global warming is not mitigated and physical changes (such as floods or droughts) have an impact on investments.

The transition risk refers to risks related to business operations and balance sheet assets that arise from measures intended to mitigate climate change, as well as from increases in the price of greenhouse gas emissions. If the transition risk materialises and society becomes more carbon–neutral, some investment assets lose their value (*stranded assets*) when all oil, gas and coal assets on the balance sheet cannot be used. This would cause significant chain reactions and could, according to the worst estimates, lead to the materialisation of the systemic risk in the financial markets.[4]

Investing is ultimately about taking a risk at the right price. In other words, successful investments usually require a successful estimate of the risk-to-return ratio of the investment. Valuation is very challenging because of the diverse nature of the climate risk. A great deal of uncertainty is related to the impacts of climate change and the measures intended to mitigate climate change, which is why it is difficult for investors to estimate the monetary impacts of climate change on investments.

Because the appropriate indicators related to the climate risk are still under development, the stock markets' ability to correctly evaluate the climate risk is also likely to be in its early stages of development. For investors, it is essential to find the answer to the following question: what are the climate risks related to the investee, and have they been considered to a sufficient degree in the company's valuation in the market?

Kirsi Keskitalo, Head of Responsible Investment, Keva (investment assets around EUR 53 billion)

Demand for Sustainable Products and Services is Increasing

There are many new sustainable investment products on the market, as sustainable investing is one of the most rapidly growing investment strategies internationally. Sustainability is a matter of reputation for both investors and investees, and neither party wants to jeopardise their reputation because of negative impacts. Private investors are also more and more interested in sustainable investing.

Sustainable development goals offer new business opportunities for companies. The Finnish pension company Keva's (2018) survey of portfolio managers revealed that even though climate change is regarded as a risk globally, it is primarily seen as an opportunity among European investors. This can be explained, for example, by the fact that European companies have the expertise and technologies to mitigate climate change. This creates new business opportunities and potential investments that may become increasingly attractive in the future. Globally, as many as 78% of people are more willing to buy a product or service from a company that is committed to the principles of sustainable development (PwC, 2015). Expectations towards sustainability are increasing, even in terms of investment products: the results of surveys conducted by several investment organisations (e.g. Barclays, Morgan Stanley) have shown that younger generations, in particular, are interested in sustainable investing.

Major institutional investors are particularly strongly committed to sustainable investing. Sustainability is often recorded in the investment strategies of pension and insurance companies, asset managers and other institutional investors. Internationally, institutional investors own a significant portion of securities. For example, institutional investors own around 80% of the shares in the ten largest listed companies in the United States.

International Frameworks of Sustainable Investment

Global frameworks harmonise and promote sustainable investing. Sustainable investment is defined by the UN Principles for Responsible Investment (PRI), and responsible business operations are guided by the Global Compact initiative, which consists of ten principles based on key international norms related to human and labour rights, environmental considerations and anticorruption. The UN Sustainable Development Goals (SDG) describe global sustainability challenges and set goals for public and private operators to address. Sustainable investing supports sustainable development goals and the Global Compact initiative.

The UN Environment Programme and the Global Compact initiative drew up the Principles for Responsible Investment (PRI) in cooperation with leading investors and experts in 2006. The PRI is an independent non-profit organisation funded by its members. It publishes several guides and situation reports each year to support sustainable investing. The PRI signatories are committed to *six principles for responsible investment*: investors include ESG aspects in their analysis and decision-making; serve as active owners; promote ESG reporting; promote the implementation of the Principles for Responsible Investment; promote cooperation with other investors; and report on their responsible investment activities. Globally, these principles had been signed by around 2,900 organisations by November 2020. In monetary terms, the Principles for Responsible Investment cover more than EUR 100 billion in investment capital.

The PRI signatories are listed by country and industry on the public PRI website and their annual monitoring reports are published on the website. Investors are removed from the PRI membership list if they neglect reporting. In addition, the PRI has minimum requirements for responsible investment. In 2019, the PRI placed around 10% of its members on a watch list, because they had not met these minimum requirements. The companies that failed to comply despite having been advised to do so were excluded from the signatories and their names were published in late 2020.

The PRI promotes sustainable investing globally. The PRI supports its international network of investors in incorporating ESG aspects into their investment and ownership decisions. It encourages members to improve their reporting practices and expects them to report in line with the TCFD (Task Force on Climate-related Financial Disclosures) recommendations starting from 2020.

The UN and the PRI have contributed to the promotion of sustainable investing. The PRI for investors, the Global Compact for investees and the Sustainable Development Goals for the private and public sectors drive various operators towards more sustainable business and more responsible investment globally.

> *We try to work globally while acknowledging that there are different regulatory environments in place across the globe, and that organisations are at different stages of development in terms of responsible investing. Our role is not only to work with the leading investors but also to get everybody across the world moving forward. Investments are global – they don't exist within just one country or region. This is one of the reasons why the PRI is based on principles rather than rules – it has to fit within those different regulatory settings.*
>
> *We work with regulators and governments across the world in an effort to ensure good regulation that will enable responsible investing. We are also trying to remove regulations that hamper its development. In the early days, we worked on the issue of fiduciary duty to ensure that investors could include ESG aspects in their investment process. Now we are working to ensure sustainability outcomes are prioritised.*
>
> Fiona Reynolds, CEO, PRI

Megatrends Behind Political Decisions and Legislation

Factors affecting political decision-making include global megatrends such as climate change, globalisation, digitalisation and population growth. In the political decision-making mechanism, phenomena are addressed at the global level and within the EU, where they have practical impacts through legislation in the member states.

> *Even if we succeed in involving the presidents, parliaments, governments and other public-sector operators of the superpowers in promoting sustainable development, it is not enough. It is too small a portion of the resources that we need to combat climate change and promote sustainable development in other respects. We need consistent thinking across societies. The impacts of governmental measures are limited, which is why it is important to involve independent operators in consistent action. This is a duty of not only the public sector but also society as a whole: the business sector, pension companies, the scientific community, non-governmental organisations and many other stakeholders play an important role in promoting sustainable development. Consumers have become aware of this, and good investors are also paying attention.*
>
> Tarja Halonen, President of Finland 2000–2012

The Sustainable Development Agenda, or the 2030 Agenda for Sustainable Development, was adopted by government leaders at the United Nations Sustainable Development Summit 2015 in New York. Its 17 goals are extensive and universal and are applicable to both the private and public sectors. It is a politically binding document, so the signatory states will increasingly promote the achievement of its goals through restrictions and incentives. Legislation (e.g. emission limits) will increase, and direct economic impacts on the business sector will arise from both positive (tax incentives) and negative (environmental and emission taxes) changes in taxation. The implementation of the 2030 Agenda plan is monitored by the national governments. Political decisions have significant direct and indirect impacts on returns on investment.

Globalisation has increased the need for the assessment of sustainability in all business operations and investing activities. As illustrated by the cases presented in this book, international business operations are increasingly presenting us with challenges related to navigating foreign business cultures. Group structures and supply chains have become complicated. Ownership is more distant and fragmented. Monitoring, audits and reporting are needed to increase transparency and trust. Many investors use sustainability analyses and tools to support their assessments. Such analyses and tools are offered by a few key global companies and a large number of smaller operators. Some investment organisations send their own sustainability surveys to companies as part of their ESG analyses. In addition, many investors seek to have an impact on companies, even through smallholdings, to actively promote sustainability requirements in global investment activities.

Digitalisation has made it easier to trace and monitor sustainability regardless of time and place. Digitalisation increases business opportunities, but it also involves sustainability risks, such as human rights issues related to information security and data privacy. Digitalisation also enables good and bad news to travel fast through non-governmental organisations and social media.

Birth rates are declining in Western countries, but people are living longer and spending natural resources excessively. The global ecosystem is also burdened by population growth in the emerging markets, where the standard of living is rising and consumption habits are developing towards Western levels. This is why solutions are increasingly sought in the circular economy and other business models that support sustainable development.

Global megatrends affect political decisions and are materialised on many levels as legislative changes, restrictions, taxes or financial incentives. Investors must be aware of large-scale developments and must seek to predict political trends. Megatrends involve not only risks but also new business and investment opportunities.

Legislation on Sustainable Financing is Increasing

Legislation related to sustainable investing is evolving, and is expected to increase significantly over the next ten years. For example, the EU has a Sustainable Finance Action Plan in progress.

The purpose of legislative reforms is to align the financing system with sustainable development goals. The financing system has been criticised for its short-term perspective and focus on quick returns. Negative risks have not been considered over the longer term (5–10 years, for example) when making decisions concerning investments and financing. The following aspects, in particular, have been presented as obstacles or hindrances to a sustainable financing system:

- The general integration of ESG into investment processes is slowed by a fragmented understanding of sustainability themes and their connection to the valuation of companies.
- Inconsistent sustainability reporting affects the quality of sustainability analysis, as the information reported by companies is not often comparable, even within sectors.
- Many investors are primarily guided by a fiduciary duty, meaning that institutional investors and asset managers must invest others' assets profitably and securely. In light of legislation, it is not entirely clear whether taking ESG into consideration is part of this duty. While it is possible to achieve outperformance through sustainable investing, not all sustainability aspects have a positive impact on companies' returns—not, at least, when examined individually and over the short term. There are also numerous sustainability-themed funds on the market that have not outperformed the market.
- Claims concerning the sustainability of investment products have not been standardised, and no statutory minimum requirements have been set for sustainable investments. This has undermined customers' trust and has aroused suspicions of greenwashing. For example, claims have been made that operators have started to market funds as sustainable without making any changes to the investment portfolio.

The purpose of the development of legislation on sustainable finance is to address these challenges and create more harmonised international practices.

Notes

1. As a rule, the investment asset data on the interviewed organisations is the latest available, from 31 December 2019 to 30 September 2020.
2. Statman and Glushkov (2009) and Deng, Kang, and Low (2013).
3. E.g. Cheng, Ioannou, and Serafeim (2014), Dhaliwal, Zhen Li, Tsang, and Yang (2014), and El Ghoul, Guedhami, Kwok, and Mishra (2011).
4. Systemic risk refers to a chain reaction caused by the serial collapse of financial institutions. The chain reaction begins when it is impossible for one operator to meet its obligations, which causes damage to its creditor. This, in turn, causes the lender to have difficulty in meeting its obligations. Generally, systemic risk refers to the risk that almost the entire financial sector is drawn into a crisis and that the crisis will expand into other sectors of the economy.

2

Methods of Sustainable Investing

There are many methods of sustainable investing. In this context, we have divided these methods into three categories: exclusion, active ownership and the integration of sustainability (ESG) into investment decisions (Fig. 2.1).

Ethical or Sustainable Investing?

Sustainable investing is often confused with ethical investing, but these two methods differ from each other in terms of investment philosophy, returns and methods. Sustainable investing has become more mainstream, while ethical investing continues to be much less common. However, the Global Compact principles and the underlying international norms are increasingly guiding both ethical and sustainable investing.

Ethical investing arises from the investor's values. *Ethical investors are willing to compromise on their expected returns in order to invest their assets in good conscience.* Ethical investors typically refuse to invest in five sin stocks: alcohol, tobacco, the arms industry, adult entertainment and gambling. Based on ethical choices, investors may also exclude other companies, such as finance companies (payment of interest), pharmaceutical companies (birth control), meat industry companies (pork or all animal-based products) and companies selling cannabis for recreational use. Initially, ethical investors often used to have a religious set of values, but their selection of investments

© The Author(s), under exclusive license to Springer Nature
Switzerland AG 2021
H. Silvola and T. Landau, *Sustainable Investing*,
https://doi.org/10.1007/978-3-030-71489-5_2

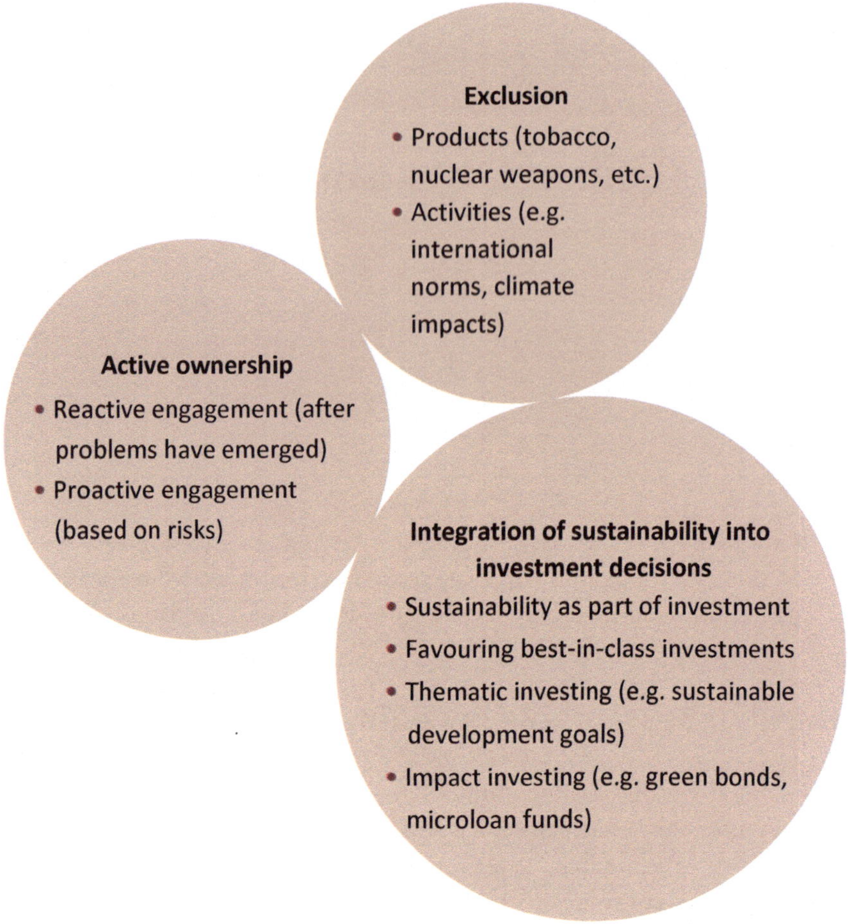

Exclusion
- Products (tobacco, nuclear weapons, etc.)
- Activities (e.g. international norms, climate impacts)

Active ownership
- Reactive engagement (after problems have emerged)
- Proactive engagement (based on risks)

Integration of sustainability into investment decisions
- Sustainability as part of investment
- Favouring best-in-class investments
- Thematic investing (e.g. sustainable development goals)
- Impact investing (e.g. green bonds, microloan funds)

Fig. 2.1 Key methods of sustainable investing

is increasingly affected by views related to environmental objectives, such as combating climate change.

Sustainable investing refers to the consideration of environmental, social and governance (ESG) factors in investing, as well as to the connection between the risks and opportunities arising from these factors and the value of the investee. Sustainable investors often refer to a set of international norms or an international framework, such as the Principles for Responsible Investment. *Sustainable investors seek good returns on their capital*, but they also seek to consider ESG aspects by favouring investees that promote sustainability. There are various methods of sustainable investing, and investors can put more weight on the methods that are suitable for them. In practice, sustainable investors can use several methods simultaneously, and there may also be overlaps. Many investors seek to prioritise various methods, in addition to seeking methods that enable them to achieve outperformance as part of their investment strategy.

Is Exclusion an Ethical or Financial Decision?

Exclusion (or negative screening) is the oldest method of sustainable investing and stems from methods of ethical investing. It used to play a more important role, but its significance has decreased now that other methods—such as active ownership and the integration of ESG aspects into stock analysis—have become more common. Exclusion originally concerned the sin stocks mentioned above, as well as controversial industries. For example, tobacco used to be considered a sin stock mainly by ethical investors. Today, however, mainstream investors are also increasingly excluding tobacco companies because of undeniable health risks. Tobacco companies have also been excluded from the scope of the Global Compact initiative, as it is estimated that tobacco kills around seven million people each year. However, despite its harmful effects, tobacco has been a profitable investment, and many investors report having lost returns because of its exclusion.

There are grey areas within the Principles for Responsible Investment and international norms, and investors need to assess the sustainability of these grey areas. Many investors exclude investments in controversial weapons, which are considered to include nuclear weapons and weapons prohibited by international treaties. Investors must also make choices concerning the definition of manufacturers of controversial weapons (for example, whether controversial weapons also include launch pads, maintenance measures or key components that may also have purposes other than those related to controversial weapons). ESG analysis services support investors in shaping these policies, but these parties may come to inconsistent conclusions.

In recent years, investors have increasingly included coal mining and coal-dependent electric utilities in their lists of questionable industries because of their negative environmental impacts and environmental risks. Since 2015, the Government Pension Fund Global of Norway has excluded investments in companies that keep mining and using coal. This decision has been made for reasons related to the climate. The exclusion of coal companies has since increased, and according to an AODP report published in 2018, coal has been excluded by 15% of the world's 100 largest pension companies. The exclusion of coal often involves a more specific definition, such as a limit for net sales, which is used to exclude a company from the investment portfolio (for example, a company will be excluded if coal represents more than 30% of its total net sales). Some Danish and Norwegian institutional investors have also excluded companies focusing on oil sands from their investments. These decisions have been made for environmental reasons.

Coal and other forms of fossil energy involve the *transition risk*, which forces investors to assess their investments in terms of both values and investment risks, and the *ultimate reason for exclusion may also be (partly) financial*. If the profitability of investment were jeopardised because of legislative changes, consumer behaviour or climate risks, this would also be reflected in these companies' cash flow statements over time because such cash flows can be predicted to continue only for a limited time in a calculation formula based on perpetual discounting. It is possible that the life cycles of the *cash flows of certain products or industries are not indefinite* but last for 5–10 years instead, for example. In addition, the elevated risk (return requirement) included in the calculation formula has an immediate impact on the value. As a result, *some of the assets* on the company's balance sheet *would lose their value (stranded assets)*.

If several investors excluded companies focusing on fossil fuels from their portfolios at the same time and the market value of these companies decreased as a result of this, new owners would buy shares at a low price in terms of the standard price-to-earnings ratio. However, the low price involves two assumptions: that future cash flows will continue unchanged, generating good returns, and that the company's market value has stabilised and will no longer decrease as a result of new divestments, for example. Investors should critically evaluate the underlying assumptions. The same *valuation paradox* also applies to other investments to be excluded, such as tobacco companies. The consumption (cash flow) of their products is decreasing in Western countries, and their performance depends on emerging markets. However, there is a risk that consumption will also decrease in emerging markets following legislative developments.

Divestment primarily serves a purpose of informing companies that there are certain activities that investors are not happy with and that they worry about. However, I don't think divestment can drastically change the price of assets in the long run, unless it gains momentum as well, for example, through changing public sentiment or changes to legislation for some products (unless we are speaking of a small company that a lot of investors don't want to invest in, based on, say, governance). For example, the sale of cigarettes has a significant impact on the price of tobacco companies, and consumer habits can change. However, the largest risk for tobacco arises from changes to legislation and not from divestment or consumers, for the time being.

Similarly, the debate related to the carbon bubble is not the only variable guiding the prices of fossil fuel companies. Instead, the valuation of shares reflects the prices of commodities (e.g. oil or coal) and the effectiveness of business models. However, the profits of coal companies cannot be expected to continue forever. On the other hand, it is impossible to say when they will end. Some coal-mining companies are still profitable, but they must improve their operational efficiency in the future and diversify into other commodities. Investors should review companies' product selections in various areas and estimate future demand for their products. Share prices are based on changing observations about how much coal will still be needed in the future.

Andreas Stang, Senior Portfolio Manager, (former) Head of ESG, PFA Asset Management (investment assets around EUR 75 billion)

Most Common Methods of Sustainable Investing

Responsible investors determine their investment strategies and choose the methods and analysis tools that they deem best suited for their purposes. According to an international study by Amel-Zadeh and Serafeim (2018), investors' most commonly used methods of sustainable investing vary by geographical region. Globally, the most common methods are *active ownership/engagement* (37%) and the *integration of ESG aspects into stock analysis* (34%), which are favoured by large and European investors in particular. These are followed by *negative screening* (30%) and *thematic investing* (21%), which is particularly popular among large and North American investors. Judging from investors' future plans, *positive screening* is expected to become the most popular method over the next five years. Positive screening is a more cost-effective and easier way to make sustainable investments than the in-depth integration of ESG aspects into investment decisions. However, based on comprehensive and in-depth ESG analysis, ESG integration is the most advanced means of sustainable investing, and it offers investors an advantage in analysing investees when combined with active ownership, for example.

Active ownership is based on the owner's goals guiding the company's strategy and operations. An active owner communicates their sustainability goals to the company's board of directors and/or management, monitors the achievement of ESG targets and addresses any issues. A responsible investor can seek to impact companies' operations by attending general meetings and having discussions with company representatives. An investor who is a member of the board of directors can contribute their expertise to the company and seek to affect the company's value creation, for example. According to research-based information, active ownership is an effective way to increase added value, as it reduces the traditional principal–agent issue. An agent problem arises when the owner hires managers (agents) through the board of directors to manage the assets of their company, instead of impacting the company's operations themselves. An active owner is better aware of the company's affairs.

The integration of ESG aspects into investment decisions means that the impacts of ESG aspects on the value creation of the investee are taken into consideration. However, there is no standardised definition for ESG integration, meaning that each investor implements ESG integration as they see best. Many institutional investors purchase ESG data, analyses and/or ratings from external service providers and use these and other sources of information in the process of making investment decisions. The integration of ESG aspects into investment decisions is an advanced and essential method of sustainable investing, and is discussed extensively throughout this book.

Favouring (or positive screening, or the best-in-class method) is the opposite of exclusion and involves positive opportunities related to sustainable investing. This method favours the most sustainable companies, using company-specific sustainability ratings offered by international service providers, for example. In the *best-in-class method*, companies are prioritised in accordance with ESG criteria *within their sectors*. In other words, it is not necessary to exclude any sectors, and various sectors may have different weights in portfolios.

Norm-based screening is also a common form of sustainable investing. It has already become something of a routine measure for many institutional investors and funds in particular. In practice, this means that investments are regularly screened for any violations of international norms. Norm-based screening typically concerns violations of the international norms related to the Global Compact initiative or breaches of the OECD Guidelines for Multinational Enterprises.[1] Many investors primarily seek to engage with companies suspected of violations of international norms, and exclusion is often regarded as a last resort if improvements cannot be achieved through engagement.

Sustainability indices take ESG aspects into consideration. There are many types of sustainability indices, and they may contain only the best companies in their sectors, or focus on such companies, based on ESG ratings. Sustainability indices often focus on large and liquid companies about which more ESG ratings and data are available (the selection of large and liquid companies also supports the better formation of the value of the index in trading). Investment strategies that use sustainability indices are suitable for both institutional and private investors, as they offer a relatively effortless way to make sustainable investments. However, when making investments directly based on an index, the investor leaves the determination of sustainability to the service provider. Indices are also used as a benchmark value for return impacts in the active selection of investments.

The ESG Leaders indexes, for example, are based on company-specific ratings produced by MSCI for institutional investors globally, and certain sectors have been excluded, such as manufacturers of tobacco and controversial weapons, as well as companies that have committed serious violations of international norms.

The Popularity of Impact Investing is Increasing

Thematic investing (or theme investing) means that certain themes are favoured in the selection of investments—that is, companies operating in certain sectors or producing certain products and services. The themes may be related to sustainable development goals, and may range from water and forests to climate change, for example. In thematic investing, the investor wants either to support the development of their chosen operations or to achieve returns on investments related to a specific theme that they see as having great potential. Thematic investing can be regarded as one form of sustainable investing, meaning that other principles of sustainable investing are not applied extensively to all thematic investments. Information about the sustainability of a thematic investment can also be obtained by assessing its ESG aspects separately.

Impact investing is a hybrid form of investing that combines returns with benefits for society. Examples of the various forms of impact investing include green bonds, which support sustainable development, and social impact bonds. These are used to finance projects that have positive impacts on the environment or a social community. Projects financed through green bonds can be related to energy efficiency, renewable energy, public transport or sustainable construction, for example. Typically, their purpose is to reduce emissions. Social impact projects often seek to prevent social problems, such as homelessness or social exclusion. In the 'original' idea of impact investing, the returns for investors depend on the improvements achieved, but this is not the case with green bonds, for example.

In monetary terms, the share of impact investing continues to be small, but it has multiplied in just a few years. With the growing demand, its effectiveness should also be examined critically, as there are practically no standardised methods for measuring impacts. The first negative impacts have been detected in Great Britain, among other places. A social impact project designed to eradicate homelessness failed in London. The project attracted public attention after its completion: the results were poor, and the people who were homeless returned to the streets (Cooper, Graham & Himick, 2016). Although this is an individual case, it reflects the novelty of the subject: the methods to measure impact are still under development, and their understanding requires more detailed case-specific studies.

Microloan funds are a form of impact investing. They invest in operators that lend relatively small amounts of money to people whose loan applications would be rejected by traditional banks. The original purpose of microloans was to help the poor in developing countries and enable them to start small businesses, but the target groups have since expanded.

Note

1. According to the OECD Guidelines, companies must comply with national laws and regulations in their operations, as well as considering, preventing and reducing adverse impacts in terms of human rights, labour rights, the environment and corruption in their own operations and those of their suppliers.

References

Amel-Zadeh, A., & Serafeim, G. (2018). Why and how investors use ESG information: Evidence from a global survey. *Financial Analysts Journal, 74*(3), 87–103.

AODP. (2018). *Pensions in a changing climate.* https://aodproject.net/changing-climate-part-3/.

Bloomberg. (2020). *The biggest ESG funds are beating the market.* https://www.bloomberg.com/graphics/2020-ten-funds-with-a-conscience/.

Cheng, B., Ioannou, I., & Serafeim, G. (2014). Corporate social responsibility and access to finance. *Strategic Management Journal, 35,* 1–23.

Cooper, C., Graham, C., & Himick, D. (2016). Social impact bonds: The securitization of the homeless. *Accounting Organizations and Society, 55,* 63–82. https://fearfulasymmetry.ca/practice/2017/6/12/measuring-social-impact.

Deutsche Bank. (2018). *Integrating ESG in company research: Tackling the industry's alpha dilemma.* Markets Research.

Global Sustainable Investment Alliance. (2019). *Global sustainable investment review 2018.* https://www.gsi-alliance.org/wp-content/uploads/2019/03/GSIR_Review2018.3.28.pdf.

Keva. (2018). Vastuullisuusraportti 2017. https://www.keva.fi/globalassets/2-tiedos tot/tama-on-keva--tiedostot/sijoitukset-talous-ja-raportointi/2017/vastuullisuusra portti_2017_keva.pdf.

Lev, B., & Gu, F. (2016). *The end of accounting and the path forward for investors and managers.*

Morgan Stanley Institute. (2018). *Sustainable signals. Asset owners embrace sustainability.* https://www.morganstanley.com/assets/pdfs/sustainable-signals-asset-own ers-2018-survey.pdf.

Morningstar. (2020). *Sustainable fund flows hit record in Q2.* https://www.mornin gstar.co.uk/uk/news/204525/sustainable-fund-flows-hit-record-in-q2.aspx.

OECD. (2020). *The OECD guidelines for multinational enterprises.* https://mnegui delines.oecd.org/guidelines/.

PRI. Minimum requirements. https://www.unpri.org/Uploads/q/t/s/PRI-Min imum-Requirements.pdf. Referenced 25 November 2020.

PwC. (2015). *Make it your business: Engaging with the sustainable development goals.* https://www.pwc.com/gx/en/sustainability/SDG/SDG%20Research_FINAL. pdf.

Statman, M., & Glushkov, D. (2009). The wages of social responsibility. *Financial Analysts Journal, 65,* 33–46.

World Economic Forum. (2018). *The global risks report 2018.* https://www.wef orum.org/reports/the-global-risks-report-2018.

Other Sources

Deng, X., Kang, J., & Low, B. S. (2013). Corporate social responsibility and stakeholder value maximization: Evidence from mergers. *Journal of Financial Economics, 110*(1), 87–109.

Dhaliwal, D., Zhen Li, O., Tsang, A., & Yang, Y. G. (2014). Corporate social responsibility disclosure and the cost of equity capital: The roles of stakeholder orientation and financial transparency. *Journal of Accounting and Public Policy, 33*(4), 328–355.

El Ghoul, S., Guedhami, O., Kwok, C. C. Y., & Mishra, D. R. (2011). Does corpo rate social responsibility affect the cost of capital? *Journal of Banking & Finance, 35*(9), 2388–2406.

Part II

Engaging with Investees

3

Active Ownership

Owners can promote companies' sustainability and good governance by making an impact at general meetings and through discussions. When the selection of investees is important primarily in terms of risk-adjusted returns (the degree of risk involved in an investment), active ownership can generally be used to make a positive impact on the real world.

Making an Impact at General Meetings

In their public principles of ownership steering, investors compile their expectations concerning the companies, as well as information about how they exercise their ownership rights. These principles generally include investors' guidelines on remuneration, the selection of the board of directors and changes in the capital structure (the scope and validity of share issue authorisations), and increasingly also sustainability related expectations. For example, Finnish employment pension insurance companies are required by law to publish their ownership steering principles.

Owners exercise formal power at annual and extraordinary general meetings. In addition, the largest owners often have an opportunity to impact the selection of the board of directors through nomination processes and/or have representatives on the board. In this context, some investors pay attention to diversity,[1] for example, and to increasing the proportion of women on boards of directors.

© The Author(s), under exclusive license to Springer Nature Switzerland AG 2021
H. Silvola and T. Landau, *Sustainable Investing*,
https://doi.org/10.1007/978-3-030-71489-5_3

Many companies discuss the key items of the agenda before general meetings, especially when they conflict with the owners' guidelines. Differing views can be discussed with the largest shareholders before the meetings. Through advance discussions, individual investors can also have more impact on the items on the agenda than they would have based on their proportionate shareholding, provided that the aspects to be promoted are essential in terms of good governance—that is, good practices that also serve the interests of the company and the other shareholders.

Recommendations by International Service Providers Have an Impact

Many investors rely on studies and voting recommendations by international service providers such as ISS (Institutional Shareholder Services) and Glass Lewis. The recommendations are based on general principles of good governance, local corporate governance codes for listed companies and the special features of the markets, as well as the service providers' own methodologies.[2] Voting recommendations in line with the investor's own guidelines are also available from service providers, in addition to weighted recommendations, such as recommendations that take sustainable investing into consideration.

Some investors automatically vote in line with the service provider's recommendations online, especially outside their home markets. For example, at Finnish general meetings, many international investors voting through share custody services (nominee register) often consistently oppose certain proposals in line with the recommendations issued by the service providers.

The cases in which service providers have recommended voting against companies' proposals have in recent years been related to the following themes, for example (in these cases, the companies' proposals have been in conflict with the guidelines issued by the service providers and/or the information included in the proposals has been incomplete):

- Disproportionately large increases in remuneration for board members compared with other companies of similar size in the same market.
- The large size of share issue authorisations (share dilution of e.g. more than 20%).
- Insufficient information about remuneration schemes or rules that go against the principles of good governance.
- Disproportionate non-audit fees paid to the auditor (e.g. more than 50% of the total fees).

Sustainability Aspects Through Shareholders' Proposals at General Meetings

Shareholders also have an opportunity to present their own proposals at general meetings if their proposals are related to matters falling within the competence of the general meeting and if the shareholder so demands in writing from the board of directors well in advance of the meeting. In Finland, even a single shareholder can have their proposal dealt with by a general meeting, while the requirements are much higher in some other countries. For example, holding a certain percentage of all shares in the company may be required. In Finland, shareholders' proposals presented by institutional investors are rare and have in recent years been related to eliminating dual-class shares, for example.

At general meetings in recent years, some sustainability proposals presented by international alliances of shareholders have been backed by a significant portion of the shareholders. In some cases, the company has also recommended that the proposal be approved. In addition, proposals are occasionally presented to general meetings by private individuals and/or non-governmental organisations. However, such proposals often fail to receive sufficient support because of their impracticality, for example.

According to the Sustainable Investments Institute (2020), the five most common ESG-related themes of shareholders' proposals in the United States in 2020 were corporate political activity, climate change, decent work, diversity and human rights. Investors called for better transparency and reporting on expenses related to companies' political activity, such as lobbying and support for political candidates. Of proposals concerning climate change, 75% were related to carbon assets risks. Proposals concerning decent work and diversity were often related to the diversity of the board of directors and the management, or sexual harassment or the status of women or employees of colour. The proposals often called for fair representation, treatment and pay. In terms of human rights, the proposals covered a wide range of themes but generally required stricter human rights policies from companies, as well as better communication about risk management.

Legislation Impacting Shareholders' Rights

EU amended the Shareholder Rights Directive (EU 2017/828) in 2017 to increase openness between listed companies and shareholders, increase shareholders' opportunities to influence remuneration for operative management and the approval of significantly related party transactions (for the board of directors or general meeting to decide on), make voting at general meetings easier for foreign shareholders and shift the focus away from short-term returns on investment. The directive concerns asset managers and institutional investors.

Legislative developments on shareholder rights in the United States have been opposite to those in Europe. The U.S. Securities and Exchange Commission (SEC) voted in September 2020 on a rule that raises the bar for submitting shareholder proposals to companies' annual ballots and increases the proportion of the vote a proposal must be backed by before it can be resubmitted. The new rule would make it more difficult for shareholders to push companies on ESG issues such as climate change, social justice and diversity. It seems that the SEC and corporate lobby groups want to stop niche issues obstructing corporate ballots. The reasons presented include 'significant' costs for companies and the other shareholders. Many investors, on the other hand, strongly opposed this proposal. The new regulations by the SEC would limit the information that shareholders are traditionally entitled to. Since the change of administration in 2021, this approach is being re-evaluated and also the US is looking at setting further guidance to promote sustainable investing.

EU Sets Requirements on Remuneration and Ownership Steering

With the amendments to the directive, shareholders now have more power over remuneration paid by companies in the EU, because the approval of remuneration policies is presented for general meetings to decide on, at least concerning remuneration for the CEO. The remuneration principles concerning the members of the board of directors and the management board have already been largely included in the agendas of general meetings. Each member state decides whether the approval of remuneration policies concerning the operative management will apply only to the CEO or the management group as a whole and whether the decision will be advisory or binding.

Pension companies, as well as other asset managers investing in listed shares and other institutional investors, are required to draw up and disclose their engagement policy. Previously, investors were largely able to independently determine the content of the ownership steering principles. With the implementation of the EU's directive, the content of the principles is determined in more detail. Accordingly, the principles need to include a description of the connection between ownership steering and the investment strategy, as well as the procedures that the owner uses to monitor listed companies concerning matters essential to them.

The exercise of voting rights and the involvement of parties issuing voting recommendations (such as ISS and Glass Lewis) must also be reported. In addition, employment pension institutions must include in the principles information about the exercise of other rights related to shares, as well as about their dialogue with investees and their other shareholders and stakeholders.

Stewardship Codes Are Becoming More Common

'Stewardship code' refers to principles that supplement statutory requirements on corporate governance. Stewardship codes are mainly intended for institutional investors that manage their customers' assets. Stewardship codes encourage institutional investors to engage with their investees, further develop cooperation between the investor and the investee, vote at general meetings, promote long-term value creation, integrate ESG factors into investment decisions and favour transparent reporting.

Stewardship codes have been evolving rapidly on a global scale. The first stewardship code was published by the United Kingdom in 2010, followed by countries around the world, from Australia to Brazil and from South Korea to Kenya. The International Corporate Governance Network has published a Global Stewardship Code to encourage institutional investors to develop governance practices across legislative boundaries, even in countries without a stewardship code. Although compliance with a stewardship code is mainly voluntary, there is often institutional pressure to comply. For example, the Government Pension Investment Fund (GPIF), the largest pension fund in Japan, requires all its asset managers to sign the Japanese stewardship code.

One of the key challenges of shareholder stewardship around the world is to make institutional investors good supervisors and active owners of their investee companies. The co-existence of soft norms (stewardship codes or principles) and semi-hard and hard law rules across the globe is necessary for the future of shareholder stewardship frameworks and their enforcement. In my opinion, the pressure caused by global financial markets is a necessary way to impact developments in countries that are not proactive in this regard. Soft norms, such as stewardship codes for institutional investors, are an even more effective way to boost sustainable business and investing than legislative rules.

Konstantinos Sergakis, Professor of Capital Markets Law and Corporate Governance, University of Glasgow

Engagement Through Dialogue

Investors have influence over companies through informal discussions. The level of success in engagement depends not only on the size of the holding and the investor's importance in society but also on other developments in the operating environment. Listening to a shareholder who promotes sustainability can also be beneficial for the company, as similar expectations and demands may be expressed by several investors, civil society operators and the authorities.

The scope of engagement ranges from individual discussions to processes with a longer term impact. Individual topics may include, for example, items on the agenda of the notice convening the general meeting or requests to report on specific aspects of sustainability, such as climate risks.

More extensive engagement is often based on an issue in the operations of the company that has attracted public attention, such as information about violations of norms concerning human rights, labour rights, environmental protection and/or anti-corruption. The goal of engagement is often to ensure that the issue is eliminated and that the company knows how to prevent similar problems from occurring in the future.

Investors also engage in proactive engagement to mitigate general risks in the industry, such as risks related to good governance, water and climate impacts. The goal of proactive engagement is often to reduce investment risks or increase the sustainability of investments.

The focus of the discussion varies in line with the investors' strategies and the criticality of the situation. The following division describes the various levels of engagement:

- *Questions*: for example, 'How do you take human rights into account in your operations?' The questions in themselves indicate to the company that the theme is important to the investor and that the company should do something about the matter.
- *Requests*: for example, 'Would you please start reporting on your operations in accordance with the UN Guiding Principles on Business and Human Rights Reporting Framework?' Compared with questions, requests are slightly more demanding, with the investor directly communicating their expectations towards the company.
- *Demands*: for example, 'Are you going to make changes/continue the undesirable activities?/ If these operations continue, we will have to sell our shares in the company'. In the case of demands, the investee must change

their ways considerably, unless it wants to operate in a manner that the investor cannot approve.

It is often said that you can have more influence through ownership than by selling your investments. After you have sold your shares, the company's guidelines depend on the new owners and there are no guarantees of a favourable approach to sustainability. In practice, excluding an investment is a key means in circumstances where change cannot be achieved through engagement (the reason for exclusion is product-based, such as the manufacture of nuclear weapons) or where engagement proves ineffective and the issues are of a type that the investor cannot approve. Some investors continue discussions with companies after selling their shares. In such cases, the goal may be an attempt to drive the situation in a better direction, to make it possible to invest in the company again in the future.

Engagement Through Investor Alliances

Investors collaborate to increase the weight of engagement and the efficient use of resources. Investor alliances usually engage with selected companies concerning a specific theme. The PRI, an organisation for responsible investment, has a web-based platform for its members to start engagement projects and invite other investors to join. Engagement through the PRI covers a broad range of themes, such as challenges related to palm oil and tax liability.

In addition, there are other investor cooperation projects coordinated by non-profit organisations. Widely known investor cooperation projects include the CDP (formerly the Carbon Disclosure Project), the Institutional Investor Group on Climate Change (IIGCC), which focuses on engagement related to climate risks, Climate Action 100+, which promotes reductions in emissions, and Farm Animal Investment Risk and Return (FAIRR), which focuses on the challenges posed by intensive meat production.

There are also many investors' joint statements and commitments that do not necessarily involve any other type of collaboration. These include the Montreal Pledge, for example, where the signatories are committed to reporting on the carbon footprint of their investments annually.

In addition to extensive cooperation channels, there is a great deal of regional cooperation involving a limited number of investors. In such groups, individual investors generally have better opportunities to participate in determining the goals and content of engagement than in extensive alliances.

Providers and Key Themes of Engagement Services

Many investors use commercial service providers for at least part of their engagement. Examples of such service providers include Sustainalytics, ISS ESG and Hermes Equity Ownership Services EOS.[3] Engagement coordinated or implemented by commercial service providers may partly overlap with the operations of large investor alliances. In addition to engaging on behalf of their customers, the service providers facilitate investors' engagement work concerning violations of international norms, as well as various themes, such as climate and water risks.

Nearly all business operations involve sustainability challenges if studied closely enough, including the supply chain and/or impacts on customers. Service providers and their partners have their own methodologies for assessing the severity and deliberateness of violations of international norms and prioritising the targets of engagement. In addition, some service providers engage in extensive discussions with the stakeholders of the investee when necessary and determine the extent to which the challenges can be resolved by the company, as well as the extent to which they require input from other operators.

Service providers can also set goals for engagement. Such goals are often related to addressing issues, preventing them from being repeated in the future and verifying the improvements that have been implemented. They also monitor companies' progress regularly and may advise investors to stop engaging when sufficient improvements have been implemented, for example, or when engagement is not fruitful and improvements do not seem probable.

As the providers of engagement services bring together a large number of investors, the goals of engagement become increasingly consistent and investors' expectations seem somewhat similar from a company perspective. In addition, many companies take enquiries from key providers of ESG services very seriously, and investors may sell their holdings if sufficient progress is not achieved and if the company is not willing to have discussions with investors.

The Role of Activist Investors in Promoting ESG

In addition to the means of engagement commonly used by institutional investors, there is a separate category of activist investors. 'Activists' refers to hedge funds that target companies based on underperformance, for example, or a specific situation. Activist investors buy large amounts of shares in these companies and may try to get their representative on the company's board of directors to bring about significant change.

Activists usually engage through discussions with the company's management and board of directors, but if private engagement fails, they can also run public campaigns to receive support from other investors. For example, activists may prepare shareholders' proposals to general meetings. Traditionally, the changes driven by activists have concerned good governance, such as the removal of clauses against corporate reorganisation and the appointment of independent board members. In recent years, other ESG aspects have also been included in the agendas of activist investors, and some sustainability proposals presented by activist investors have also been supported by major long-term institutional investors.

> *ESG topics chosen by activist investors will be chosen according to financial materiality. That could be either disclosures related to climate change in the oil and gas industry or social issues in the textiles industry. I think the most interesting example over the last year has been the collaboration on Apple engagement. In May 2018, the pension fund CalSTRS – with a strong reputation in sustainability – and the activist investor JANA Partners (hedge fund) sent a letter to Apple about concerns over technology addiction. There has been growing concern over the long-term impacts of the compulsive use of smartphones and tablets, especially for young people. Following the campaign, Apple announced new functionalities to help customers control the time consumption of their products.*
>
> Hugo Dubourg, Co-Head of ESG Research, J. P. Morgan

Academic research has shown that activist investors have a positive impact on the returns generated by the investee. After the involvement of activist investors, the target companies improved their operating results and generated positive risk-adjusted excess returns, while the market value of their shares has increased (e.g. Denes, Karpoff, & McWilliams, 2017; Greenwood & Schorb, 2009).

Case: Shareholder Resolutions on Climate at the General Meetings of Shell and BP

In 2015, a group of international investors filed shareholder resolutions with Shell's and BP's Annual General Meetingswhere the investors requested wider climate reporting and action. These were among the first sustainability-related shareholder resolutions that were supported by company management.

According to Stephanie Maier, who at the time was Head of Responsible Investment Strategy and Research at Aviva Investors, the support of company management for these resolutions was based on a strong relationship with the companies. These strong relations were built on past engagement, notably the 'Aiming for A' coalition,[4] and included collective engagement coordinated by the Institutional Investor Group on Climate Change (IIGCC) and bilateral engagements that many investors had conducted. Maier explains that the companies saw that the requests regarded something that they should be doing and that they could meet the requirements of the resolutions.

Maier describes the role of a common voice of investors as follows:

Collaborative engagement can be extremely effective where the company recognises that there is broad investor support for action. Shareholder resolutions can be used as part of this signalling to drive progress.

These **resolutions received the support of more than 90% of investors** at the Annual General Meetingsof Shell and BP. Says Maier, '*Since the resolutions we have seen an improvement in the reporting of Shell and BP, including a clearer articulation of their business strategies. However, there is still progress that needs to be made and there will always be an element of interpretation concerning the extent to which the companies are delivering on the resolution. The fact that the shareholder resolution was supported by the management was a game changer, clearly putting climate risk on the corporate agenda.*'

Shell and BP were targeted with these resolutions because oil and gas are a key sector in the transition to a low-carbon economy.

'*We wanted to set the expectations for climate risk assessment and reporting more broadly and mobilise a larger shareholder base,*' Maier explains. To co-file a shareholder resolution in the UK, at least 100 different shareholders or 5% of the company's shares must be included, and strict technical requirements related to the filing process must be followed.

These resolutions had a wider impact, as other industry players, such as **Total** and **Equinor** (previously Statoil) took action in line with the resolution requirements. Maier explains, '*These other companies recognised that this type of reporting was sensible, and they went ahead. The fact that the shareholder resolution was supported by the management of two majors sent a clear message to the rest of the sector.*'

The impact of the resolutions expanded beyond the energy sector. In the following year, similar resolutions were co-filed at three mining companies (*Anglo American, Glencore* and *Rio Tinto*). Both the oil and gas and the mining resolutions referenced the IIGCC investor expectations for those sectors. A number of these expectations were also reflected in the TCFD recommendations, thereby influencing this new standard of climate reporting as well.

Summary

Collaborative engagement at general meetings can be an effective tool. It is worthwhile for investors using this method to combine their efforts even prior to the general meetings and to prepare carefully the items regarding which they are seeking change. Both companies, Shell and BP, changed their practices, and this caused a chain reaction. As a result, other companies in the industry started applying the same principles. This made the impact of investor activity even more significant. A company also benefits if investors present their views collectively, meaning that the company does not need to consider a wide variety of views expressed by different parties.

Background Information

This case description is based on an interview[5] with Stephanie Maier, when she was Director of Responsible Investment at HSBC Global Asset Management, as well as on public information. Maier has also chaired the work of the IIGCC's Corporate Programme since 2014 and is on the Global Steering Committee of Climate Action 100+.

Case: Stora Enso's International Challenges Brought Sustainability to the Core of Strategy

Sustainability challenges in the Finnish forestry products company Stora Enso's operations have been subject to public debate since the beginning of the 2000s. The company's land use in Brazil and its land acquisitions in China have provoked discussion. However, the most significant stakeholder reactions were not witnessed until 2014, when it was discovered that child labour was being used in a supply chain in Pakistan. Between 2014 and 2017, the company made major changes to its management of sustainability and accelerated its implementation of sustainability measures, which had begun in the 1990s. The company began to communicate more openly and invested significant resources in sustainability, making sustainability the focus of its business strategy. The company's sustainability issues, the public attention and the changes implemented by the company are illustrated in Fig. 3.1.

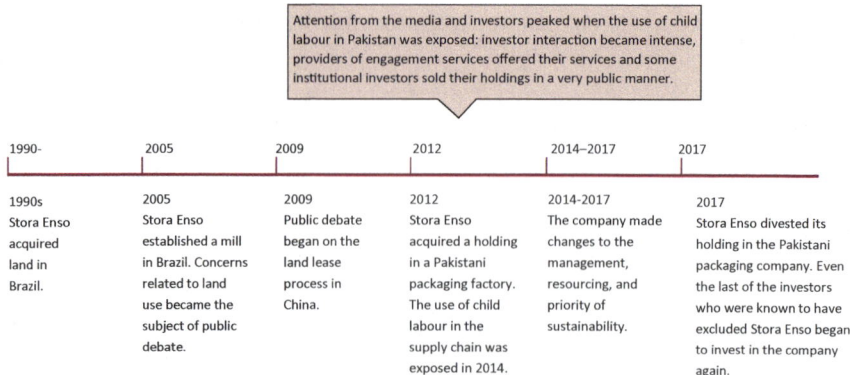

Fig. 3.1   Stora Enso's sustainability timeline

Controversial Publicity for Disputes Over Land in Brazil

Stora Enso established Veracel, a joint venture, in cooperation with Aracruz (later Fibria), a Brazilian forestry company. The lands were purchased from Odebrecht, which had bought them in the 1990s. The acquired lands had originally been part of the Mata Atlântica rainforest area on the eastern coast of Brazil. The rainforests had been cut down for the highway from Rio de Janeiro to the Amazon. At the time, cattle breeders moved northwards and cleared rainforests for grazing. However, the forest land was not suitable for cattle breeding, and the farmers ended up selling the lands. Veracel turned some of the lands into tree plantations, while turning around half of the lands back into rainforest to facilitate biodiversity between the tree plantations. A pulp mill was built in the area in 2004, and the growing economic interest increased the publicity value related to land acquisition from the beginning of the 2000s.

From Stora Enso's perspective, the challenges arose from long-term political issues and conflicts related to land use in Brazil. In Brazil, the invasion of privately owned lands is a long-term social challenge that affects various land users, such as mining and agricultural companies. Landless workers' movements have also invaded Veracel's lands illegally. To find local solutions, Veracel seeks to engage in continuous dialogue with these movements, as well as supporting the land-sharing initiative in the region. The initiative includes reserving a land area of 16,500 hectares for the use of the landless workers' movements participating in the initiative, as well as providing socio-economic support for agricultural operations and the promotion of literacy, for example.

Some landless people were dissatisfied, and their representatives travelled to Helsinki to attend Stora Enso's Annual General Meetingto make the issue public, as well as to make investors aware of the situation.

Challenges Related to Land Acquired Through Intermediaries in China

Stora Enso rented land in China in the late 2000s. The company used intermediaries, which is a common way for foreigners to acquire land in China. However, this led to difficulties in some areas. The intermediaries were supposed to engage in dialogue with village communities, as they knew the locals, as well as whether they had any land to lease out. Intermediaries were also used for practical reasons: transferring money was difficult in China at the time.

Some of the land was acquired through intermediaries as follows: the leasing out of the land was supported by two-thirds of the members of the village community, as required by Chinese law. However, some intermediaries turned out to be unreliable: it was discovered that the approval of two-thirds of the members of the village community had not been gained, or that the money had not been submitted to the community. There was also disagreement over land for which the approval of two-thirds of the members of the village community had been secured. Views differed, even within families, on what should be done, and the minority were not necessarily very happy with the leasing out of the land and were very vocal about their opinion. Furthermore, the locals were not always happy with the monetary compensation, as Stora Enso leases forest land and not arable land, which is more valuable. When the locals became aware of the rent amounts paid for arable land, they began to regard the lower amounts paid for forest land as a problem. The general increase in the prices of leased land also caused dissatisfaction, because the original lessors of the land did not benefit much from the increase. The situation concerning land ownership was somewhat similar to that in Brazil, as reliable maps were not available and the villagers did not know where the borders of the lands were located.

The case became public in 2009. At that point, Stora Enso had already begun to think about ways to shorten the land lease contract chains and improve the system. Stora Enso hired local lawyers as employees to review all agreements and amend agreements that involved discrepancies. Incomplete land lease agreements were rectified. Agreements that could not be rectified were terminated, and the land was returned to the lessors.

In addition, the company started a separate negotiation process with the Chinese government to voluntarily give up some of the land, because the company's business plans had changed and the land was no longer needed. Stora Enso initially intended to build a chemical pulp mill and a consumer packaging board mill in the area, but its strategic plans changed, and the company eventually built a board mill and a chemo-thermomechanical pulp mill. The company's chemical pulp capacity exceeds its own needs by more than two million tonnes, meaning that chemical pulp for its Beihai mill in China can be supplied from its other plants, such as its Veracel joint venture mill in Brazil.

Suspected Use of Child Labour by a Pakistani Subcontractor Made the Company a Centre of Controversy

In 2012, Stora Enso acquired a minority stake in Bulleh Shah, a packaging board mill in Pakistan. The company's packaging division hired an in-house sustainability expert, as the region was regarded as a high-risk area because of human rights risks. A report on human rights risks prepared by consultants for Stora Enso revealed risks related to the use of child labour in the company's supply chain. Operations in Pakistan had already started when the report was covered by the media. The purpose had been to ensure sustainability at the mill before focusing on the supply chain. There ended up being no time for this, however, because a Swedish television channel ran a story on the issue.

Stora Enso's position as a partly state-owned company added to the controversy: the debate escalated to the level of national politics in Finland, all the way to the relevant government ministry. Stora Enso took immediate corrective measures. The parts of the supply chain where child labour had been used were discontinued. Child labour had been used in the sorting of waste paper. The primary purpose of this function had been to promote the recycling of raw materials in Pakistan while also producing recycled materials for the company's own production. However, the raw material was not necessary for the business operations, and after the function had been discontinued, the raw material was acquired from other sources, which also improved its quality.

In 2015, the International Labour Organization (ILO) and Stora Enso started a public–private partnership (PPP) to strengthen Stora Enso's global principles and in an effort to promote decent work. An important part of this cooperation was to gradually eliminate the use of child labour in Stora

Enso's value chains in Pakistan. Stora Enso also established a school for the children who had worked in the supply chain, and is committed to funding the school until 2023. The company intends to continue funding the school in line with the original plan, even though Stora Enso has sold its holding in the Pakistani company and no longer operates in the country. The company considers funding the school to be part of a responsible exit. The reasons behind the divestment of the unit include changes in the customs regulations: the packaging board can now be imported to Pakistan at lower tariffs. This made the competitive situation more unfavourable for Stora Enso, as well as making the production of packaging materials unprofitable in Pakistan, and there were no longer grounds for continuing the company's operations in this high-risk market area.

Sustainability Has Been Brought to the Core of the Investor Debate: Continuous Dialogue and Investor Trips

The challenges in Brazil and China had already prompted many of Stora Enso's investors to ask about corrective measures. However, the attention paid to the company peaked when the issues in Pakistan became public.

The company has organised visits for its shareholders to Brazil, China and Pakistan. Most of the participants have been from the home countries of major shareholders: Finland and Sweden, as well as Norway to some extent. A trip to Pakistan was made soon after the media controversy had begun, because the company wanted to offer investors an opportunity to see how the people worked on-site and in what kinds of conditions. According to Ulla Paajanen, SVP, Head of Investor Relations at Stora Enso, the investors seemed to appreciate the transparency and understand the context better after the trip. The visits were also learning experiences for Stora Enso's management, who had an opportunity to see what kinds of aspects are important to investors.

Around ten sustainability-focused investor trips have been organised since 2006. In addition, six or so round-table investor meetings have been held since 2013 to further clarify the situation and the corrective measures. The company has also organised several online presentations to discuss sustainability themes, and these continue to be part of regular investor communications.

According to the company, the questions posed by institutional investors reflect the fact that many of them use the same service providers—this has made their questions more consistent. However, there are differences between investors: the better an investor knows the company and the more closely they interact with the company, the better their understanding of the company seems to be. According to Paajanen, the fact that Finnish institutional investors are more pragmatic and act more rationally than investors from other countries is particularly noteworthy—while emotions run high for some investors. Paajanen says that Finnish institutions in particular want to see that the issue is addressed in the first place, that developments are moving in a better direction and that risk management is improving.

However, the pressure from customers was occasionally evident, even in Finnish investors' activities. Says Paajanen, '*These investors must also have had customers who questioned the decisions made by their portfolio managers and refused to have their money invested in what they deemed a questionable operation. After all, the customers saw the emotional side of things in the media. Perhaps in some institutions, the customers seemed to have more confidence in the investment asset manager (investor) handling the dialogue so well that changes will take place in Stora Enso's risk management and the money will continue to be ethically invested.*'

Private investors mainly presented Stora Enso with questions related to sustainability at general meetings. The focus of the questions differed somewhat from the institutional investors' approach and was largely related to the individual level.

Active Dialogue Started by ESG Service Providers

With the publicity given to the Pakistan case, GES (now part of Sustainalytics[6]) and ISS ESG, two providers of ESG services, contacted Stora Enso and engaged in active dialogue. Stora Enso had open discussions with these service providers. Paajanen felt that the service providers did not directly disclose to the company how they rated sustainability and its development at Stora Enso or what recommendations they were giving to their customers with regard to Stora Enso.

Paajanen also noticed a clear difference between the operators: one of the operators spent more time on analysis and was more objective, while the other conducted media analysis, focusing more on the claims made in public.

The Investors Used the Same Service Providers, Which Was Reflected in the Questions They Posed

According to Paajanen, the investors' questions to Stora Enso were more sophisticated than those posed by the media and some non-governmental organisations: the investors looked more rationally at how the issue was handled. Paajanen says that the investors also understood that international companies can operate in line with sustainable development and thereby also improve the conditions in the emerging markets.

According to Paajanen, the questions presented by the investors were very similar: '*The questions were based on guidelines provided by sustainability rating agencies. In my opinion, this is a good example of how closely individual companies can be monitored. In particular, the investors requested detailed and practical explanations of how the risk was being managed, how we had organised and allocated resources to our sustainability functions, what we were doing in practice, how we were auditing our supply chains and what kind of ethical principles we had in place for our suppliers. To this day, we continue to report on how many of our suppliers have signed the Supplier Code of Conduct, for example.*'

Paajanen emphasises that the service providers' views are always their own, and that investors should form their own opinions: '*Investors should not commit to just one rating agency. Instead, their risk assessment should be based on at least two views. There are also investors who use only one rating and do not conduct any research of their own.*' In practice, the use of several international service providers that assess violations of international norms is quite rare among investors. This is because of the cost of such services, among other reasons. Investors can form their own views by studying various sources of information, such as other sustainability analyses and the information provided by the company, for example.

The discussion was intense, and there was also concern about Paajanen's feelings: '*People tried to tell me many times that they had nothing personal against me – the investors even seemed to be a little sorry,*' says Paajanen.

The Sustainability Crisis Culminated During the Annual General Meeting in 2014

Stora Enso's Annual General Meetinghas been used as a forum for civil society dialogue: a person who intends to give a critical address at the meeting buys one share or attends the meeting as the assistant of a person who has bought a single share for this purpose.

Says Paajanen, '*The 2014 Annual General Meeting was a powerful experience: the CEO had resigned that morning, but he presided over the meeting in a matter-of-fact manner. The discussion at the Annual General Meeting was hardcore. Emotional and inappropriate addresses were given by a few private investors in particular: there were serious accusations and allegations towards the representatives of the company. There were also non-governmental organisations present to ask about land ownership issues and forests. The institutional investors were more constructive. They asked about corrective measures, and some of the Swedish institutional investors also stated publicly that investor relations had been managed well. The CEO's review was also praised: the material was considered concrete and illustrative.*'

Stora Enso's principal owners—Solidium, a holding company owned by the State of Finland, and FAM, a Swedish holding company owned by the three largest Wallenberg foundations—expressed their views at Stora Enso's Annual General MeetingAccording to Kari Järvinen, CEO of Solidium, both of these companies emphasised the importance of good corporate social responsibility management, with Stora Enso expanding into the emerging markets. The principal owners reaffirmed their support for Stora Enso's transformation strategy while also stressing the importance of sustainability as a key competitiveness factor.

Expansion into the emerging markets comes with a great deal of responsibility. Stora Enso invests in China, India, Brazil, Pakistan, Uruguay and other emerging markets. … In the emerging markets, corporate responsibility is even more significant than usual. … A company's sustainable success calls for strong ties with local communities in all countries of operation and for the company's operations to be perceived as a positive resource in each country of operation.

… It is completely impossible for Solidium to approve the use of child labour. … This is also a key issue in terms of responsible ownership. The UN Universal Declaration of Human Rights and the ILO Declaration on Fundamental Principles and Rights at Work are key guidelines that we respect. Stora Enso is also committed to respecting the principles of these key declarations.

As long-term owners, we expect Stora Enso to find a sustainable solution to the child labour issue in the subcontracting chain of its joint venture in Pakistan in line with a schedule that ensures the well-being of the children concerned in the best possible way. We also expect the company to communicate about its plans and developments in the situation more actively and openly than before. … Solidium and FAM are currently looking into how we can best support Stora Enso as owners in the future.

… All shareholders should keep in mind that the good management of corporate responsibility is a key indicator of competitiveness for companies over the long term. Before long, it will also create value for all shareholders.

Some Investors Sold Their Holdings Because of Sustainability Issues

According to Paajanen, the controversy also had an impact on Stora Enso's share price, and this impact materialised on the day of the Annual General Meetingafter the CEO had resigned. The share price continued to decrease throughout the autumn of 2014, with certain sustainable development funds in particular selling their holdings, but there were also investors who wanted to buy shares in the company. Some investors had sold their holdings earlier, while others sold their holdings later in 2014 in response to the fact that one of the two ESG service providers who had interacted closely with Stora Enso lowered the company's rating to the worst risk category.

Some investors divested their holdings very publicly, announcing their decisions by means of press releases, while others informed Stora Enso directly about having sold their holdings. For example, the Swedish pension fund AP7 announced on its website in late 2014 that it had sold its holding in Stora Enso, and that it had blacklisted the company. Other investors did not announce their divestments until after they had started to invest in Stora Enso again. For example, the Church of Sweden announced in 2017 that it could invest in Stora Enso again. According to Paajanen's calculations, no more than ten investors announced that they had divested their holdings in Stora Enso completely or in their sustainable development funds: '*Investors who know Stora Enso also know that we address issues and improve our management of issues. Commercial operators market funds based on their investees, which is why reputation management is important for them. This also affected how quickly holdings were sold and how quickly various operators started to invest in Stora Enso again.*'

According to Paajanen, the greatest impact on the company arose from publicity and reputation risks, rather than sustainability issues having directly affected the operating conditions in the target countries, for example.

The same aspects also affect investors' assessments. For example, when calculating return on investment, the financial impact of material costs related to the packaging board for a small unit is minor.

Open Communication and a Strong Commitment to Sustainability Were Key in Managing the Crisis

Paajanen now acknowledges that resources should have been better allocated to sustainability when Stora Enso expanded its business operations into Pakistan in 2014. According to Paajanen, in hindsight, the company should have communicated about the situation in Pakistan before the investment decision was made, as part of the first press release concerning the acquisition, because the risk of child labour was already known at that point and it would have been better for the company itself to report on risk management in advance.

Paajanen says that the following key changes helped Stora Enso overcome the crisis, as well as affecting the normalisation of the situation:

1. *Open and proactive communication*
   As the dialogue with investors became more intense, Stora Enso wanted to be as transparent as possible and provide investors with information in advance. The company included a section on sustainable development in its interim reports from the second quarter of 2014. The company also sought to answer questions from operators serving investors as well and accurately as possible.

2. *Strong resourcing and increasing the weight of sustainability in the company's management*
   Back in 2014, the sustainability team was still part of the communications unit. As a result of the crisis, the company implemented an organisational change: it established a separate corporate responsibility unit, as well as establishing the position of Executive Vice President, Sustainability, who is a member of the Group Leadership Team and has experience in similar matters. The company also appointed a sustainability director for each of its divisions, in addition to increasing the allocation of resources to the sustainability team. Paajanen emphasises the importance of hiring highly competent and motivated people because sustainability is largely about what people are doing. The company's board of directors had established a Sustainability and Ethics Committee a little earlier to monitor and guide the implementation of sustainability.

3. *An extensive study on human rights with suggestions for corrective measures*
   Stora Enso conducted a study on risks in cooperation with the Danish Institute of Human Rights. According to the Institute, the study was more extensive than any other earlier study conducted by a company globally. The company also communicated the key results of the study to investors openly. The report identified a number of needs for corrective measures. A plan was prepared to address the issues, and its implementation began immediately. Stora Enso also prepared and published new human rights principles, as well as cooperating with the International Labour Organization concerning the principles.

The new risks announced by the company no longer caused similar controversy, meaning that investor communication and media attention had peaked in connection with the case in Pakistan.

4. *Further development of processes to assess sustainability risks*
   To prevent similar incidents from recurring, Stora Enso further specified its processes to assess the risks before making investment decisions (the due diligence process). Today, the probability of materialised risks is assessed more accurately, and intended investments have also been abandoned because of sustainability risks.

Regaining Investors' Trust Required Time and Effort

According to Paajanen, the media and non-governmental organisations created an impression in public that Stora Enso was doing nothing about the sustainability issues. This misunderstanding had to be corrected for investors. Investors started to invest in Stora Enso again at different times, with the exclusion lasting for 1–3 years, depending on the investor. The last investors returned in late 2017 when the business operations in Pakistan had been divested.

When we communicated the improvements we had made, we began to receive messages from investors that they had been granted permission to invest in Stora Enso again in all funds. It felt wonderful to see that our work was appreciated. The ESG service providers also discontinued their active dialogue with us, one as early as 2016, and the second announced in 2017 that they would remove Stora Enso's high-risk rating. We also received positive feedback on our open interaction.

Investors Have Supported the Company's Transformation in Sustainability

Although changes in the company take place in accordance with the guidelines provided by its board of directors and management, Paajanen also stresses the importance of the need to seek feedback from investors and to listen to it. Investors have contributed to changes in the company and have also offered their expertise to help the company.

Following the controversy, we paid special attention to the better implementation of sustainability in business operations. Today, Stora Enso works to make sustainability its top priority. We have a good core: a renewable raw material. In addition, we need to take care of our operations in line with the principles of sustainable development.

According to Paajanen, many investors are well informed, which is important, because such investors can share best practices between companies. In particular, investors with major holdings in Stora Enso have expressed an interest in knowing Stora Enso well as an investee. Generalists—that is, experts who monitor a large number of companies and themes—seem to have less time to study individual investees. For this reason, they need to rely more on external sources, which often generalise too much.

The Dialogue with Investors Has Normalised

At the peak of the sustainability debate in the media, Stora Enso had to respond to claims made in public. Having learned from this, the company now seeks to make all information publicly available in advance, either on its website or in its interim reports, to reduce its news value. '*Openness is increasingly important today,*' says Paajanen.

Communication about sustainability has been part of the company's day-to-day investor relations for a while now. Stora Enso organises an online presentation on sustainable development for investors each year after the publication of its sustainability report. The company also holds ESG meetings, as well as seminars and conference calls for investors, in addition to organising an ESG-themed roadshow, during which the company meets investors in various countries. Stora Enso has also renewed its sustainability report to make it clearer, more concise and increasingly transparent. As a result of this work, Stora Enso won a national award for its sustainability report in Finland in 2015. One of the grounds for granting the award was related to the successful management of the sustainability crisis and to communicating about the crisis by means of reporting.

Paajanen says that Stora Enso no longer receives questions from investors about old cases. Stora Enso now steers its sustainable development agenda more independently, as well as continuously developing its work related to climate change, stakeholder dialogue and human rights.

The general meetings have also resumed their normal course, and the discussion has largely calmed down. At the 2018 Annual General Meeting there were two people present who wanted to discuss Brazil. In 2017, no questions were posed by investors concerning sustainable development. Compared with 2014, the 2018 Annual General Meeting was an hour shorter—the company's difficult years of sustainability crisis were over.

Paajanen is not very worried about similar events recurring, because the company is now in a better place: '*We are working hard to promote sustainability and have better resources, which also makes us better prepared for any future challenges. However, we must remember that when the controversy happened, demand for paper was decreasing significantly, and we were making major investments to transform Stora Enso into a company of renewable raw materials. We had our hands full. Now the major investments have been completed, and we can develop structures and processes based on the current situation.*'

Today, investors are increasingly interested in opportunities related to Stora Enso's sustainability. For example, they want to know when bioplastics will be introduced into the market. The procurement of raw material from sustainably managed forests is also an important topic—and one of continuous discussion.

Stora Enso has engaged in new forms of green financing, where the price of the loan is affected by the achievement of greenhouse gas emission targets.[7] The company has also created a framework for green financing and has issued its first green bonds.[8] Sustainability is increasingly part of the company's day-to-day operations.

According to Paajanen, a positive risk should be materialised instead of negative risks, now that plastic is being replaced with other materials. In the company's view, **anything that is made based on fossil fuels today can be made from wood tomorrow**. Stora Enso sees itself as a renewable materials company, with sustainable development at the core of its strategy.

Says Paajanen, '*Sustainability themes are highlighted more than before. They have also become mainstream in investing and have been included in mainstream investors' questions for companies. When I started at Stora Enso in 2002, investors only had separate sustainability units and funds, but the situation began to change gradually after the financial crisis. In my opinion, sustainability should be at the core of the strategy, and should not be separated from investing.*'

Summary

The materialisation of the sustainability risk does not serve the interests of the company or the investor—no one wants to find themselves caught up in media controversy. The negative impacts can be related to reputation, or even to business opportunities or financial profits. Fixing the issues arising from a crisis requires time and a great deal of extra work from both parties. The case of Stora Enso shows that companies should screen for potential sustainability risks in advance. If a potential risk materialises, the company must address the issue immediately, communicate about it openly and build cooperation with its stakeholders. Companies must have clear instructions and an action plan and trained employees in place for any crisis situation where even an individual material sustainability risk emerges.

The case also shows that investors' reactions and demands can have a significant impact on support for the corrective measures implemented by the company. However, investors should also analyse the level and means of risk management in the investee in advance and ask the management how they have prepared for the materialisation of any sustainability risks, for example. If the information is not publicly available, the responses will indicate whether the company's management considers the matter to be important at all.

The Perspective of an Engagement Service Provider: Sustainalytics Has Engaged with Stora Enso on Behalf of Investors

The engagement process that Stora Enso describes is typical when it comes to situations that are potential or actual severe breaches of international norms. GES (acquired by Sustainalytics in 2019) then typically aims to have an in-depth dialogue with the company, with participation from its institutional investor clients. Stora Enso was very open to such a dialogue. There are many Nordic institutional investors in Sustainalyticss' client base, which most likely made the process more intense, but also more focused and effective in finding ways to resolve the issues at hand.

The questions detailed by Stora Enso accurately describe Sustainalytics' approach. For Sustainalytics, it is very important that the company not only takes measures to address the actual situation, such as the issues that Stora Enso experienced in Pakistan, but that it also takes proactive measures to prevent similar situations in the same and other countries of operation. The goal is to reduce future risks and make the company more attractive to investors. In the case of Stora Enso and Pakistan, this meant that we wanted to see that audits were in place in the supply chain, that the situation for children who had their work taken from them was addressed (which Stora Enso managed by providing school for them) and that Stora Enso would complete its corporate and local human rights assessments and transparently report results and mitigation measures related to the risks identified (which they did).

We also wanted Stora Enso's corporate management to demonstrate its commitment to human rights due diligence, particularly in terms of preparedness when entering new high-risk markets. The company made several changes in its senior management, as well as improvements in the area of human rights (led and supported by senior management). We thereby concluded that this requirement was also fulfilled by the company.

We are always open to providing companies with our assessments, at any given time. *When we first contact a company, the company is informed about Sustainalytics' role and the aim of the prospective dialogue. Sustainalytics' Global Standards Engagement does not result in ratings. We make a distinction between the* **research phase**, *during which we collect information to understand what has happened and what the company is doing about it, and the* **engagement phase***, when we already have a fairly good understanding of the situation and focus on suggesting improvements. If we have substantial sources confirming the allegations, we can also confirm that the company in question can be associated with a violation of international norms. Companies are informed about this. The confirmation does not, however, mean that we recommend our clients to divest from the company. Quite the contrary – we nearly always engage with the company until the situation has been resolved.*

Decisions to exclude a company are always made at the investor *level and not by Sustainalytics. We discontinue our engagement – and notify our clients and the company – only in rare cases, when the company is unresponsive and shows no or poor progress in resolving the situation. In such situations, it is quite likely that many of our clients will divest. In some particular cases, some of our clients may divest while dialogue is ongoing, but this is never our advice. In the case of Stora Enso, we engaged the company until we assessed its responses as being satisfactory.*

With regard to Stora Enso, we were pleased to see a focused and relatively quick response to the issue in Pakistan. We encourage the company to continue open and constructive dialogues with investors.

Stina Nilsson, Associate Director, Sustainalytics

Background information

The description of the Stora Enso case is based on an interview with Ulla Paajanen, SVP, Head of Investor Relations. In addition, we have used public material. Paajanen has 18 years of experience in investor relations at Stora Enso. During this time, she has seen how, following heavy criticism, the company has included sustainability in the focus of its business strategy, as well as seeking to become a company that sets an example in sustainability for others. At the same time, Paajanen has witnessed the mainstreaming of sustainable investing.

GES was a sustainable investment and engagement service provider. The company was acquired by Sustainalytics in 2019. The comment provided by Sustainalytics has been prepared by Stina Nilsson, who was responsible for the Stora Enso engagement process.

Sustainalytics screens public sources of information (including the Internet) for potential severe and/or systematic violations of international norms, especially the UN Global Compact Principles and the OECD Guidelines for

Multinational Enterprises.[9] When severe situations (incidents) are identified and linked to a specific company, Sustainalytics enters into dialogue with the company. Among the types of engagement methods used by Sustainalytics are meetings with the company, round-table discussions with investors and the company/companies, on-site visits, follow-up dialogue over email, etc. At the time of writing this book, Sustainalytics was involved in active dialogue with 37 companies regarding instances of child labour discovered in their supply chains.[10]

Case: KLP Engages with Maersk on Responsible Ship Recycling

'*Ship-breaking is called the most dangerous work on the planet because of the high risk of injuries and casualties. The shipping industry is one of the largest industries in Norway, and KLP is one of the largest institutional investors in the country. Therefore, it became important for us to engage with shipping companies to reduce the negative impacts of ship dismantling,*' says Marte Siri Storaker, Advisor, Responsible Investments at KLP.

In 2014, KLP first started to have discussions concerning ship scrapping practices with companies listed on the Oslo Stock Exchange or otherwise linked to Norway.[11] Prior to that, not many investors had focused on ship recycling in Norway or elsewhere. KLP received information from non-governmental organisations about ship-breaking at the same time as news coverage emerged about Norwegian shipowners that had sent ships to beaches in Asia.

The Danish shipping company A.P. Moller Maersk (later Maersk) became KLP's focus for engagement in 2016, when the news broke out that the company had begun to dismantle ships on beaches (beaching) in India.

Shipowners Use Beaching to Receive Higher Compensation

To gain a more in-depth understanding of ship recycling, KLP commissioned a report from the International Law and Policy Institute (ILPI) in 2015. The report focuses on the practices and legal framework connected to ship-breaking on beaches in South Asia. The report defines beaching as follows:

*With beaching, the ship is sailed "… onto a tidal flat at spring tide" on sites
with a large tidal gauge. There is no clear definition of beaching, but the Norwegian Shipowners' Association defines it as dismantling ships without using fixed
installations for the collection and handling of dangerous and polluting waste.*

Shipping companies no longer own the ships when they are dismantled.
When a ship reaches the end of its life cycle, it is sold to a cash buyer—that
is, a company that specialises in the process of buying and selling ships to
yards for dismantling. The business of buying ships is based on the fact that
they still contain valuable raw materials, such as steel. The price a company
receives for the ship reflects two aspects: the *amount of steel the ship contains*
(the steel is recycled and sold) and the *cost of dismantling*.

Beaching is the cheapest way to dismantle a ship. The price paid for the
ship by the cash buyer reflects the fact that the difference in price that the
shipowner receives for the ship can amount to USD 3–7 million, depending
on whether the ship is beached or broken up using safer and more sustainable
methods such as dry docks.[12]

Maersk Decided to Recycle Ships in India

Maersk has sent ships to be dismantled in India since 2016. Storaker recalls
the situation:

*Maersk used to send ships to recycling yards in China and Turkey, but in 2016 they
started to send ships to Alang in India for beaching. In 2016, news also broke about
two additional cases concerning Maersk's end-of-life ships. The first case concerned
a ship owned through a joint venture that was sent to Bangladesh for beaching. The
second case concerned the contractual language in Maersk's charter contract,
which incentivised the maximisation of profits, which effectively means recycling at
sub-standard yards – standards for the dismantling process were not mentioned at
all.*

Alang in India and the Chittagong area (Sitakunda coastal strip) in
Bangladesh are the largest ship-breaking sites in the world. Both areas employ
mostly migrant workers from within the countries. In 2014, around 40,000
workers from north-west Bangladesh worked in Sitakunda. In Alang, there
were around 35,000 migrant workers from other parts of India who worked
in the yards directly, and additional workers indirectly, through the related
industries. Between 1983 and 2013, an estimated 6,318 ships were beached
and dismantled in Alang.

The practice of beaching is widely criticised due to the high level of health, safety and environmental risks. According to the report commissioned by KLP, which describes the situation up until 2015, the challenges faced in Alang include the following:

- *Accidents were common, and safety measures were lacking*. From 1983 to 2013, around 470 workers died in accidents in Alang. The fatality rate of Indian ship-breaking yards is around six times higher than that of the Indian mining industry.
- *The living conditions were sub-standard*. Workers resided in or close to the yards in shanties, lacking basic facilities such as clean water, sanitation, electricity, drainage systems, schools and teachers for children, ambulances and hospitals with the capacity to treat potentially fatal incidents.
- *Ship-breaking impacts the oceanic ecosystem that surrounds the work-site*. For example, some fish species had disappeared completely, and the general number of fish had decreased at the Alang beach.

Based on the report commissioned by KLP, improved conditions were identified at some ship-breaking yards in India, to the extent that some have received a *statement of compliance* with international norms. Also, the creation of a ship-breaking workers' training centre was underway.

'*Even today, Alang is a closed area where representatives of non-governmental organisations or reporters are not allowed – which is similar to the situation in many other ship-breaking facilities around the world. But if you look up a satellite view of Alang on Google Earth, for example, you will see a coastline full of ships on the beach*,' says Storaker.

Weak International Regulation Enables the Dismantling of Ships in Substandard Conditions

Ship recycling has not traditionally been subject to international standards. Calls for international regulation have come to ensure the protection of human rights and environmental standards, as the industry has shifted from highly regulated developed nations to countries with weak regulatory and enforcement systems.

Currently, the only international regulation applied to ship recycling is the *Basel Convention on the Control of Transboundary Movements of Hazardous Wastes and their Disposal*, as ships are viewed as hazardous waste. However, the convention was not drawn up to regulate challenges specific to ship-breaking, and it falls short of addressing the related problems.

In 1995, the parties of the convention agreed to incorporate a ban on the export of ships to non-listed countries for final disposal, but this amendment has not entered into force.

In 2009, the International Maritime Organization (IMO) adopted the ***Hong Kong International Convention for the Safe and Environmentally Sound Recycling of Ships***, which has yet to come into force. According to the convention, ships to be sent for recycling would be required to carry an inventory of hazardous materials specific to each ship. Meanwhile, the convention has been criticised for not banning the beaching method.

In Europe, regulation has been developed to implement these conventions, as well as helping the development of a European control system for the ship recycling industry. However, the implementation has fallen short historically: while end-of-life ships are prohibited from being exported from the EU for recycling in non-OECD countries, shipping companies have been able to get around this by changing the ship's flag state and steering the ship outside OECD waters (e.g. to Morocco) before it is sold to be dismantled. In addition, the recycling capacity in OECD countries has been estimated as being insufficient.

Storaker explains the difficulty of the situation, as the current regulatory environment has made the sustainable disposal of vessels voluntary for shipping companies:

> *It is difficult to regulate the shipping industry by law, as it is such an international business, and the price differences that you can receive from selling the ship to South Asia or Turkey are huge. We have deemed it really important to find a way to engage with these shipping companies to make them understand that this is not a viable way to scrap ships in the long run.*

KLP Started Investigating Maersk's Situation After the News Broke Out

KLP started engagement when Maersk sent ships to be dismantled in Alang, India. It was important for KLP to understand why the company had decided to do this, and what mechanisms they had in place to manage the risk of adverse impacts on the environment and human rights.

KLP's responsible investment team used several sources of information to investigate the case: the company, the media, non-governmental organisations, service providers and other stakeholders. After the initial assessment of the information, KLP contacted the company: '*For us, it is most important to have a dialogue with the company, based on the information assessed, to discuss and understand what has happened,'* Storaker explains.

Storaker describes why KLP decided to engage with Maersk directly through its in-house responsible investment team:

No one seemed to be putting the topic high on the agenda at the time when we decided to begin engaging with the company. Meanwhile, KLP already had experience in engaging on the topic of ship recycling. Maersk is one of the largest companies in the shipping industry and an industry leader when it comes to sustainability. Many of the smaller Norwegian companies look to Maersk for examples of best practices. For these reasons, it became very important for KLP to engage with Maersk.

KLP Seeks More Transparency from Maersk Over Ship-Recycling Practices

Maersk explained on its website why the company decided to start sending ships to be dismantled on the beaches of Alang in India:

In 2016, Maersk began sending ships to selected yards in Alang, India, based on two considerations. Foremost was the fact that a number of leading yards in Alang had begun upgrading their facilities and practices in a way that put them close to compliance with Maersk's standards for safety, human rights and the environment. Secondly, while Maersk had been applying its own voluntary standard since 2009, which implies leaving money on the table every time it sends a ship for recycling, this had not proven effective in driving a solution to this industry problem.

From KLP's perspective, the starting point for the engagement with Maersk seemed better in comparison with some other industry peers, as Maersk had already accepted that it has responsibility for the ships through the scrapping process. In addition, the company had a policy in place for scrapping entailing audits of yards before, during and after recycling, as well as Maersk staff being present on-site for supervision. These requirements were stipulated in the contracts with the buyers, including cash buyers.

KLP started an engagement process with the goal of encouraging the company to become more transparent about the difficulties and progress they experienced in Alang. Storaker explains, *'It is difficult for an investor to assess the facts prevailing on-site in India, so the burden of evidence rests with Maersk to show that it is possible to scrap ships responsibly in Alang.'*

KLP Observed Progress Between 2016 and 2020

KLP engaged in dialogue with Maersk in 2016 and has had several conversations with the company since. KLP also sent a letter to the management concerning their practice for ship recycling and policies for the sale of ships nearing the end of their life cycle. Throughout the process, KLP has also had discussions with a large number of stakeholders, including the Norwegian Shipowners' association and non-governmental organisations.

Attention towards Maersk has come from several directions:

- *Non-governmental organisations*, such as the NGO Shipbreaking Platform, have put this topic high on their agenda. KLP has had several discussions with them, but no pressure to divest Maersk has been put on KLP.
- *Several investors and engagement service providers* have approached Maersk, some in cooperation with KLP. In 2017, for example, KLP hosted a seminar where Dutch banks invited Scandinavian banks to join the Responsible Ship Recycling Standards (RSRS) initiative.
- In 2016, *Danish opposition parties* called on the government to halt Maersk's ship-beaching practices.

Storaker explains the impact of various stakeholders:

Our direct influence is difficult to measure. I believe and hope that the combined pressure from investors, the media and non-governmental organisations has them on their toes, and that they know that there is little acceptance for errors in India.

At the time of the first interview, in October 2018, KLP was relatively happy with the dialogue they had had with Maersk. Says Storaker, '*From our point of view, Maersk has been open to engagement, and positive steps have been taken. Maersk has adopted a new policy to limit the risk of unsustainable ship recycling. In addition, the company has started to report on activities at the yards in their sustainability reports, such as findings during audits and general information about the yards.*'

Maersk's new policy limits the risk of unsustainable ship recycling. This policy includes new contract terms, which are based on the value of the vessel at the time of sale. As publicly reported by the company:

1. *If the value is low (less than 25% of the highest recycling price), Maersk will not divest but will recycle the vessel according to its standards.*

2. *If the value is higher (25–40% above the highest recycling price), the new owner will be required to operate the vessel for a further two years or to recycle it in accordance with Maersk's standards. When the vessel has been operating on behalf of others beyond a period of 24 months, Maersk can no longer take on this extended responsibility.*
3. *If the value is high (more than 40% above the highest recycling price), the vessel can be resold without restrictions, as there is no financial incentive for the buyer to recycle at that point.*

In 2020, KLP has excluded five companies for beaching ships at substandard yards in Bangladesh and Pakistan.[13] Maersk was not on the list of excluded companies, as KLP views Maersk as one of the most transparent companies in the shipping industry and acknowledges that they do a great deal of work to ensure that the yards comply with human rights. Storaker also believes that Maersk has probably contributed positively to the on-site conditions in India. However, the question remains of whether it is at all possible to scrap ships in a responsible way in this area.

Storaker considers the results of the engagement as average and concludes:

Ideally, Maersk would not have put its stamp of approval on Indian yards. However, the policies that they put in place for the sale of vessels in 2016, and the fact that they have started to report on progress, are important steps forward. KLP would still like to see more transparency in the yards in Alang.

KLP Put the Engagement with Maersk on Hold as It Waited for Changes in the EU Regulation

In 2018 the engagement with Maersk was put on hold, because KLP was waiting for the result of the *EU Ship Recycling Regulation* that entered into force in 2019. According to the regulation, commercial ships registered in an EU member state can only be recycled at safe and reliable facilities that have received the EU's approval. However, companies could still avoid implementing the EU regulation by using flags of non-EU countries on their ships, meaning that the ships are registered outside the EU.

Storaker explains the importance of the change as follows: '*When the applications have been processed, it will become clearer whether Indian yards hold a standard that is acceptable and whether the risks related to human rights and the environment can be properly managed.*'

Many Indian yards have applied to be included on the EU's list of ship-recycling facilities but had not been included at the time of the interview in November 2020. There have been on-site inspections, and these yards are not currently in line with the technical standards and have received feedback on what needs to be in place for them to be able to be included. Information about the on-site inspections is available on the EU's website. KLP has been in dialogue with DNV GL, one of the advisors used by the EU, to conduct on-site inspections to learn more about what their understanding is of the Indian market for recycling ships.

KLP has had a follow-up conversation with Maersk regarding the fact that the Indian yards have so far not been approved. However, the process of approval is still ongoing, as the yards have the opportunity to correct what is missing in terms of compliance with the EU Ship Recycling Regulation and reapply for the list.

Says Storaker, '*It is important for us to understand how Maersk will comply with the EU list, as they have previously announced they may disregard it. If the yards that Maersk is currently using are not approved by the EU, KLP will enter into dialogue with Maersk to understand what processes this will trigger with regard to their policies for the scrapping of ships.*'

KLP Visits Alang

In 2019, KLP was able to visit Alang. Together with a responsible ship-recycling consultant, KLP visited several yards. Says Storaker: '*This gave us a clear picture of the situation and the developments in India. We were pleased to see with our own eyes that the demand for responsible ship recycling was real, and that the yards doing work for companies engaged in responsible ship recycling, such as Maersk, Stolt-Nielsen, TransOcean and more, all had improved standards. KLP notes that engagement has a positive effect from investors to companies and from companies to improved standards on the ground.*'

Storaker continues: '*Sadly though, the standards in India vary tremendously. Side-by-side on the beach are yards that have worked hard to improve their facilities and in contrast yards with very poor standards. Very few yards have adopted these improved standards, and most of them still have a long way to go. KLP therefore continues to engage in dialogue with shipowners recycling ships in India, Pakistan and Bangladesh – asking about policies, practices, the yards used and continuous supervision and results.*'

KLP Views Ship-Recycling Practices Primarily as an Ethical Question

Storaker estimates that from an investor perspective, the company earns more money by selling the ships to India, even though it has to spend more money in the process regarding sustainability considerations. While the practice itself does not necessarily have a negative impact on returns, it increases risks connected to the company.

For KLP, the topic of ship-breaking is primarily an ethical question; therefore, it has not assessed the financial implications in detail. Storaker explains that there may be some implications nonetheless:

> *Even though something might look like it earns the company more money in the short run, I believe this is not as clear in the long run. The legislation and regulations will, at some point, include the practice of beaching, and the company will have to adapt to higher standards. In addition, the company is headquartered in Denmark and also relies on attracting customers and talented employees in order to generate profits. In a society steadily more concerned about the social impacts of companies, the practice of beaching may very soon be looked at as being intolerable.*

KLP does not deem it very likely, though, that Maersk will be held legally responsible for the environmental damage caused by the buyers of its ships. As emphasised by Storaker:

> *Maersk is one of very many companies that send ships to the beaches. It would be difficult to single them out. The problem is that since these legislations are not international, shipping companies can easily avoid them. However, there are cases in Europe where companies are being prosecuted for selling ships to India, Pakistan or Bangladesh. In Norway, there is the case of a ship called Harriet, which was taken to court. The ship was in Norway when its engine broke down and it had to be rescued. On board, they found documents indicating that the ship had been sold for scrapping in Pakistan, and that it was not on its way to be repaired, as the shipowner had reported. Ships are considered hazardous waste, and are not allowed to be exported as such outside the OECD under the Basel Convention. There has been a similar case in the Netherlands as well.*

Company Point of View: Maersk Develops Sustainable Practices in Collaboration with Recycling Docks

At Maersk, we take our responsibility for the vessels we have owned very seriously. Since 2009, we have had a responsible ship recycling policy in place that is based on – but goes further than – the Hong Kong Convention and matches the scope of the EU regulation. It includes all the relevant labour and human rights, anti-corruption and social aspects, as well as downstream waste management and does not allow contact in the area within the tidal range with blocks from primary cutting as these areas can include several types of habitats with various species of life, such as seastars, sea urchins, and many species of coral. Substandard yards if Afghanistan, Pakistan and India allow the cutting of blocks from the deck of the vessels to happen in that area, polluting it. Of the global tonnage, around 90% is still recycled under sub-standard conditions, mainly in South Asia.

The beaching method is less capital intensive but can offer higher prices as it taps into an effective and efficient circular economy with around 98% of the ships being reused in one form or another, the prices [received for recycled ships] are higher. This is part – but a minor part – of the reason [for the price difference]. The real reason for the price difference is the inherent demand for steel-scrap at the domestic markets with almost no costs of delivering the material to the customers (last-mile costs) in these countries. This is important, as the last mile delivery tends to be complex and it is by far the most expensive part of the process. You get a lot of money for used steel in India and Bangladesh – more than 98% of the vessels broken there are reused. This is important in terms of understanding why these industries operate in these places and why they are so difficult to move.

There is virtually no tonnage in the world which is broken in dry docks. In Turkey, the vessel is also landed directly on the coast and with primary cutting takes place over open water.

For years, we could not find providers in South Asia that could live up to our standards. And for decades, virtually no progress has been made in what is clearly one of the worst aspects of the shipping supply chain. But five years ago, a number of Indian yards (prompted by the Japanese government in particular) began to upgrade their practices, obtaining statements of compliance with the Hong Kong Convention. We had the yards audited by Lloyd's Register and began to work with a few of them to close the gaps in order to comply with our standards and thus break to the same level of quality that we maintain in Turkey. Our hope was that this would induce other yards to invest and upgrade, that other shipowners would follow us and that an improvement momentum could be created in Alang.

After decades of no progress, the results have exceeded our imagination. When we break ships in Alang, we always have our own staff supervising the process, we have the right to stop the work at all times and we have Lloyd's Register and Elevate to conduct independent audits. Currently, we responsibly recycle in two yards to the same level as in Turkey, and we have ten other yards pre-cleared to do the same. But more importantly, we see a race to the top where yards compete not only in terms of price but also in terms of quality, with more than 80 out of around 120 yards holding statements of compliance with the Hong Kong Convention and many others in the process of being upgraded.

As part of our commitment to the wider Alang development, using our local implementing partners, we have for over the past two year run a mobile health unit aimed at addressing the health care gaps in the area and a training project aimed at mitigating health risks through raising awareness.

By accepting a lower price compared to the non-responsible alternatives and working on-site to create a model for how to do this, we believe we have played a role in creating this momentum and a feasible responsible alternative has been created. Thereby have significantly increased our leverage beyond our own sphere of control.

Going forward, we remain committed to work with industry stakeholders to support yards globally to achieve a sustainable solution for compliance with the EU Ship Recycling Regulation and thereby increase actual capacity on the EU List.

Ole Graa Jakobsen, VP, Head of Fleet Technology, Maersk

Summary

Based on this case description, we conclude that investors can also address activities and operations that they consider unethical, even if the primary motive is not financial. Responsible ship dismantling and recycling practices tend to increase costs, and the financial benefit is related more to avoiding the potential materialisation of sustainability risks. KLP's example shows that an investor can request companies to change their business practices that are considered unacceptable and can, along with other issuers, have an impact on the environmental, health and safety procedures and training related to ship dismantling.

Maersk's experiences demonstrate how solving complicated sustainability challenges can require using the company's leverage in relation to suppliers and working at the grass-roots level. The goals of a company and an investor can be similar to one another. However, from the investor's point of view, adequate transparency is also essential: an investor wants reasonable reassurance that the operations meet their sustainability requirements.

Background Information

Kommunal Landspensjonskasse (KLP) is Norway's largest life insurance company. It provides pensions and finance and insurance services to municipalities, county authorities, healthcare companies and public-sector and private-sector businesses. The KLP Group manages around EUR 75 billion in assets in total. KLP invests in Maersk as part of its passive equity investments and fixed income and hedge funds, totalling around EUR 9 million. While KLP also uses an external service provider for some of its engagements, Maersk is one of the companies where KLP's in-house ESG staff have engaged with the company directly.

This case description is based on an interview with and information provided by Marte Siri Storaker, Advisor, Responsible Investments at KLP, as well as on a report commissioned by KLP on ship recycling, publicly available information and the response provided by Maersk's Ole Graa Jakobsen, VP, Head of Fleet Technology including a contribution from John Kornerup Bang for the first edition of the book, at the time he was serving as Director, Head of Sustainability Strategy.

Notes

1. The criteria for diversity on boards of directors are most advanced in Great Britain, for example, where the boards of the 100 largest listed companies (FTSE 100) must have at least one person of colour or a representative of another ethnic minority as a board member in 2021 (Parker Review, 2017). The same requirement will concern the 250 largest listed companies in 2024.
2. Service providers must disclose more detailed information about their research methodologies and the preparation of voting recommendations on their websites when the amendments to the EU Shareholder Rights Directive comes into effect in 2019.
3. Hermes EOS is a unit of Hermes Investment Management that focuses on insurance.
4. The shareholder proposals presented to the Annual General Meetings of Shell and BP were part of the 'Aiming for A' engagement campaign. The 'Aiming for A' coalition consists of CCLA (one of the UK's largest charity fund managers), the Local Authority Pension Fund Forum (LAPFF, a British joint engagement initiative) and the largest members of the Church Investors Group and Rathbone Greenbank Investments. The coalition was formed in 2012, with the goal of achieving the best possible environmental rating (A) for the UK's ten largest electricity companies and fossil fuel companies with CDP. Focusing on environmental reporting, CDP is an investor initiative to assess companies annually. CDP publishes what is known as the 'A List' of companies that lead the way in reducing environmental impacts in their respective sectors.

5. The interviews related to the case descriptions were generally conducted between September and November 2018 and were updated between October and November 2020 as applicable.
6. In January 2019, Sustainalytics announced that it had acquired the business operations of GES.
7. A revolving credit facility is backup for a financial instrument, such as a bank loan or a bond, in case problems emerge with the primary means of credit. In such cases, a revolving credit facility serves as an option to secure the necessary funding.
8. Stora Enso issued its first green bonds in February 2019.
9. Sustainalytics looks for information about serious violations of human rights (including labour rights), serious environmental damage and corruption involving large amounts of money and/or senior management. Sustainalytics has detailed criteria for assessing the severity of the cases. At first, the discussions with companies focus on understanding the situation and the company's view. If the situation continues, Sustainalytics recommends improvements to resolve the situation.

   Where the cases are related to human rights, Sustainalytics bases its assessment and recommendations on the UN Guiding Principles on Business and Human Rights. This means that Sustainalytics requires companies to respect human rights, implement a due diligence obligation to reduce human rights risks (exercise particular care to ensure respect for human rights) and apply a compensation process to manage any negative human rights impacts. Sustainalytics uses these criteria to set goals at the beginning of engagement processes.
10. Sustainalytics also has experience in numerous discussions concerning child labour where the situation has been resolved. However, not all cases of child labour are reported, which is why the GES also contributes to proactive initiatives aiming to address the risk of child labour in agricultural supply chains, for example. Agriculture is the sector with the highest use of child labour.
11. Ship-breaking is a practice used by several shipping companies. In KLP's view, policies for scrapping ships are worth discussing with all shipping companies. KLP tracks which of the companies in its holdings send ships to the beaches of South Asia and engages with companies on their policies for selling ships for scrapping. This is because KLP sees these companies as being at risk of violating KLP's guidelines for responsible investing on human rights and environmental damage.
12. The ILPI report commissioned by KLP also describes the better methods for ship-breaking: 'With the dry-dock approach (also referred to as "docking" or "dry-dock recycling"), the ship is placed in a dock, the water is pumped out and the ship is dismantled piece by piece. Pier breaking (also known as the "alongside" or "top-down" method) consists of securing the ship alongside a pier and removing pieces with a crane, starting from the top. Slipway recycling (or "landing") entails sailing ships against the shore at sites with little to no

tide. The ship is then dismantled using a mobile crane from the shore or from barges.'

13. The excluded companies were Evergreen Marine Corporation Ltd., Korea Line Corporation, Precious Shipping PCL and Thoresen Thai Agencies PCL and Nordic American Tankers.

References

Denes, M. R., Karpoff, M. R., & McWilliams, V. B. (2017). Thirty years of shareholder activism: A survey of empirical research. *Journal of Corporate Finance, 44,* 405–424.

Greenwood, R., & Schorb, M. (2009). Investor activism and takeovers. *Journal of Financial Economics, 92*(3), 362–375.

Sustainable Investments Institute. (2020). *Special report: 2020 mid-year review summary social, environmental & sustainable governance shareholder proposals in 2020.* https://siinstitute.org/reports.html.

Other Sources

Dittmar & Indrenius. (2018). *Government proposal regarding the implementation of EU's second shareholders' rights directive published.* D&I Corporate Advisory Alert. https://www.dittmar.fi/insight/government-proposal-regarding-the-implementation-of-eus-shrd-ii-published/.

European Commission. (2017). *Shareholder Rights Directive: What is new?* ec.europa.eu/newsroom/document.cfm?doc_id=45719. Referenced 25 November 2020.

Finlex. (2018). *Act on earnings-related pension insurance companies.* Available in Finnish at https://www.finlex.fi/fi/laki/ajantasa/1997/19970354. Referenced 25 November 2020.

Finnish Government. (2017). *Working group on shareholders' rights.* Available in Finnish at https://valtioneuvosto.fi/hanke?id=c8f1d3b9-8895-4f69-9364-616b46 9b9d81. Referenced 25 November 2020.

Knuts, M., Raade, P., & Kanervo, J. (2018). SHRD II: Osakkeenomistajien oikeudet -muutosdirektiivi – markkinaharmonisaatiota runsaalla liikkumavaralla [*Amendments to the Shareholder Rights Directive—Market harmonisation with considerable leeway*]. Thematic article by Director's Institute Finland. Available in Finnish at https://dif.fi/teema-artikkelit/q1-2018-hallitus-ja-johto/shrd-ii-osa kkeenomistajien-oikeudet-muutosdirektiivi-markkinaharmonisaatiota-runsaalla-liikkumavaralla/. Referenced 25 November 2020.

Ministry of Finance. (2018). Kysymyksiä ja vastauksia osakkeenomistajien oikeuksista [*Questions and answers about shareholder rights*]. https://vm.fi/documents/10623/6304750/Usein+kysyttyjä+kysymyksiä+ja+vastauksia+osakkeenomistaj ien+oikeuksista/217e8436-38a1-4949-9535-6aca7e0c4806/Usein+kysyttyjä+kys ymyksiä+ja+vastauksia+osakkeenomistajien+oikeuksista.pdf.

Ministry of Finance. (2018). *Working group on shareholders' rights. Working group memorandum.* Available in Finnish (English abstract) at https://vm.fi/docume nts/10623/7263094/Osakkeenomistajien+oikeudet+-työryhmä+-+työryhmämuis tio/553e6576-e06c-4395-b075-5ed96a1d563d/Osakkeenomistajien+oikeudet+-työryhmä+-+työryhmämuistio.pdf?version=1.0. Referenced 25 November 2020.

Securities Market Association. (2015). *Corporate governance code.* Available in English at https://cgfinland.fi/wp-content/uploads/sites/39/2018/04/hallinnointi koodi-2015eng.pdf.

The Parker Review. (2017). *A Report into the Ethnic Diversity of UK Boards.*

Part III

Sustainability in Investment Analysis

4

Sustainability as Part of Qualitative Analysis

Investors assess the risks and opportunities related to ESG aspects: the environment, social responsibility and governance. This is commonly referred to as the integration of sustainability into investment decisions. The goal is to achieve better returns with a more controlled risk (improving the risk-to-return ratio) and/or manage the investor's reputation. In practice, this means that the return potential may otherwise be the same for different companies, but some companies are subject to higher ESG risks. In other words, an investor benefits if they can identify an investment that offers similar returns with a lower risk.

We have outlined the process of ESG analysis in Fig. 4.1. The figure includes the key phases of the ESG analysis process, as well as references to the chapters of this book in which the topic is discussed.

Sustainability in Traditional Investment Analysis

In recent years, sustainability aspects have, to some extent, become part of traditional investment analyses that banks offer their customers. These analyses prepared by banks are widely available to portfolio managers who make investment decisions, as well as to the analysts who support them. For this reason, the development of traditional investment analysis plays a key role in the mainstreaming of sustainable investing and the integration of ESG aspects into the normal investment process.

© The Author(s), under exclusive license to Springer Nature
Switzerland AG 2021
H. Silvola and T. Landau, *Sustainable Investing*,
https://doi.org/10.1007/978-3-030-71489-5_4

Defining materiality	• Key ESG factors for the sector (Chapter 4) • Changes in the operating environment and sustainability trends (Chapter 11)
Preparation of an ESG analysis	• The company's processes, ESG performance and sustainability management (Chapters 4, 5 and 9) • Past sustainability problems (Chapters 4 and 5) • The future viability of the business model (Chapters 9 and 11)
Investment decisions	• Analysis of ESG information and its connection to financial statement analysis and valuation (Chapter 4) • Comparison with the investor's requirements (Chapter 4) • Assessment of engagement needs (Chapter 3)

Fig. 4.1 Process description of ESG analysis

In traditional investment analysis, the sustainability perspective is currently taken into consideration as a downside risk – that is, potential negative materialisation. In risk analysis, the perspective should be expanded to cover the materialisation of positive risks by identifying a company's excellent level of sustainability as a competitive factor that increases the probability that its net sales and profitability will develop more favourably than expected (positive risk). After all, an investor always runs the risk of not owning shares in the company (opportunity cost) and thereby losing potential returns. In other words, risk analysis must be conducted in both directions, even in terms of sustainability.

A good example of this is the Finnish forest industry, which is often analysed only in terms of negative risks. Their analysis should cover the opportunities to use renewable and biodegradable (wood) fibre in packaging and biomaterials, for example. Consumers are increasingly expecting that the products they purchase (and/or the packaging) are made from renewable and recyclable materials, and the legislation in various countries is being amended to restrict the use of non-degradable (plastic) materials to a growing extent. In addition, pulp production is more than self-sufficient in electricity, very much so, which is rarely considered from any other perspective than financial performance.

Rami Vehmas, Senior Portfolio Manager, Ilmarinen Mutual Pension Insurance Company (investment assets around EUR 50 billion)

Sustainability Ratings and Specialised Analysis

In addition to traditional investment analysis, institutions that are more advanced in sustainable investing usually use company-specific ESG analyses prepared by service providers. Sustainability analyses classify and rank companies, as well as providing background information about their sustainability risks, opportunities and their management, and past sustainability issues that have been subject to public attention.

As yet, there is no single internationally approved standard for preparing sustainability ratings and analyses. In practice, this means that service providers have their own methodologies for compiling their ESG ratings, with a focus on various sustainability aspects. *Sustainability risks are highlighted in the analyses*; nevertheless, the sustainability rating of a company manufacturing wind turbines, for example, relative to other technology companies, improves somewhat when opportunities related to renewable energy and climate change are considered.

Providers of sustainability analysis services include *MSCI*, an international provider of index and analysis services, and *Sustainalytics*, which focuses on ESG services, among other companies. Unlike banks, these research organisations that prepare reports do not broker securities (such as shares and corporate bonds) in the companies that they analyse. Although banks may own some of these companies that prepare sustainability analyses, they have separate operations, meaning that the sustainability rating agencies are more independent of the companies subject to analysis.

Understanding the Ambiguity of Sustainability Ratings Is Important

Utilising ESG ratings and reports increases investors' understanding of corporate responsibility. The strengths of ESG reports prepared by international service providers include the underlying systematic methodologies that enable companies in the same sector to be examined consistently. The assessments take into account the key aspects related to the companies' operations and their management, covering countries of operation, products manufactured and services provided, as well as any other special features of the sector, for example.

The performance of companies in the same sector is compared, and this comparison includes key indicators, such as energy and water consumption and accident frequency. On the other hand, in interpreting the data from the ESG analyses, it is good to understand that the definitions of sectors are usually broad and that the company is also compared with somewhat different types of operators. In this comparison, **some companies may seem more risky because of the nature of their operations alone**: for example, pharmaceuticals of a certain type may generally have more adverse effects, and consequently, more product safety risks may be related to their manufacturers than to companies producing basic medications.

The data from the ESG analyses is based on the public reporting of the investees, as well as on media monitoring and any additional reports provided by the companies (however, not all companies correct any errors or omissions). The content of sustainability reporting is not very highly standardised. In other words, if a company fails to report on an aspect deemed material by a service provider, this does not necessarily mean that there are deficiencies in the company's operations in this respect. Furthermore, the ratings do not recognise differences in the levels of requirements between countries, although the legislation may be so strict in practice in some areas that compliance in itself may mean a relatively good level of sustainability.

Differences between countries affect ESG ratings. Based on their ratings, companies operating in the United States, for example, may seem less sustainable than their European peers. This may partly be because of the fact that public disputes lower the scores, and many companies in the United States are subject to general class action suits, which are common in the country.

In addition, **large-scale misconduct is difficult to identify in the analysis unless it is otherwise exposed**. If a company is outright lying, finding out about misconduct is difficult unless the incident is detected during an official inspection, for example. In other words, not all key sustainability aspects are apparent from public sources, and even some companies controlled by the Mafia have been claimed to have the highest sustainability ratings.

For investors using ratings, it is good to understand that **ESG ratings are averages of very different sustainability aspects**. Therefore, risks in one area of sustainability may be balanced by good performance in another area. However, a significant risk in even a single area may turn out to be a critical risk for the entire investment in practice. For this reason, investors who only follow sustainability ratings may overlook some material sustainability risks.

Sustainability Ratings Help Investors Identify Risks

Sustainability analyses by service providers are compilations of **large amounts of company-specific ESG information in a concise and easy-to-read format to support the investment decision**. In addition, ESG ratings help investors focus their own resources for sustainability analysis on the highest-risk companies. Monitoring the sustainability ratings of investments, as well as changes in the sustainability ratings, can help investors pay attention to high-risk companies in particular, in addition to providing background information for more in-depth analysis.

> *One of the mining companies in our portfolios had a low ESG rating, and we noticed that a lot of governance weaknesses had been identified. The company had a high exposure to corruption (operations in corrupt regimes and weak processes to deal with these challenges), lack of transparency in how transactions were being dealt with and past association with illegal activities in high-risk regions – for example, the company had obtained mining licences that had been put into question. We were not comfortable with the risks, and decided to sell our holdings in the company and invest in a more sustainable one in the same sector. This has turned out to be the right call, as the company was soon hit by scandals globally that have affected their business and share price.*
>
> Even though the starting point for this analysis was the ESG score and especially the governance score, we also studied information from another service provider about controversies related to international norms and assessments, for example, and news from Bloomberg. It is also worth highlighting that this is not just a number but qualitative data that has to be read – and you also need to figure out how to interpret the information.
>
> Andreas Stang, (former) Senior Portfolio Manager, Head of ESG, PFA Asset Management

Preparation of an in-Depth ESG Analysis

The preparation of an in-depth sustainability analysis begins with the identification of ESG themes that are material in terms of investment analysis. In choosing perspectives, investors can use sustainability reports prepared by service providers, for example, or sustainability reports by companies and the Sustainability Accounting Standards Board's (SASB,[1] 2018) definitions of material sustainability themes (26 issues in total, presented in Fig. 4.2). The SASB has defined key ESG-related sustainability indicators that are material from companies' financial perspective for 11 sectors and 77 sub-sectors.

In addition to sustainability ratings and analyses prepared by service providers, in-depth sustainability analysis usually involves companies' sustainability reports, third-party reports (if available), discussions with corporate management and sustainability ratings, as well as other ESG analysis tools.

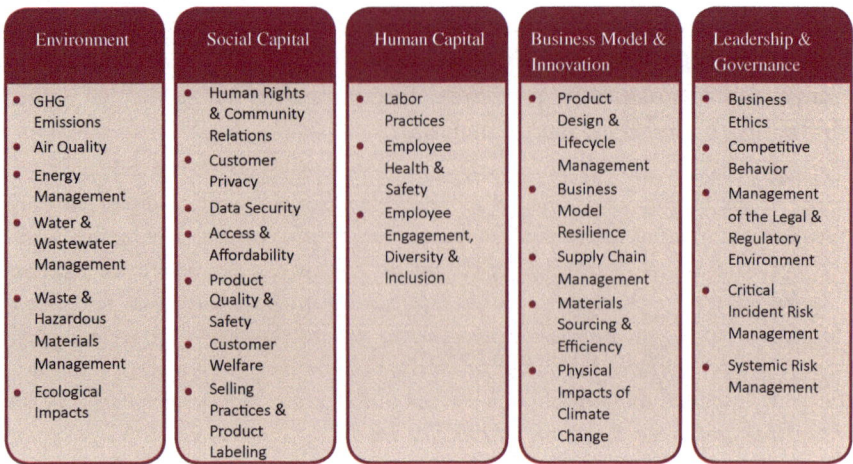

Fig. 4.2 Material sustainability issues defined by the SASB (©2021. Reprinted with permission from The SASB Foundation. All rights reserved)

Sustainability Reports Prepared by Companies: How to Recognise Material Information

Reports prepared by companies help analysts gain a better understanding of the company's level of sustainability and their goals. They usually provide information about the sustainability impacts of business operations that the company deems material, as well as information about their management, goals, measures implemented during the reporting period and the direction of development.

The format of sustainability reports is not standardised, and their quality and coverage vary between companies and markets. The EU has a directive concerning public-interest entities (PIE), which requires the companies to report non-financial information. The directive obligates the companies to disclose certain matters concerning the environment, employees, social impacts, human rights and the prevention of corruption and bribery, as well as their business models and operational risks and their management. However, companies can choose the format in which they present the information to be reported and the indicators they use for this purpose. In many other markets, there is no such reporting obligation, and voluntary sustainability reports in the emerging markets are not usually as high quality as in industrialised countries.

Sustainability reports contain both qualitative and numerical information to support analysis. However, the standardisation of sustainability figures is still in progress. These figures are affected by the assumptions and choices made by each company concerning baseline years, the (emission) conversion factors used in the modelling and the coverage of the data collected. In addition, the quality assurance processes and controls related to collecting sustainability figures are often lighter compared with financial figures, meaning that the published figures may contain major errors even for this reason. Some listed companies, large ones in particular, have their sustainability reports verified by a third-party auditor or consulting firm.[2] Still, the published versions may contain errors.

Table 4.1 provides examples of questions for the preparation of a sustainability analysis of a company in the manufacturing industry sector. Public sources do not often provide answers to all questions that are material in terms of the analysis, and an opportunity to present additional questions may significantly improve the quality of the analyses. However, it is good to note that major institutional investors often have the best opportunities for meetings with corporate management.

External Sources of Information

Many parties—such as non-governmental organisations, independent research organisations, UN institutions and investigative journalists— examine selected companies. Some of these reports are publicly available. The reports can focus on a specific sustainability issue or more broadly on the company's sustainability, usually in terms of its shortcomings. These reports may also be useful in investment analysis, as they provide more detailed information and another perspective on the company's operations and/or any sustainability challenges in the value chain. Some of these parties producing reports are also open to discussion directly with investors or their representatives.

In addition, some companies have third parties prepare more extensive reports on the sustainability of their operations or specific cases. Some companies make the key results of such reports available to investors, which in itself can increase trust towards the companies' operations and problem-solving skills.

Source criticism is also necessary in interpreting information provided by third parties.

Table 4.1 Examples of questions for an ESG analysis of a manufacturing industry company

Topic	Sample questions	Guidelines for interpreting answers
Strategy	• How is sustainability taken into account in the company's strategy? • Are the defined priorities relevant from a business perspective?	• Developments in the operating environment and sustainability trends affect companies. There are differences between companies in how well they take sustainability into consideration in their strategic choices
Goals	• What kinds of goals has the company set for its operations and how have the key indicators developed in terms of the goals? • What are the underlying factors? Does the company report on improvement measures, for example, or reasons for its unfavourable development?	• By examining companies' goals, investors can understand the focuses of sustainability measures and seek to interpret how much the company invests in the management and development of sustainability aspects • From outside a company, it is challenging to assess whether the reported figures are good or bad and whether the targets set are ambitious. Indicative information may be obtained from comparisons of figures between companies in the sector (for example, from analyses offered by service providers)
Management systems	• What sustainability management systems and certificates does the company have in place with regard to environmental management, quality and occupational safety, for example? • What is the coverage of the certificates and is there a plan to increase their coverage?	• The use of management systems indicates to investors that the company's operations comply at least with certain international standards and that third parties conduct audits regularly in its locations. However, management systems do not in themselves guarantee that all aspects of responsibility are being taken into account • If the coverage of the certificates is only partial, it is important to understand whether certificates are missing in high-risk countries, for example, where they are not essential because of the nature of the operations, or in new units acquired through corporate arrangements that have not yet been certified

(continued)

Table 4.1 (continued)

Topic	Sample questions	Guidelines for interpreting answers
Sustainability issues	• Has the company had any major failures or inconsistencies in sustainability that have become public? • What does the company state about reducing negative impacts and preventing similar challenges in the future?	• For example, frequent minor accidents may suggest that processes may not be working adequately • Reports are channels for companies to present their own perspectives, and the omission of any failures covered by the media gives a somewhat questionable impression
Ethical business principles	• Does the company have a whistle-blowing channel for employees and partners to report suspected misconduct anonymously? • How many incidents are reported each year and on what topics? What measures have been implemented based on them?	• A very small number of reports may mean that the whistle-blowing channel is not widely known or is not trusted • If there is no official whistle-blowing channel or it is not effective (for example, the company does not respond to reported cases), misconduct may not be detected until much later, during audits conducted by the authorities or through leaks to the media, for example
Other special features of the business operations	• Do the company's operations have other special features that involve sustainability risks? • How are specific risks taken into account in the company's operations?	• Specific sustainability risks may be related to operations in high-risk countries and/or conflict areas, challenging international projects and development needs related to new units acquired through corporate arrangements, for example

Management Meetings and Requests for Additional Information

Sustainability reports and third-party reports do not usually meet the information needs of the analysis exhaustively. However, they help investors send more relevant requests for additional information to companies and make more effective use of short meetings with management: the discussion can start at a level where the basics are already known and key questions have been prioritised in advance.

Sustainability reports usually focus on the past, while investment analysis seeks to predict the future. This is why reports are studied for indications of what may happen in the future, and the information is combined with normal investment analysis, which is forward-looking.

Discussions with companies can increase understanding of their sustainability levels, ambitions and future plans. The analysis examines how companies' processes support ensuring that the level of sustainability is good and improves further—the management's attitude also comes into play here. If sustainability is not one of the management's focuses, negative future risks are higher than in circumstances where the company is committed to promoting the implementation of sustainability. For example, a high accident frequency in the past does not necessarily mean that the company will have accidents frequently in the future.

Direct dialogue with companies, if possible, also helps investors clarify any discrepancies or inconsistencies in the reports. For example, some companies may report investments in energy efficiency, but according to the report, their energy consumption has increased. In some cases, the context is not provided: a company may report measures to reduce its water consumption but does not disclose in which operations water is used and how significant water consumption is in terms of the sustainability impacts and risks to the company's business operations.

The following questions help investors assess sustainability based on the answers provided by the company:

- How comprehensive are the answers given by the management to the questions? Do the answers improve when the same question is asked the next time—in other words, is the company making progress?
- Are the answers consistent with the reported information or between different representatives of the company?
- At what organisational level are sustainability aspects reviewed? What sustainability issues are on the senior management's agenda?
- How competent are the company's representatives in sustainability issues and what is the level of ambition?
- What is the company's own understanding of its development needs related to sustainability? What measures have been planned and implemented to promote them?

Sustainability Analysis Affects Valuation and Investment Decisions

Risks and opportunities related to sustainability can be identified based on sustainability analysis. Sometimes the risks seem so significant that the investment is no longer attractive. In such a case, the cost of a materialised risk would be higher than the expected returns. Based on analysis, the company may also involve risks that would have a decisively negative impact on the investor's reputation, which makes the investment unviable. Some investors directly exclude companies with the poorest sustainability ratings from their investments based on their own assessments or ratings produced by service providers.

There is no established way to include sustainability aspects in valuation. Costs related to negative sustainability impacts, including the cost of financing, can be taken into consideration in modelling, as well as cash flow growth and expected returns as positive opportunities. Alternatively, *the return requirement set for the company can be increased in valuation based on sustainability risks*. In such a case, the extent of the adjustment is discretionary, as there is no specific formula for its determination.

Analysts and portfolio managers assess investments in their own ways based on common valuation methods. It is essential to understand the impacts of sustainability risks and opportunities on costs, cash flow growth and earnings. Investment institutions seek to harmonise guidelines and practices to make it easier for analysts and portfolio managers to implement the sustainable investment strategy in practice.

The valuation of companies will remain similar in the future. However, the factors affecting future cash flows are likely to include an increasing number of ESG aspects that will need to be identified and that will have a positive or negative impact on future cash flows. And the ESG aspects that will affect future cash flows are already having an impact on the pricing of securities.

When analysing the production of equipment related to winter sports, for example, or the long-term demand outlook for companies focusing on winter travel, investors cannot ignore the shortening of winters due to global warming, as well as the ensuing decrease in total demand. A shorter season reduces demand for companies' products and services and is also likely to reduce the availability of debt financing.

Mika Leskinen, Chief Investment Officer, FIM (investment assets around EUR 8 billion)

Case: An Analysis of ABB to Illustrate ESG Analysis

We have prepared an analysis of ABB's sustainability based on public information, which is amply available. Many institutional investors also use service providers to collect sustainability data for analysis. In addition, institutional investors often have an opportunity for discussion directly with the management.

Our analysis is based only on publicly available information. This means that the company may have mechanisms in place to manage the risks we have identified, but it has not reported on these mechanisms. The company is responsible for providing information about its operations in such a way that it is possible to form an accurate picture of its sustainability and the related impacts, risks and opportunities.

A summary of our analysis of ABB is presented in Table 4.2. It covers key sustainability aspects related to the company and their possible impacts on returns.

From Initial Analysis to Investment Decisions

Depending on the investor's goals, resources and other opportunities, the analysis can be deepened by presenting more detailed questions to the company and having discussions with analysts, for example. Additional information helps the investor evaluate whether all the detected risks are related to the company's operations or whether they arise from shortcomings in reporting, and whether something essential has not been identified in the analysis based on public information.

For investment decisions, the various sustainability aspects related to ABB's operations should be prioritised. This means considering how much weight to put on the diverse range of aspects detected during the analysis and assessing them in relation to *the company's operations and financial outlooks.* In practice, the investor must decide how essential they consider the company's positive environmental impacts to be in terms of eco-efficiency and climate change, and how significant they find the detected risks and the related uncertainty.

The modelling of the costs related to ESG risks is challenging and therefore relatively rare. For example, if it was considered necessary for a company to further develop its supplier audit system and make it more systematic, additional costs would arise. Few companies openly share how much it would cost to develop audit systems and other processes—and information about such costs is not publicly available even about benchmark companies that comply with best practices. Assessing the probability and impacts of possible reputation losses is also challenging.

Table 4.2 Summary of an ESG analysis of ABB

Classification: ● Operations seem sustainable   ● Potentially material risks   ● Potentially significant risks

ABB – BUSINESS OPERATIONS PROVIDE SOLUTIONS TO ENVIRONMENTAL CHALLENGES			
SUMMARY – KEY ESG ASPECTS TO CONSIDER BEFORE MAKING AN INVESTMENT DECISION			
Eco-efficient solutions are part of ABB's core business: nearly 60% of its net sales are related to improving customers' energy efficiency and enabling clean technology solutions. **Key ESG risks to investments are related to compliance with sustainability principles in international operations.** ABB has made several acquisitions in recent years, which increases the need to implement company-wide standards in all operations.			

ESG OPPORTUNITIES			
THEME	LEVEL	CURRENT SITUATION	POTENTIAL IMPACTS ON REVENUES
Impacts of Products and Services	●	Nearly 60% of ABB's net sales come from its eco-efficiency portfolio. The company has a strong focus on clean technology innovation.	Several megatrends are bringing growth opportunities for the company (e.g. climate change, automation and sustainable transport).

ESG RISKS			
THEME	LEVEL	CURRENT SITUATION	IMPACTS ON REVENUES
Ethical Business Principles	●	ABB has comprehensive principles and a certified anti-bribery programme, including training (98% coverage), as well as a whistle-blowing channel for reporting misconduct. However, the cases exposed in 2017 and 2019 (two corruption investigations and significant embezzlement by a South Korean employee) raise questions about the effectiveness of the processes.	• Potential legal expenses and fines • Potential future failures could lead to losses, disruptions and reputational damage
Responsible Procurement	●	ABB has a sustainability programme for high-risk suppliers, which includes training, on-site assessments and monitoring. However, the company does not report details on the coverage of annual measures, such as the number and content of completed audits.	• Potential costs related to the improvement of audit and monitoring practices in response to stakeholders' expectations • Possible delivery interruptions and delays arising from social problems
Harmful Materials	●	ABB maintains a public list of prohibited and restricted materials, which also concerns its suppliers. In addition, the company reports on reductions in terms of the harmful chemicals that it still uses. Further information would be required to understand the significance of the harmful chemicals that the company still uses and the impacts of any future prohibitions and/or restrictions.	• New restrictions could increase costs and/or affect quality
Environmental Management	●	Since 2018, the company has been implementing an organisation-wide management system with ISO 14001 certification on environmental management. At the end of 2019, the coverage of the new system was 65%, while the goal was for all operations to be covered by the new system by the end of January 2020.	• Potential costs of environmental remediation
Health and Safety	●	ABB's new management system has ISO 45001 certification on health and safety, and the number of accidents in relation to hours worked has decreased over the past five years.	• Potential operational disruptions, legal expenses and compensation

Opportunities: Focus on Clean Technology and Innovation

Headquartered in Switzerland, ABB is a technology company with operations in more than 100 countries. The company is listed on the Zurich, Stockholm and New York stock exchanges. Its four business areas—Electrification, Industrial Automation, Motion, and Robotics & Discrete Automation—serve customers in the energy, industrial, transport and infrastructure sectors. Eco-efficiency solutions represent ABB's core operations: nearly 60% of its net sales come from improving the energy efficiency of customers' operations and enabling cleantech solutions.

The company has shown ambition to remain at the forefront of cleantech innovation. The solutions developed by ABB are related to more sustainable transport (e.g. fast charging points for electric vehicles), more intelligent and greener electricity networks (e.g. platforms for digital and green electricity networks, solar power conversion applications) and automation systems for homes and industry that can improve energy efficiency, to name a few examples. In 2018, ABB placed eighth on a *Fortune* magazine list of companies that are changing the world significantly through their positive social impacts.[3]

Risks: Compliance with Sustainable Business Principles in International Operations

Ethical Business Principles

ABB has comprehensive anti-bribery principles, a certified anti-bribery programme with related training (98% coverage in 2019) and a whistleblowing channel for reporting suspected misconduct anonymously. However, publicly expressed suspicions raise questions about the effectiveness of these processes.

The authorities in the United Kingdom and the United States investigated the company from 2017 for bribery and corruption concerning its earlier cooperation with Unaoil, a consulting firm registered in Monaco. According to information published by the media, ABB collaborated with the investigating authorities in the United Kingdom. In the spring of 2020, the authorities decided not to press charges against ABB, unlike the case with two other companies that had previously cooperated with Unaoil.

In 2019, it was revealed that *the authorities in the United States were investigating suspect payments to Eskom Holdings SOC Ltd., a South*

African electricity company. ABB seems to have identified and self-reported these incidents to the authorities in the United States and South Africa. There is only limited information available about the cases from public sources, and the information involves uncertainties because of the ongoing investigation. In the analysis, it is not possible to predict the scope of the possible sanctions very reliably. A rough idea can be established by studying how much the sanctions have been in relation to net sales in similar cases before, and by assessing in which countries the company may have to respond to charges. The probability of a conviction should also be assessed.

An employee of the South Korean subsidiary disappeared with 100 million dollars. According to information published by the media, the embezzlement was not detected until this employee of the company's financial department had disappeared. The immensity of the amount is illustrated by the fact that the stolen funds correspond to around 4% of the Group's net income in 2016 and, according to estimates, up to 20% of the annual net sales of the South Korean subsidiary. The company and its auditor have come to the conclusion that the crime was made possible by insufficient division of duties: a single individual was able to transfer the money without needing to have the transfer approved by another person. According to information published by the media, the embezzler served as the contact person for reporting ethical issues at the South Korean subsidiary. However, it is not known whether this had an impact on the developments.

Judging from reports, the studies conducted and measures implemented by the company focused on South Korea, where the case was investigated and the senior management was replaced. The investor would need to find out whether the control mechanisms are globally intact so that similar incidents will not happen again. ABB should also ensure that all suspected cases will be reported effectively to its headquarters.

Additional information about the use of the ethical whistle-blowing channel would help the investor assess the risks related to the company's operations in more detail. Based on the public information available, it remains unclear whether the incidents are isolated or whether there is reason to suspect a broader problem in the sense that the principles drawn up by the parent company have not been sufficiently implemented in global operations. The assessment is made more difficult by the fact that the company does not report on the following aspects:

- How many cases are reported annually through the whistle-blowing channel?

- Which topics are the received reports related to? The sustainability report discusses complaints related to harassment and discrimination, but there are no mentions of any enquiries concerning other topics.
- Where are the complaints processed? Are they always reported to the parent company?
- How is it ensured that employees around the world are aware of the whistle-blowing channel and trust it?
- How is information collected in countries of operation where data privacy is not generally trusted?

Responsible Procurement

ABB has a sustainability programme for high-risk suppliers, which includes training, on-site assessments and monitoring. However, only general descriptions are available about the practical implementation of the sustainability programme. *More detailed information is lacking about the coverage of annual measures*, for example, such as the proportion of suppliers covered by the programme, as well as the number, content and implementation method of audits (e.g. which party does the auditing and according to which standard).

Judging from public information, ABB has invested in promoting the implementation of human rights in its operations. The company has operations around the world, and it has suppliers in high-risk countries such as Saudi Arabia and the United Arab Emirates, which have challenges related to migrant labour. The report refers to human rights by mentioning separate human rights principles and two annual training campaigns. As a new development, ABB has started to provide training to an in-house Human Rights Champions Network with the aim of implementing its principles into practice. To assess its human rights risks, ABB reports that it conducts reviews in line with the UN guiding principles on business and human rights. Based on the company's reports, it is not quite clear how comprehensive its assessments have been so far. To support the analysis, it would also be useful to have more information about the key results of the reviews and any corrective measures.

ABB has reported to the authorities in the United States that it uses *conflict minerals*, some of which may originate from the Democratic Republic of the Congo. The company's measures seem appropriate, including supplier surveys and participation in the Responsible Minerals Initiative, a multi-sector sustainability initiative.

Sustainability issues cannot be completely avoided in international business. Some types of issues are inevitably discovered if operations are examined closely enough. Studies by non-governmental organisations and other third parties are good examples of this. However, even minor issues appear much worse if it seems that the company is indifferent or has weaknesses in its processes.

Harmful Materials

ABB maintains a public list of prohibited and restricted materials, which also concerns its suppliers. The company also reports on reductions in its use of harmful chemicals. A group-level programme on material compliance management, established in 2019, and 55 location-specific programmes give the impression that the company has clear processes and plans in place to reduce the use of harmful materials. The company also provides concrete examples of investments that have resulted in reduced emissions.

Although the company may not necessarily be able to provide information about all the harmful materials that it uses, the *company-level plan on harmful materials is reassuring in the sense that the company is prepared for possible future restrictions and would be in a better position to adapt to any changes*. For the investment analysis, it would also be interesting to obtain information about the significance of the harmful chemicals that the company still uses, as well as opportunities for their reduction and the impacts of any future prohibitions and/or restrictions on its business.

Environmental Management

Since 2018, the company has been implementing an organisation-wide management system with ISO 14001 certification on environmental management. At the end of 2019, the coverage of the new system was 65%. The goal was for all operations to be covered by the end of January 2020. This can be seen as a positive development: although the level of certification had previously been relatively high (75% in 2017), it *remained unclear* based on public information *whether certification was missing where it was not necessary*, or from recently acquired companies (that had not yet been certified), or whether certification had purposefully not been obtained in some areas (such as high-risk countries).

It is also worth noticing that the company only discusses significant spills in a table at the end of the report, with no mentions elsewhere in the report. In 2019, there were 26 significant spills. These included oil and chemical spills, emissions into the air and other spills. However, the limit for a significant spill is relatively low (e.g. spills with a cost impact of more than USD 10,000). In other words, the scale of these challenges and whether they can be regarded as relatively ordinary is unclear. It would be more illustrative if the company divided the spills into categories, such that by reading the report, the investor could tell whether any of the spills had been financially and/or environmentally significant.

Unlike most of the sustainability report for 2019, the figures related to spills, recycled and reused water and discharged water have not been assured by a third party. This raises questions about whether the company has weaker data collection processes for these figures, which would also mean that there may be more errors—or whether the figures are less material, which would also be a reasonable explanation for the lack of more detailed information. While assurance increases the reliability of the information, it does not guarantee that the information is completely accurate.

Health and Safety

In terms of health and safety, the company's operations seem rather good: ABB's new management system has ISO 45001 certification on health and safety. The accident frequency rate has decreased over the past five years. This indicates that the company has taken successful measures to improve occupational safety. To support the analysis, it would also be enlightening to understand in more detail what were the causes of fatal accidents in particular and whether similar incidents could be prevented more effectively in the future.

Other Themes Reported by the Company in Addition to Material Risks

ABB reports on the carbon footprint of its operations, and its emissions seem to have decreased year by year through projects to improve energy efficiency, for example. However, because of the nature of ABB's operations, it can be assumed that its most significant climate impacts are generated through its customers.

Water risks can also be interpreted as being excluded from key risks. The company reports that it operates in some areas with high water risks. However, water use does not play a significant role in its operations. For more detailed analysis, it would be beneficial to understand in which operations the company uses particularly large amounts of water, whether its water discharge has negative impacts on local natural environments, and whether such operations are located in areas with a shortage of water (high water risk). The figures related to water discharge vary considerably between different years, without comprehensive explanations. More information about the quality of water discharged without treatment would also be beneficial for the analysis.

An ESG Analyst's View: ABB Is at the Forefront of the Low-Carbon Energy Transition

The key reason why ABB is investable in all our sustainability funds is the fact that the company enables a sustainable global energy transition, and that most of its net sales come from products related to sustainability. The company provides solutions to key challenges of the expansion of renewable energy production that are related to storage and effective distribution.

In our view, ABB's most significant ESG risks are related to possible breaches of its internal guidelines or the legislation, as controlling global business operations and a large number of employees is a constant challenge. **The value of the orders the company receives may be very high, and such orders are often related to the public sector. These aspects expose the company to a high risk of bribery and corruption, cartel formation and local-level fraud.** *In addition, while ABB has a significant link to fossil energy production, many of its products and services can also be used in renewable energy production. ABB delivers building elements (components) to major dam projects and other large-scale energy infrastructure projects that may have a negative impact on local communities and the environment. There is a risk that ABB can be accused of contributing to such sustainability problems, particularly because the company has maintenance and other service agreements on construction sites. We consider ABB's climate risks to be limited, because the company has a strong climate strategy.*

The sustainability issues that ABB has faced are not exceptional, considering the scope and nature of its business operations. Nevertheless, there is always an ***internal reason within companies for incidents****, even if the illegalities are conducted by a single individual. The underlying structural reasons may be related to the control of subsidiaries. Then again, ABB has a high number of subsidiaries, and it may be extremely challenging to keep them under control in any case and apply the same rules universally.*

So far, nothing has been revealed that would cause us to no longer want to invest in the company. We sell our holdings in a company if it is deemed to be in systematic and serious breach of international norms, or if other reasons are revealed that go against our initial justifications for investing in the company (for example, if a company in which we invested for environmental reasons contributes to systematic environmental destruction in its operations, supply chain or customers' operations). However, as long as the incident is isolated, we would like to know more before making any decisions.

We regard ABB as a company that has succeeded in adjusting its business operations for the future. **ABB is an old, large and traditional company, but it is also at the forefront of the low-carbon energy transition.**

Anita Lindberg, Senior ESG Analyst, Skandia Asset Management (around EUR 65 billion in investment assets)

The Company's View: Responses by the Sustainability Unit at ABB to the Questions that Emerged During the ESG Analysis

1. **What are the key sustainability opportunities and risks related to ABB?**

With its pioneering technologies, ABB contributes to meeting many of the underlying targets of the UN Sustainable Development Goals (SDGs). ABB's structured analysis identified seven SDGs where we can have the most impact. ABB's products, services and solutions promote not only SDG 7 (affordable and clean energy), which is one of our core businesses, but also SDGs 6, 8, 9, 11, 12 and 17.[4] The 2017 Sustainability Report provides many case studies that show evidence of our impact. ABB's greatest contribution to the reduction of greenhouse gas emissions is through energy-efficient and renewable energy products, systems and services.[5]

Based on the feedback from our most recent stakeholder meeting, we have identified that our key ESG risks are related to responsible sourcing, human rights and integrity. Each of these areas has a specific programme in place to minimise the business risk, as covered in our 2017 Sustainability Report.

2. **What is the number and more detailed scope of your annual supplier audits?**

ABB conducts a risk review of its suppliers on an annual basis, and supplier audits are carried out based on the results of the review. The scope of supplier audits for ABB is global. From 2018, supplier audits are conducted in 17 high-risk countries (new countries may be added to increase coverage). Suppliers are selected for sustainability audits based on risk screening in accordance with the following:

a. *Geographical risk: risk of labour/human rights violations; safety/environmental risks prevalent in the country where the supplier is situated*

b. *Category risk: environmental and safety hazards involved in the manufacturing of the material*
c. *Economic risk: business risk.*

Supplier on-site audits are conducted based on 42 parameters across labour/human rights, safety, the environment and local legal requirements in all 17 countries of operation. In all cases of non-compliance, ABB facilitates the preparation of a corrective and preventive action plan, along with root cause analysis. To help suppliers improve their operational standards, a variety of supplier training programmes, capacity building events and support sessions are conducted before and after the audits.

   ABB also collaborates and implements special programmes with suppliers to find innovative solutions for chronic problems (which are usually influenced by socio-economic and cultural practices).[6]

3. **Can you provide details concerning the whistle-blowing hotline: Are the reported cases always assessed at the headquarters? At the South Korean subsidiary, was the thief in reality the person responsible for addressing ethical concerns?**

   All cases reported via the whistle-blowing hotline are forwarded to the Office of Special Investigations at Group level. The office is responsible for the investigations. Regarding the South Korean subsidiary, the entire leadership team was replaced. The people involved in the embezzlement were not responsible for addressing ethical concerns in the country of operation.

4. **Have the measures taken with regard to the embezzlement case been focused solely on South Korea or have reviews/changes been implemented throughout global operations to ensure control over subsidiaries, for example?**

   Following the unfortunate embezzlement scheme that was exposed in our South Korean subsidiary in February 2017, the company took swift and decisive action. We identified the relevant control issues, remediated the material weakness in our internal controls and replaced the management team in South Korea. No other country was affected. After the theft was discovered, compensation decisions were made that reduced the level of annual short-term incentive payments to ABB employees, as well as the Long-Term Incentive Plan pay-out for senior executives.

5. Were any of the reported spills material?

The spills were in the amount of around USD 80 million net of insurances recoveries.

6. The potential negative impacts of energy infrastructure projects and dams on local communities have not been discussed at all in ABB's sustainability report. Is this also a risk area that ABB recognises, and are there processes in place to manage these risks?

For many years, ABB has been working to embed sustainability topics in its due diligence and risk management processes. These processes include project risk reviews, which cover energy infrastructure projects and dams. Sustainability aspects covering potential environmental and social risks are part of the risk review process.

7. What is the role of and risk related to harmful materials in terms of ABB's business operations? How material is this topic for ABB?

At ABB, we require all operations to actively phase out hazardous substances and replace them with less hazardous alternatives, which should be introduced as soon as technically and economically feasible. To help us manage this risk, we have compiled the ABB List of Prohibited and Restricted Substances. The list applies to all our operations, including goods supplied to ABB, product development, production processes, products, packaging materials, service operations and construction sites.[7]

We have a network of experts who monitor, interpret and inform our businesses about new and forthcoming restrictions on hazardous materials.[8] This helps our supply chain management, product managers and R&D units plan for the timely phase-out of substances and materials and/or the change of suppliers. We have also launched a cross-functional material compliance team, with a mission to facilitate a standardised and systematic approach to the increasingly complex material compliance regulations we face in our global markets, based on best practices. The team has assessed current efforts in the business units, communication with suppliers and customers, standards, guidelines, tools and training, as well as internal and external support. The team has also worked with ABB's divisions to develop and issue new global standards and guidelines, together with new, globally available webinar training packages on the REACH Regulation and the RoHS Directive.

Summary

This sustainability analysis of ABB is based on publicly available information. This means that any investor with basic ESG analysis skills can assess the sustainability of their (current or potential) investees in a similar manner. The critical examination of the ESG factors identified during the analysis reveals opportunities, risks and issues that investors should be aware of. The case also illustrates the importance of comprehensive reporting for investors. If a company does not report (sometimes there is a justified reason) comprehensively and transparently on all material sustainability aspects, it should disclose the reason for the lack of such information. Otherwise, investors may misunderstand something or be left with an insufficient view of the company's level of sustainability and the related risks.

ABB's responses to the questions we posed indicate that direct dialogue with a company can supplement the information that is available and thereby improve the quality and descriptiveness of the analysis. Even if the company cannot answer all the questions arising from the analysis, it may be able to clarify its situation and processes more extensively than publicly reported information. Direct dialogue also makes it possible to correct any misunderstandings that are based on information reported by the media, for example.

Background Information

Our analysis is based on ABB's global business operations as a whole. We studied the company's sustainability reports for 2017 and 2019, annual reports for 2016 (with regard to South Korea) and 2019 (with regard to Unaoil and Eskom), website and reports to the authorities, as well as information published by the media about the sustainability problems and issues detected in the company's operations.

The case description also includes a comment by Anita Lindberg, Senior ESG Analyst, Skandia Asset Management, on ABB's sustainability risks and opportunities, in addition to responses by ABB's sustainability unit (Sustainability Affairs, Zürich, Switzerland) to questions we posed based on the analysis.

Notes

1. The SASB is an organisation developing the standardisation of sustainability reporting in the United States.
2. A verifier ensures that there is no reason to believe that material errors have been made or that material information has been excluded from reporting. Around 20% of Finnish companies had their reported sustainability information assured by a third party in 2018.
3. Fortune magazine prepared its 'Change the World' list in cooperation with FSG, a non-profit consulting firm; the Shared Value Initiative, a collaboration platform seeking business solutions to social challenges; and Michael E. Porter, Bishop William Lawrence University Professor at Harvard Business School. The companies included in the list must achieve measurable social impacts and socially beneficial business results, as well as having significant innovation operations.
4. Sustainable Development Goal (SDP) 6 is 'Clean water and sanitation', SDG 8 is 'Decent work and economic growth', SDG 9 is 'Industry, innovation and infrastructure', SDG 11 is 'Sustainable cities and communities', SDG 12 is 'Responsible consumption and production' and SDG 17 is 'Partnerships for the goals'.
5. One of ABB's 11 sustainability measures is to monitor the performance of its eco-efficiency portfolio. This portfolio achieves the most significant positive impacts during operation in three areas: energy efficiency, renewable energy and resource efficiency. The company seeks to increase the share of the eco-efficiency portfolio, aiming at 60% of ABB's total net sales in 2020 (53% in 2014).
6. The following video illustrates the positive impacts of this type of collaboration: https://www.youtube.com/watch?v=IKfsloFZu-4&t=6s.
7. In addition, the list helps ABB comply with statutory requirements, as well as ensuring that human health and the environment are taken care of throughout the value chain. Legal compliance is also one of ABB's global terms and conditions for suppliers, in addition to being part of its Supplier Code of Conduct, which the company has developed as additional guidance for suppliers to help them better understand their responsibilities.
8. With regard to hazardous materials, ABB is subject to the EU REACH legislation, the EU ROHS directive, California's Proposition 65 and the China RoHS.

5

ESG Analysis Tools for Assessing Listed Shares

Numerous tools are available for sustainability analysis that makes it possible to systematically compare ESG aspects between investments. Analysis tools have their strengths and weaknesses, which is why the use of several different sustainability analysis tools and a diverse range of information sources may provide a more comprehensive understanding of the sustainability of investments.

In recent years, the selection of data and tools for sustainability analysis has increased rapidly, particularly with regard to the assessment of climate impacts.

During my more than 10 years in ESG research, there has been a tremendous change in the availability of ESG data. When I started, you had some data, and then you had to realise what could be analysed based on that. Now there is loads of data, and you need to decide what the key questions are that you want to under-stand and then choose what data to use. In my view, it is most important to focus analysis on the key sector-based sustainability trends that are impacting companies.
Andrew Howard, Head of Sustainable Research, Schroders (investment assets around EUR 545 billion)

We have compiled a selection of key sustainability analysis tools in Table 5.1. We determine the types of analysis tools based on two focuses:

- Time perspective
- Interpretation of data.

© The Author(s), under exclusive license to Springer Nature Switzerland AG 2021
H. Silvola and T. Landau, *Sustainable Investing*,
https://doi.org/10.1007/978-3-030-71489-5_5

Table 5.1 Key types and focuses of sustainability analysis

		Time perspective	
		Past	Future
Data interpretation	Reported figures	• Carbon intensity[29] (ISS ESG, MSCI, S&P Trucost) • Green/brown exposure (S&P Trucost, ISS ESG, MSCI) • Sustainable development investments (MSCI, FTSE Russel)	
	Summaries and conclusions	• Sustainability ratings (broad ratings: MSCI, Sustainalytics, theme-/sector-specific ratings: CDP*, Corporate Human Rights Benchmark CHRB*, Coller FAIRR Protein Producer Index*) • Violations of international norms (ISS ESG, Sustainalytics, MSCI) • Environmental costs (S&P Trucost)	• Preparedness for climate change (CDP*, Transition Pathway Initiative TPI*) • Climate scenarios (2° Investing Initiative[30]*, Carbon Tracker*, Mercer)

In brackets: examples of organisations that provide various types of sustainability analysis tools. Non-profit operators are marked with an asterisk

Time Perspective: Past or Future

Most of the sustainability analysis tools used by investors focus on historical figures and other information. Because the purpose of investment analysis is to assess companies' future sustainability risks and opportunities, the examination of historical information does not provide all the material information for ESG analysis. A good or poor level of sustainability in the past does not guarantee that the situation will remain the same in the future. Forward-looking analysis tools, which have developed rapidly in recent years, support investors in assessing companies' future sustainability impacts and operating conditions.

Many of the ESG analyses and tools that focus on the past have been developed by commercial service providers. In the development of forward-looking analysis opportunities, a key role has also been played by non-profit organisations based on investor alliances and/or public funding. Commercial operators usually update ESG analyses and information at least annually and provide them in a format that is easy to integrate into investors' information systems. Many non-profit operators are developing research that benefits the entire sector and that is often at least partially free for all to use.

Interpretation of Data: Reported Figures or Summaries and Conclusions
Investors have access to compilations of information reported by companies, or raw data, as well as summary reports produced by service providers. Summary reports include more interpretation of what the collected data means and how various data sets are weighted to draw conclusions. However, service providers also determine boundaries for the data to be collected in terms of the reported figures, as well as the underlying assumptions for the modelling of data (in this case, modelling concerns particularly figures that the companies have not reported themselves).

Comparison and Selection of ESG Analysis Tool Providers
Evaluating the modelling methods applied by service providers is laborious and requires a great deal of special expertise and understanding, as well as familiarity with the origin and consistency of the data. Service providers may end up with different key figures and estimates even when assessing the same company, depending on their sources, interpretations and any oversights. Some of the background information for analysis and the methodologies used for editing are protected based on competition data. In other words, the reliability of the data cannot be fully assessed from the outside because of limited transparency.

The differences between ESG analysis tools are illustrated by a case described by the *Wall Street Journal* (WSJ, 2018) concerning the Exxon-Mobil oil company. Sustainalytics rates the company as the most sustainable of five oil companies, because Sustainalytics gives social responsibility a weighting of 40%. According to Sustainalytics, ExxonMobil has strong principles concerning labour, the supply chain and local communities. MSCI rates ExxonMobil at the second-lowest level of sustainability in relation to the other five operators, with a weighting of 51% for environmental aspects and only 21% for social responsibility. The WSJ observes that MSCI applies a small number of material indicators to each company, and each of these indicators has a significant impact on the total score, while Sustainalytics has a larger set of indicators, and part of its assessment is also based on analysts' views.

In addition to assessing quality when selecting service providers, the coverage of the analysis tools of the investment universe is often assessed, as well as the suitability of the tools for the investor's goals, such as whether quantitative or qualitative analysis is preferred and whether the goal is to identify new sustainability opportunities and sustainable investments or manage risks. The providers of ESG tools are continuously developing their methodologies, and new types of tools are being introduced into the market. *Occasional assessment of the offering helps investors find the best partners*. To assess the quality of ESG analyses and tools, key portfolio companies can also be asked for their views on how well various service providers have understood their material sustainability aspects.

The assessment models related to ESG analyses are evolving, and the reported data involves uncertainties. Investors need analysis for a broad investment universe; however, broad-based analysis methodologies have been harmonised and may therefore seem somewhat mechanical, and not all material company-specific aspects are necessarily taken into consideration. Nevertheless, many investors find it *worthwhile to pay for sustainability analysis, as it offers a more comprehensive overview of the risks, opportunities and impacts of investments*—despite the uncertainties involved. At the same time, it is good to be aware that traditional (financial) investment analysis is also uncertain, as it includes assumptions and subjective forecasts, although the related calculation formulas are well-established.

Historical Reported Figures

Carbon Intensity

Of the individual indicators describing climate impacts, carbon intensity is commonly used among investors. This is because information is widely available and carbon intensity in relation to financial indicators enables investments to be compared between companies in the same sector, as well as enabling the reporting of the climate profile of the portfolio. For many institutions, the assessment of carbon intensity has been the first step towards a more systematic examination of the climate impacts and risks related to investments.

Identifying the carbon intensity of the investment portfolio, as well as the companies that have the most significant impact in this respect, can help investors recognise some of the climate risks related to their investments. For example, attention may be paid to particularly high weightings (a significant proportion of the total investment) for certain energy-intensive companies. In certain circumstances, carbon intensity can be a useful indicator that supports investment decisions. However, it is an unsophisticated indicator for assessing climate risks, which usually needs to be examined more broadly as part of further analysis.

The carbon footprint is generally reported as **carbon dioxide equivalents (CO_2e)**. This means that the various greenhouse gases are compared based on their impact on global warming. In addition to carbon dioxide, methane and nitrous oxide are key greenhouse gases included in the figures, but some service providers also include other greenhouse gas emissions. Carbon foot-printing involves many choices (related to emission conversion factors and the coverage of the figures, for example) made by the reporting companies, as well as by service providers modelling figures for investors. Making choices is necessary for the calculations, but it also affects the comparability of various companies' carbon footprint figures and how well the calculations describe the actual impact on climate change.

The calculation of carbon footprint figures is typically based on the Greenhouse Gas (GHG) Protocol, which is an international standard, among other guidelines. The GHG protocol divides greenhouse gas emissions into three scopes (Fig. 5.1):

- Scope 1 includes direct emissions (fuels and refrigerants used by the company).
- Scope 2 includes indirect emissions from purchased energy.
- Scope 3 includes indirect emissions related to products purchased by the company, outsourcing, business travel, etc.

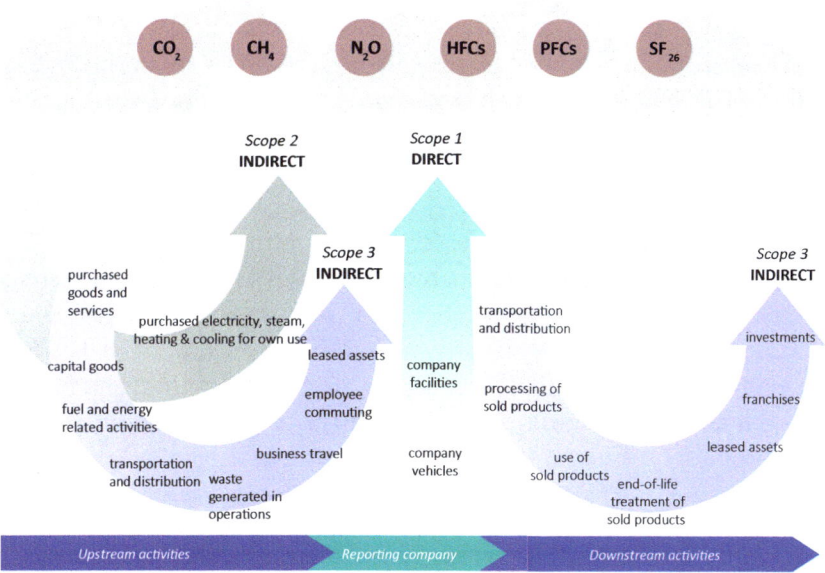

Fig. 5.1 Greenhouse gas emissions in accordance with the GHG Protocol (*Source* GHG Protocol)

In assessments used by investors, *carbon intensity* means the carbon footprint in proportion to the financial key figure. The use of financial key figures enables comparisons between companies in different sectors. They also differentiate the assessment of low emissions from production volumes. For example, a manufacturer of luxury cars may seem more efficient than a manufacturer of lower-priced cars, because the former can generate more net sales from a smaller number of cars. In addition, there are three options for the selected financial divider: portfolio value-weighted,[1] net sales and amount of euros invested (market value).[2] Depending on the chosen comparison figure, the carbon intensities of investments and their development differ, even when assessing the same investments and portfolios.

In interpreting carbon intensity figures, it is *important to understand the calculation logic of the figures and how the company's sector and business operations affect the figures.* As yet, investors have more commonly used carbon intensity figures that only include Scope 1 and Scope 2.[3] One of the reasons behind this is that companies' reporting on Scope 3 emissions for investors is generally limited and continues to be based on rough modelling that involves sector-specific averages, for example, and/or only part of Scope 3 emissions, such as suppliers' emissions. Because of the lack of Scope 3 reporting, carbon intensity best describes climate impacts for companies in cases where a significant part of the emissions consists of Scope 1 and Scope 2 emissions (e.g. electricity companies). In many sectors, however, most of the emissions are at Scope 3, meaning that investors using carbon intensity figures need to know what has been included in the calculations.[4]

The most common carbon intensity figures used by investors include information *only about the negative climate impacts of business operations.* However, many companies also have positive impacts on their customers' emissions (carbon handprint), among other aspects. On closer examination, it has been discovered, for example, that the particularly high carbon intensity of a sustainability fund in the technology sector was due to a significant investment in a solar panel company. The considerable emissions caused by the manufacturer of solar panels had been included in the carbon intensity figures, but the climate impacts generated during the use of the panels are not materialised until the customer's emissions decrease as a result, and had therefore been excluded from the scope of the calculation. Case-by-case assessment is important.

Carbon intensity figures do not directly reflect *companies' exposure to the increase in costs caused by emissions trading schemes and carbon taxes.* The pricing of emissions is also affected by political decisions: for example, which of a company's countries of operation have an emission trading scheme in place[5] and what sectors are covered by the scheme, whether a company is compensated for the costs arising from emissions trading, etc. In addition, the *market forces* affect who ultimately pays for emissions when some companies can transfer the rising cost of coal to their customers (e.g. in the form of electricity price increases). In other words, the use of carbon intensity figures in the assessment of changes in the prices of emission allowances is not straightforward. The analysis is further complicated by the fact that companies do not usually specify in their reports what proportion of their emissions is covered by emissions trading schemes.

Green/Brown Exposure

There are indicators that illustrate companies' exposure to operations and technologies based on 'clean' fuels (green) and fossil fuels (brown). Such indicators are used to compare companies in specific sectors. Indicators of this type include, for example, electricity companies' energy distribution (sources of renewable/fossil energy), car manufacturers' technologies (internal combustion engine/electric/hybrid) and material companies' exposure to fossil fuels (oil and gas drilling, mining operations focusing on coal, holdings in underground reserves of fossil fuels).

Information about green/brown exposure can be used in analysing risks and opportunities, identifying investments that are in line with the investor's views, excluding certain companies (such as coal producers and users) and monitoring the achievement of the targets set by the investor (such as the development of the proportion of renewable energy).

In analysis, it is key to understand that not all the information collected by service providers comes from companies' reports. Instead, some of the information is based on modelling and adjustments. For example, some electricity companies report the energy sources they use only in terms of their own production plants (in line with the financial reporting boundaries). However, in terms of environmental figures, many investors expect the energy sources used by part-owned companies to also be included in the figures. Service providers need to evaluate the combined figures, and this can lead to different interpretations between service providers.

Sustainable Development Investments

Many investors seek to identify investments that benefit from the opportunities related to sustainability and global challenges in their business operations—while also financing a cleaner and more sustainable world as part of profitable investment activities. The UN Sustainable Development Goals (SDGs) are used as a framework for determining sustainable development solutions.

The Sustainable Development Goals include 17 goals and 169 sub-goals to be achieved by 2030. These goals are related to broad challenges in society that need to be addressed by governments, companies and other operators. Providers of sustainability analysis services have interpreted the opportunities related to these goals in terms of investments as far as applicable. For example:

- *'Good health and well-being'* (Goal 3): As an investment, this can mean a pharmaceutical company that develops and produces medications for globally significant diseases as part of its business operations.
- *'Climate action'* (Goal 13): As an investment, this can mean the production of renewable energy technologies and the provision of energy efficiency products and services to customers.

As yet, only a few companies separately report the share of net sales or numerical targets related to sustainable development solutions. Providers of sustainability analysis services have developed methods for the modelling of net sales figures related to sustainable development goals. Such databases enable investors to screen potential investments, compare the relative share of sustainable development between companies and monitor the share of sustainable development solutions in their investments.[6]

Until now, some of the sustainability analysis tools have been limited in the sense that they only describe the amount of net sales and not the actual, real-world impacts of sustainable development generated by the companies as investments. For this reason, some investors have developed their own tools to quantify and report on the sustainability impacts of investments.

Case: PGGM's Analysis Tool for Investing in Sustainable Solutions

PGGM, a Dutch asset manager of pension investments, was given a target to increase investments in companies that provide solutions related to sustainable development goals. *'PGGM works to drive the changes needed to overcome the challenges ahead while also positioning ourselves to help our clients with their long-term obligations towards their beneficiaries,'* explains Rogier Snijdewind. Senior Advisor, Responsible Investment at PGGM.

The work began by identifying which companies in PGGM's current investment portfolio provide sustainable solutions. Four focus areas were determined for PGGM's investments in sustainability solutions: climate change, water scarcity, food security and healthcare. To increase these invest-ments, PGGM built an actively managed sub-portfolio, which currently represents more than EUR 3 billion invested in around 80 companies (this equals around 5% of PGGM's listed equity investments).

Getting the information about companies' exposure to selected sustain-able development goals requires a great deal of original analysis. Says Piet Klop, Senior Advisor, Responsible Investment at PGGM, '*We looked at the revenues of companies from sustainability solutions provided by the MSCI and FTSE Russell, as well as any other information sources we could find, such as company websites. We started off with a long list of companies that could poten-tially qualify as an "investment in solutions". To narrow the list further, we set criteria requiring that a company eligible for our sustainability solutions portfolio would either have to generate at least 50% of its sales from one or more area of sustainability solutions in PGGM's focus areas or have a significant market share of one or more of those solutions. The importance of the second criterion can be explained with an example related to Siemens, which is the largest provider of wind turbines in the world, even though wind turbines represent only 10% of the company's revenue. As a result of this analysis, we created an investable universe of roughly 350 companies.*'

Decisions related to the taxonomy of sustainable solutions are illustrated in Fig. 5.2. Figure 5.3. provides an example of the concrete content of the taxonomy.

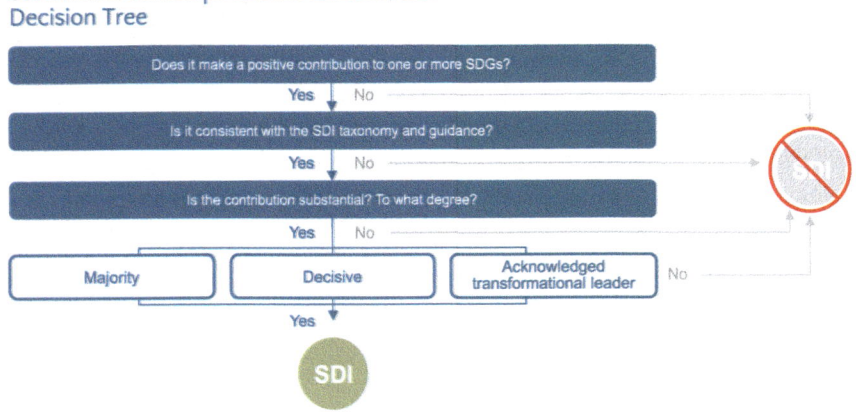

Fig. 5.2 Decision tree to define investments in sustainable solutions (*Source* PGGM and APG)

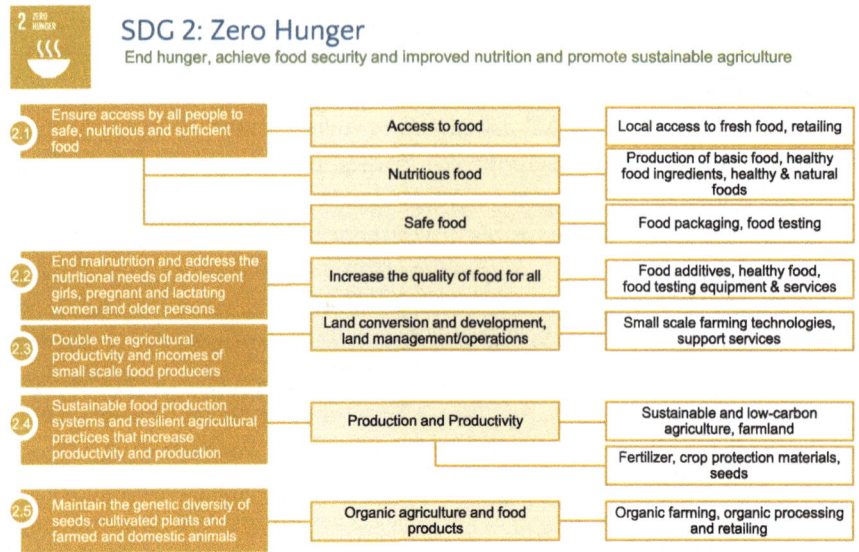

Fig. 5.3 An example of the sustainable development taxonomy with regard to SDG 2: Zero hunger (*Source* PGGM and APG)

Reporting on Impacts Required a New Tool

PGGM wanted to go deeper than just estimating pure revenue exposure by assessing the actual impact of the companies on sustainable development. However, many of these companies do not provide information about positive impacts. This is why PGGM's external fund manager partnered with the Harvard School of Public Health, the City University of New York and Wageningen University to model the positive impacts of particular companies. The work included coming up with conversion factors to estimate the impacts of different solutions based on sales figures. In practice, this means looking at a manufacturer of wind turbines and defining how much carbon emissions they avoid per unit of revenues, for example. This so-called conversion factor is then used to approximate the impact of comparable companies.

The impacts that PGGM is able to measure today range from water saved (m^3) and emissions avoided (million tonnes of CO_2) to increases in agricultural yields (tonnes) and number of patients with (improved) access to healthcare.

The work is an ongoing process. Says Klop, '*There are around 100 different solutions related to our four sustainable solution focus areas, and we now have conversion factors for 80 of them. The idea is to continue to improve those conversion factors. However, you can only improve them up to a point, as for further improvement, you need disaggregated corporate data that is competition-sensitive.'*

Adds Snijdewind, '*In addition to these revenue-to-impact models, we challenge companies to measure and report on their impact themselves. By measuring their own impact, companies can adjust their strategy. This will elevate impact from an accidental result to one of the companies' strategic non-financial targets (as an addition to the existing financial ones).'*

In addition, PGGM encourages companies to collaborate with each other. Says Snijdewind, '*Impact measurement will benefit tremendously from a consistent approach. This is why we also engage with investee companies to ask them to collaborate on setting up sector-specific and industry-wide indicators. By having companies collaborate on developing such indicators, odds will increase that this approach will be adopted by the entire sector, that the comparability will improve and that the risk of greenwashing will decrease. We are currently seeing the first positive signs of such collaborations in some sectors, for example, in the pharmaceutical sector.'*

Assessing Companies' Net Contribution to Sustainability Is Complicated

When selecting investees, you have to balance a range of impacts and ESG considerations. Says Klop, '*For example, if you take companies contributing positively to food security, they may use a lot of water – and investors have to navigate to balance positive and negative impacts, as well as downside risks.'*

Another key aspect to consider is that the same products and services (e.g. technological appliances) will not be considered as a sustainable development solution everywhere, but impacts are rather defined by their context.

> *For example, the actual impact of wind power as a climate solution is very different between France, where it would replace nuclear energy, and Poland, where it would replace coal-generated power. And it gets even more complicated for healthcare: would any healthcare improvement contribute to the sustainable development goals or would this be the case only in countries where people currently don't have access to healthcare, for example, comparing the situation between Finland and Bangladesh?*

Developing and refining decision rules takes time. Says Klop, '*You need to define each solution separately. For example, building a new road can be a positive sustainable development contribution in Sudan, but perhaps not so much in Sweden.'*

Summary

Based on PGGM's experience, we conclude that an investor can be ambitious and develop new analysis methods in collaboration with other experts in the field (e.g. companies, research organisations and service providers) to model and measure new phenomena for which tools are not yet available. Developing analysis of this scale requires significant resources, but can also take the whole field forward. Measuring sustainable development is a new and unstructured topic, which is why a systematic methodology (in this case, a decision tree) is required for getting started. After this, companies will need to produce rather comparable data on different impact metrics. As a result, an investment organisation aims to identify the kinds of companies among investees that produce net positive solutions to sustainable development challenges.

Background information

PGGM manages approximately EUR 246 billion in assets for Dutch pension funds. PGGM is the in-house asset manager of their largest client, PFZW. The taxonomies defining sustainable solutions to the SDGs were developed as a cooperation between the Dutch pension investors PGGM and APG. They have shared the bulk of the work online, so the results are available for anyone to define the positive impacts of their own investments.

This case description is based on interviews with PGGM's senior responsible investment advisors Piet Klop and Rogier Snijdewind. They are part of PGGM's responsible investment team, which consists of 12 experts.

Summaries of Historical Data and Conclusions

Sustainability Ratings

Investors have access to broad sustainability ratings that combine various perspectives. They often consist of subcategories of themes that are material for the sector of the company to be rated, such as the management of water risks and the sustainable procurement of raw materials, as well as employee relations.

In addition to broad sustainability ratings, investors also have access to individual themes and sectors, such as company-specific ratings focusing on climate impacts, human rights or the production of meat and fish.

Violations of International Norms

Many investors in Europe, for example, require their investees to address any sustainability issues and comply with the Global Compact initiative in particular, including its underlying international norms concerning human and labour rights and the prevention of environmental damage and large-scale corruption.

Suspected cases of companies' sustainability issues become public through the media and non-governmental organisations' reports. Many of the suspected cases are ultimately not investigated[7] by an official body, such as the OECD National Contact Point, which is why investors have to assess which cases are particularly serious. Providers of sustainability analysis services help investors identify cases where there is reason to believe that the company has violated international norms, as well as helping them determine the severity of the cases.

The norms of international law are agreements between states and have therefore not been prepared with investor analysis in mind. For this reason, service providers and investors must use discretion in determining in which cases companies can be held accountable for violations of international norms—in other words, which allegations are sufficiently credible and in which cases the company is also responsible for the impacts caused by other operators in the value chain, especially by suppliers, subcontractors or customers. Different service providers may interpret the same cases differently, and investors may also come to different conclusions.

In assessing violations of international norms, one issue that gives rise to differing interpretations is related to the ***responsibility of the financier***. Banks can be held responsible for project financing directed at non-compliant projects. General financing for operations, on the other hand, is not usually considered to be in violation of international norms, as the lending is targeted at the company's operations as a whole and not directly at an individual controversial project. There are also other forms of financing, and investors and service providers may have differing interpretations concerning individual cases and the responsibility of the financier.

The responsibility of each operator must be determined to identify which companies are found guilty of violating international norms. Service providers usually determine a specific ownership share that limits the responsibility of various group companies for issues caused by another unit. In addition, responsibility for products does not usually end with their sale, as the manufacturer can also be held accountable, at least to some extent, if they manufacture products for a purpose that violates international norms.

The assessment of improvements achieved is particularly important in determining when the development has been sufficient and the company is no longer being held accountable for violations of international norms. Some service providers closely monitor the details of the improvements implemented and, for example, the views of third parties, while others may rely more on official decisions and wait for guidelines provided by, for example, the OECD National Contact Point on any violations of the instructions and whether the issues have been resolved.

Some service providers issue recommendations for investors and assessments related to cases concerning the need and opportunities for engagement, as well as reporting on the progress of engagement and development measures.

Environmental Costs

The environmental costs of business operations, such as the consumption of natural resources and negative impacts on the environment, are often partly borne by society. Such impacts are known as externalities.[8] In addition, environmental damage can lead to legal proceedings, in which case companies have to pay for the damage afterwards.

Few companies report comprehensively on the negative impacts of their operations in monetary terms, and the rough modelling of these figures requires the combination of company-specific data with estimates of costs for society. For example, data on air pollution (particulate matter emissions) caused by business operations can be combined with the related healthcare costs. However, proving that a causality is an externality of an individual company is rare in practice (for example, that asthma among the residents of nearby areas is caused by an individual company), and the state may bear the costs related to public health. The assessment of externalities is based on a large number of assumptions, which are also affected by the standard of living in the countries of operation: the price of a similar externality may vary between countries.

In the analyses, environmental costs are compared with the companies' financial key figures, such as net sales and the EBITDA, and investors can assess risks related to business operations based on this. In interpreting the results, it is key to assess the likelihood that the company will have to bear more of the costs of the negative environmental impacts of its operations in the future.

Case: Evli Bank's ESG Tool

In 2015, the Finnish Evli Bank set a goal for portfolio managers to consider sustainability aspects in investment processes related to both equities and corporate bonds. To achieve this, the company deemed it paramount for portfolio managers to have easy access to sustainability information. For this reason, the company developed a tool that combines sustainability information with fund holdings.

Evli designed and implemented an ESG tool through cooperation between quantitative analysts, portfolio managers and the person in charge of sustainable investing. According to Outi Helenius, Head of Sustainability, the ESG tool is intended for portfolio managers, which is why they were asked to share what sustainability aspects they consider important.

The Sustainability Tool Collects Key Data for Portfolio Managers and Customers

The ESG tool provides portfolio managers with an overview of the sustainability of a fund, even at a quick glance. In addition, fund-specific reports on sustainability information are published on the company's website. In other words, the portfolio managers see the same information in their tool that has been presented in public ESG reports (Figs. 5.4 and 5.5), as well as more detailed company-specific information.[9]

Evli's sustainability tool uses sustainability data acquired from MSCI. The data includes information about the company's sustainability rating, the share of any controversial sectors of its net sales and information about ESG issues. Based on the data provided by MSCI, Evli has colour-coded companies' sustainability ratings, as well as any companies that have violated international norms. For example, for Global Compact principles, the codes are green (pass), yellow (MSCI watchlist) and red (fail).

The ESG Tool Contains Information About Companies' Sustainability and Potential Problems

The tool enables Evli's portfolio managers to examine funds' sustainability choices from various perspectives:

Sector-specific ratings: The tool shows the distribution of the fund's investments by sector, as well as the sustainability ratings of companies selected in accordance with the sector (Fig. 5.6).

Company-specific information about sustainability and potential problems: The tool contains company-specific information about sustainability ratings and any issues related to companies' operations, for example, as well as theme-specific information about the management of climate impacts

Summary

The fund's ESG Scores

Overall score	A
Environment	BBB
Social Responsibility	BBB
Governance	A

Thermometer of the fund's ESG Scores

Excellent
Very Good
Good
Average
Satisfactory
Weak
Very Weak

Rating	%
AAA	4.3%
AA	18.4%
A	24.0%
BBB	17.3%
BB	0.0%
B	2.6%
CCC	0.0%
Not rated	33.3%

Holdings rated B or CCC

ESG rating	Company	Weight
B	Troax Group AB (publ)	2.6%

The fund's ESG Scores are market value-weighted averages of the MSCI ESG ratings. The ESG ratings of the fund's underlying companies measure and analyse companies' material risks and opportunities arising from environmental, social and governance issues.

Company-specific ESG ratings are weighted averages for sustainability aspects that are material for each sector. Within their respective sectors, companies are rated from the best (AAA) to the worst (CCC). Theme-specific ratings (environment, social responsibility, governance) reflect the weighted average of the ratings that each company has received for the area in question and that have affected the companies' overall scores in terms of sustainability ratings.

Fig. 5.4 Summary of the ESG profile of the Evli Swedish Small Cap fund on 3 September 2018. *Note* The Evli website provides access to ESG reports on funds. The reports include the sustainability ratings of funds, their distribution and the classification of funds in accordance with how well they comply with the Global Compact principles. More detailed information about the sustainability of fund investments, such as distribution by sector, as well as the ESG scores of individual investments and notes about minor sustainability issues, can only be accessed by Evli's sustainability team

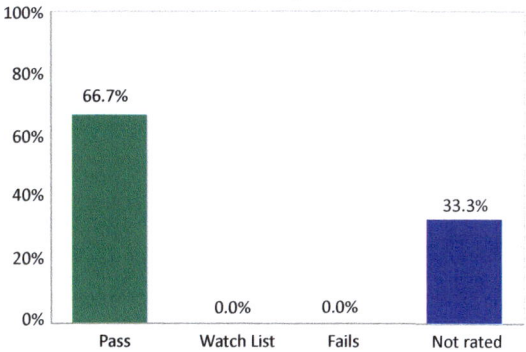

The classification indicates whether the investees of the fund comply with the Global Compact initiative for corporate social responsibility. The principles are based on the UN Universal Declaration of Human Rights, the ILO Declaration on Fundamental Principles and Rights at Work, the Rio Declaration on Environment and Development and the UN Convention against Corruption.

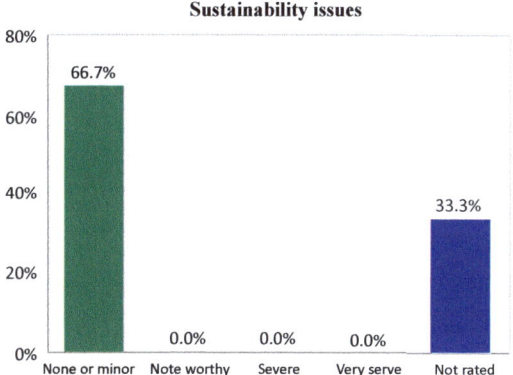

The screening of sustainability issues indicates whether the investees of the fund have notable controversies related to their operations and/or products, as well as describing the severity of the social or environmental impacts of the controversy.

Fig. 5.5 Summary of the Evli Swedish Small Cap Fund's compliance with the Global Compact principles, as well as sustainability issues, on 3 September 2018. *Note* Reproduced by permission of MSCI ESG Research LLC ©2021 MSCI ESG Research LLC All rights reserved

and any use of child labour (Table 5.2). In addition, portfolio managers have access to longer explanations concerning the underlying ratings information.

'*Thanks to the company-specific information included in the tool, our portfolio managers are aware of why a specific company has a poor rating, for example, or what any violations of the Global Compact principles are related to, and can use this information when making investment decisions,*' says Helenius

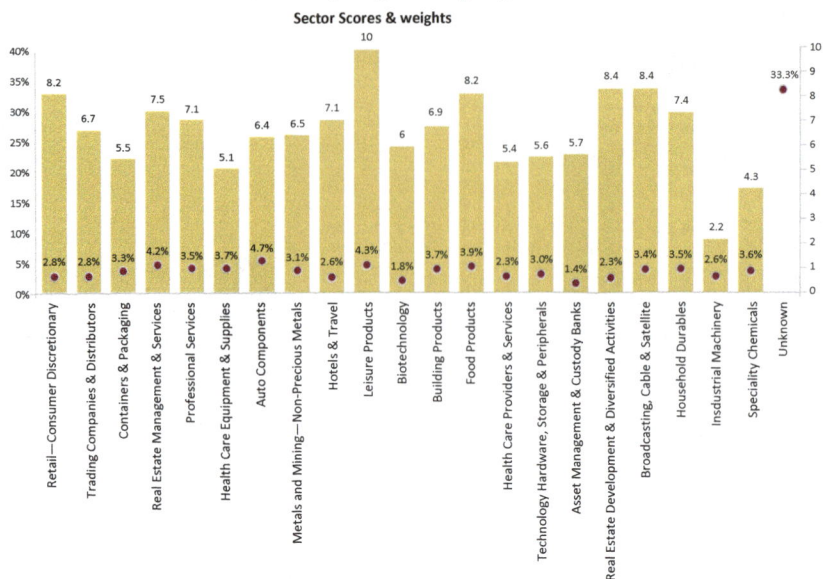

Sustainability ratings and weightings of sectors

In Figure 5.6, the average sector-specific ESG rating of the investees is presented above the columns (scale 1–10). The ratings are based directly on company-specific performance, risks and opportunities in areas of sustainability that are material for the sector. The tool also shows the weight (in terms of monetary amounts) of investments made in various sectors in proportion to all of the fund's investments.

Fig. 5.6 Sector distribution and sustainability ratings: Evli Swedish Small Cap Fund, 3 September 2018. *Note* Reproduced by permission of MSCI ESG Research LLC ©2021 MSCI ESG Research LLC All rights reserved

Controversial operations: The tool also provides portfolio managers with extensive information about various controversial products and services, such as whether the fund has invested in companies that generate at least part of their net sales from what are known as controversial operations, including tobacco, alcohol, weapons and adult entertainment.

The information also makes it possible to set a limit for net sales if there is a need to exclude from the fund any controversial operations, such as companies that generate more than 20% of their net sales from business operations related to alcohol.

The Process of Sustainable Investing Is Built Around the Analysis Tool

According to Evli's experiences, comprehensive ESG data and the use of the ESG tool make operations more efficient: they help the company target analysis resources, as well as enabling portfolio managers to see immediately why a specific investment has a poor sustainability rating, for example.

Table 5.2 Sector distribution and sector-specific sustainability ratings: Evli Swedish Small Cap Fund, 3 September 2018[a]

INDUSTRY	Score	AAA	AA	A	BBB	BB	B	CCC	Not Rated	Total
Retail - Consumer Discretionary	8.2		2.8 %							2.8 %
Trading Companies & Distributors	6.7			2.8 %						2.8 %
Container & Packaging	5.5				3.3 %					3.3 %
Real Estate Management & Services	7.5		2.5 %	1.8 %						4.2 %
Professional Services	7.1			3.5 %						3.5 %
Health Care Equipment & Supplies	5.1				3.7 %					3.7 %
Auto Components	6.4			4.7 %						4.7 %
Metals and Mining—Non-Precious Metals	6.5			3.1 %						3.1 %
Hotels & Travel	7.1			2.6 %						2.6 %
Leisure Products	10.0	4.3 %								4.3 %
Biotechnology	6.0			1.8 %						1.8 %
Building Products	6.9			3.7 %						3.7 %
Food Products	8.2		3.9 %							3.9 %
Health Care Providers & Services	5.4				2.3 %					2.3 %
Technology Hardware, Storage & Peripherals	5.6				3.0 %					3.0 %
Asset Management & Custody Banks	5.7				1.4 %					1.4 %
Real Estate Development & Diversified Activities	8.4		2.3 %							2.3 %
Broadcasting, Cabel & Satellite	8.4		3.4 %							3.4 %
Household Durables	7.4		3.5 %							3.5 %
Industrial Machinery	2.2						2.6 %			2.6 %
Speciality Chemicals	4.3				3.6 %					3.6 %
Unknown									33.3 %	33.3 %
Total		4.3 %	18.4 %	24.0 %	17.3 %	0.0 %	2.6 %	0.0 %	33.3 %	100.0 %

In addition to the data provided in Figure 5.6, Table 5.2 presents sector-specific relative sustainability ratings, which are described in letters. Unlike numerical values, the ratings CCC–AAA have been scaled in accordance with the sector in such a way that each sector has companies with both high and low ratings.

In addition, company-specific ratings for the fund's investments are available in the version of the tool that is intended for internal use, including not only the overall score but also theme-specific sustainability scores (the environment, social responsibility and governance), as well as information about when the ratings were last updated. Any detected violations of international norms, as well as less serious sustainability issues, have also been described specific to each company. In addition, as special themes, Evli has included in the tool information about any company-specific issues related to child labour and climate aspects. Evli's portfolio managers also have access to brief company-specific descriptions as part of the same tool, as well as to more extensive company-specific sustainability reports through an online portal.

[a]Reproduced by permission of MSCI ESG Research LLC ©2021 MSCI ESG Research LLC All rights reserved

Evli's sustainable investment team reviews the sustainability information related to each fund quarterly. Sometimes the monitoring reveals companies that have, according to the service provider's interpretation, violated international norms, for example. In such cases, the portfolio manager is required to provide the sustainable investment team with an explanation of why the portfolio manager has invested in the company in question and what is their view of the suspected norm violation.

Companies' violations of international norms are processed by Evli's sustainable investment team, which evaluates both the cases and the justifications provided by the portfolio manager for the investment decision. The sustainable investment team can decide to initiate engagement measures or require a portfolio manager to divest investments. Evli also has a sustainable investment executive group which meets every three months or so. The executive group decides on principles and practices related to Evli's responsible investment. The executive group consists of the Chief Executive Officer, the Chief Investment Officer and the heads of the following units: Legal, Risk Management and Compliance; Institutional Clients; Private Clients; Equities; Fixed Income; Discretionary Mandates; and Sustainability. The executive group does not have a designated chair, and decisions are taken jointly, by vote if necessary.

Helenius highlights the importance of internal and external monitoring: '*As a result of this process for dealing with violations of international norms, combined with public reporting online, portfolio managers are more aware of ESG factors and take them into consideration as part of investment decisions.*' Before the issue is processed by the sustainable investment team, the portfolio manager may also sell the holding in the company if the risk begins to seem particularly high as part of a more extensive assessment.

In addition to processing violations of international norms, Evli's sustainable investment team regularly examines the sustainability scores of funds and compares them with the ESG scores of benchmark indices used for monitoring returns. This makes it possible to evaluate whether the portfolio managers have chosen, from among potential investments, companies with higher or lower ratings on average.

The sustainable investment team also compares sustainability ratings between Evli's funds. Says Helenius, '*The comparison of sustainability between funds is not as meaningful as the comparison of the funds' ratings with indices. For example, funds investing in the emerging markets have relatively low sustainability ratings, as companies operating in the emerging markets receive lower scores in MSCI's assessments, because they involve higher sustainability risks. For this reason, we cannot require emerging market funds to have sustainability ratings as good as those of other funds.*'

Evli's sustainability team reviews ratings in general and assesses companies with a poor score on a case-by-case basis. However, Evli has not determined criteria for addressing investments with a poor score, as a company with a low score may be committed to improving its sustainability-related processes and practices, meaning that its current sustainability rating does not reflect its outlook in terms of sustainability. Therefore, the portfolio manager is responsible for assessing the sustainability of potential investments before the investment decision is made.

Sustainability Analysis Requires Several Sources of Information and Interpretation

For Evli, the sustainability tool lays the foundation for the process of sustainable investing. However, it is not the only source of ESG analysis. Using sustainability ratings in connection with investment decisions is voluntary for the company's investment team, and portfolio managers also use other sources of information at their discretion—what is most important is that sustainability aspects are considered.

Helenius describes the role of the ESG database as follows:

> *The ESG database alone is not a sufficient source of information for sustainability analysis, because we cannot expect the data to be absolutely correct. It is a relatively mechanical way to assess investments that focuses on risks and historical data in particular. Portfolio managers also use other sources of information, such as traditional investment analyses produced by banks, as they see fit. In addition, direct discussions with companies also provide a more broad-based overview.*

Company-specific ratings are not available for all investments, but the portfolio manager is responsible for looking into ESG even in these cases. The sources used for assessments vary between portfolio managers. The portfolio manager of the Evli Swedish Small Cap Fund says that they use data collected by the Bloomberg investment information service from sustainability reports and several ESG data providers. Sustainability aspects are part of quantitative and qualitative assessments made by portfolio managers. In addition to using the data included in the ESG tool, Evli's sustainable investment team monitors certain climate change indicators for funds, such as the carbon intensity of investments, the proportion of coal revenue in companies' net sales, possible fossil reserve holdings and low-carbon assessment ratings.

The following example illustrates the ***ambiguity of sustainability analysis***. It concerns a European infrastructure company involved in global construction projects.

- The ESG service provider used by Evli had noted that the company did not comply with the Global Compact principles in connection with its hydropower plant construction project in Ethiopia.

- The hydropower plant built by the company is managed by an Ethiopian state-owned electricity company. An international non-governmental organisation filed a complaint with the OECD about the construction company's operations. The complaint concerned suspected non-compliance with the OECD Guidelines for Multinational Companies.
- According to the complaint, the river was not overflowing in the same way as before, now that the hydropower plant was in operation. In addition, changes in the water level meant that the land along the river could no longer be cultivated in the way that it had been cultivated by the indigenous population.
- Because of the complaint, the company had been downgraded to the lowest category—that is, a violator of international norms—in the analysis used by the ESG tool.
- Evli's sustainable investment team assessed the case, and it was decided that the company should be contacted. Discussion with the company went well, and after telephone and email conversations, the company provided Evli with all the documents related to the case that the company had submitted to the OECD, proving that it had conducted environmental impact assessments in line with the OECD Guidelines. The company also explained that diversion gates had been installed in the hydropower plant to enable water level management in the river.
- Evli stated that it did not deem the builder responsible for the hydropower plant operator not using the diversion gates and therefore decided to allow the investment.
- After studying the case, 18 months later, the OECD court in the company's domicile interpreted the case to the same effect as Evli and released the company from liability. A year later, the record of the company's non-compliant operations was removed from the data in the ESG tool, when the service provider drew the same conclusion.

Evli also paid attention to the fact that not all ESG service providers had deemed the infrastructure construction company to have violated international norms. This illustrates how these cases leave considerable room for interpretation. This is also a challenge for Evli in the sense that some institutional clients use different service providers, and these service providers occasionally highlight cases of violations of international norms that have not been detected during the analyses used by Evli. In addition, Evli can engage concerning violations of international norms about which reliable information has been provided by customers—however, such companies are not visible in Evli's ESG tool, as the tool is based solely on the database of the service provider used by Evli.

The criteria for the selection of an ESG service provider include not only quality but also practical aspects, such as the coverage of the data in relation to Evli's investments, as well as the fact that the data is provided in a format that makes it possible to use the same database internally and for customer reporting.

The ESG Analysis Tool Has Been Further Developed

In the first phase, Evli's fund-specific tool was created in an Excel-based format and contained only information about the funds' current investments. The tool has been further improved since its launch in 2017. The data included in the tool has been exported to the portfolio management system, which enables a portfolio manager to view sustainability ratings in the same system when assessing potential investments. This also makes it possible to build real-time controls for sustainability-related exclusions.

In 2020, the ESG tools were completely renewed and transferred to the PowerBI analytics programme. One of the improvements was to include the benchmark index ESG information for each fund, which enables portfolio managers to better compare data against the benchmarks. In addition, climate-focused sustainability data from MSCI and data related to controversies have been purchased from another ESG data provider, ISS ESG. Both of these data sets have been included in the new tools.

Sources of forward-looking data for sustainability analysis will be explored next. Says Helenius, '*I would like portfolio managers to be able to assess how well investments perform in a 1.5-degree world. Individual indicators – such as the carbon footprint and the proportion of coal revenue in net sales, as well as companies' holdings in fossil reserves – do not show this.*'

Summary

Evli's example shows that even a Finnish investment organisation with reasonable human resources is able to implement and harmonise sustainable investing in terms of portfolio management and investment decisions. The effective targeting of analysis resources is important, particularly in smaller investment organisations. Evli has developed a relatively simple and visual model to be used as a tool by portfolio managers, based on their needs. This enables the sustainable investment strategy of the investment organisation to be taken into account by portfolio managers in their day-to-day operations. The model saves time for the sustainability team, as portfolio managers immediately see the most common reasons for companies' sustainability ratings, allowing discussion time to be used for more in-depth assessments.

In addition, open communication on the investment organisation's website helps customers study the sustainability information related to funds.

> **Background information**
>
> The Finnish Evli Bank manages around EUR 13 billion in investment assets across 28 funds. The case description is based on an interview with Outi Helenius, Head of Sustainability at Evli. This description discusses fund reporting and the first version of Evli's ESG tool, as well as further developments since its introduction. The case description concerns Evli's funds that engage in what is known as fundamental analysis—that is, selecting investments based on company-specific analysis. Evli also has factor funds, where the investment philosophy is based on the use of certain factors combined with systematic ESG practices through the best-in-class approach, climate-related indicators and exclusion. These funds also use the same sustainability data as has been discussed in this chapter.[10]

Forward-Looking Summaries and Conclusions

The previous section dealt with ESG analysis tools focusing on the past. Tools that support forward-looking sustainability analysis are discussed next.

Preparedness for Climate Change

To identify future company-specific climate risks and opportunities, it is essential to understand how well climate change considerations have been taken into account in companies' strategies and business operations. As yet, company-specific analyses focusing on future climate risks and opportunities are best available for certain sectors with high climate impacts, such as electric utilities, cement manufacturers, forestry and mining companies and the chemical industry. The assessments concern the fight against climate change in particular, as well as the related changes in companies' operating environments and requirements. The reports also provide some information about concrete changes caused by climate change, such as risks related to the sufficient availability of water.

Climate Scenarios

Climate scenarios can be used in modelling future climate profiles and risks of investments. Scenario modelling helps investors outline various options concerning the *future climate impacts* of investments and the *financial impacts of limiting climate change* on companies as investments. For the time being, investors have access to analysis tools for modelling environmental impacts in particular. However, even in this respect, advanced analysis is available for only a few sectors, mainly covering electricity companies, the automotive industry, mining operations and the extraction of fossil fuels.

Scenarios focusing on future environmental impacts assess the impacts of companies' business operations on climate in the coming years and how these impacts are reflected in relation to various global warming scenarios—that is, by how many degrees would the global temperature increase if the companies in the investment portfolio represented their entire sector's climate impacts. The modelling takes into account the companies' initial situation and their known investments, as well as the modelling of future technologies and energy sources that would lead to different global warming scenarios.

In practice, the scenario modelling of environmental impacts means that, for example, electric utilities' production capacity for various energy sources at the time of examination, as well as their known investments, are compared with the two-degree scenario of the International Energy Association (IEA). It describes how energy production would be formed in the coming years from various energy sources in a world where global warming was limited to a maximum of two degrees. When the company-specific information is made proportional to the investments, it is possible to roughly estimate whether the investments are in line with the two-degree target at a specific point in time in the future.

Analyses use various time perspectives and usually concern at least the next five years. In practice, the situation keeps changing—for example, more coal-fired power plants may be closed than is known at the time of the analysis. Political decisions and rapid technological development (a technology becomes more affordable) may significantly change companies' plans, but such developments are difficult to predict. Investors may also make changes to their holdings, even if analytical tools do not take this into account.

In scenarios focusing on financial impacts, the emphasis is on how limiting climate change would affect the financial returns on investments. Such assessments use a specific (shadow) price for all companies' greenhouse gas emissions (e.g. EUR 100 per tCO_2e), for example, and examine how the price would affect returns on investments.

Modelling climate scenarios for investments helps investors outline the *future* climate profile of investments, but the modelling methodologies and the initial data used vary between operators and, as yet, only consider relatively rough differences between various technologies, fossil fuel sources and geographical areas. However, the tools are developing rapidly, and their use may already be an interesting addition to other sources of information.

Combination of Various Sustainability Aspects in Analysis

In addition to applying commonly used sustainability ratings and analyses, investors have adopted other ESG analysis tools in recent years. The use of multifaceted data is based on an increased understanding of the fact that the mere assessment of risks and impacts arising from the company's processes is not enough in sustainability analysis. Future operating conditions are also affected by development costs and sustainability trends, such as the much-discussed climate change, that is independent of the companies.

*At Swedbank Robur, our sustainability analysis takes a holistic view of companies, incorporating a range of important aspects, their interlinkages and combined overall impact on business operations. In addition, portfolio management is about predicting the future, and more information about the future can be obtained by examining the direction in which a company is headed and at what speed. In terms of this model, challenging developments include the **emergence of super-weighted aspects**, such as climate change in particular, or the rapid unpredictable changes caused by the Covid-19 pandemic. Different analytical approaches can lead to vastly different conclusions. For example, in terms of climate, do investors penalise a steel production company for its high carbon emissions, or do they support the company because of its best-in-class offering of sustainable products and low-carbon R&D commitments?*

We believe that these products, capex (capital expense), momentum and organisational aspects need to be considered together in order to land on the right decision, rather than taking the silo approach and basing investment decisions only on individual figures, such as current carbon emissions. The purpose of our analysis is to take these various aspects into consideration and give them appropriate weight.

Shane Chaplin, Sustainability Analyst, Swedbank Robur
(investment assets around EUR 100 billion)

Notes

1. Weighted carbon intensity is the indicator recommended by the international TCFD framework for climate reporting.
2. Market value may fluctuate even more than net sales, even without a direct connection to production volumes. For this reason, changes in carbon intensity do not necessarily reflect changes in production efficiency.
3. In countries (e.g. the Main List of the London Stock Exchange) where the calculation of carbon footprints is required by law, it is mandatory only in Scope 1 or in Scopes 1 and 2. The quality of data and the availability of data from the supply chain continue to pose challenges in Scope 3.

4. Scopes 1 and 2 may be sufficient, but they do not provide a comprehensive overview. It is best to assess case by case when Scope 3 is significant. The increasing use of purchased services and outsourcing also 'outsources' emissions to Scope 3. Some service providers report on their direct emissions beyond the GHG Protocol, including biogenic emissions from biomass combustion, for example, in addition to fossil emissions. The inclusion of biogenic emissions has a significant impact on the carbon intensity figures of forest companies, for example, but does not take into account the fact that the raw material is renewable and that the wood sequestered carbon from the atmosphere during growth (this is known as the carbon sink effect).

5. For example, EU emissions trading covers around 45% of all greenhouse gas emissions generated in the area. There are regional differences between emissions trading systems in their coverage (which sectors are included) and pricing (the prices of allowances vary, as does the number of free allowances issued to companies).

6. The share of sustainable development investments is reported in key sustainable investment surveys: the PRI, which is widely supported by investors, and the AODP (Asset Owner Disclosure Project), which concerns major institutional investors. The standardisation of the indicator is in progress, and each investor currently uses discretion in terms of which solutions are sustainable development solutions, what are the criteria for sustainable development investments (e.g. the extent to which the investee's business operations should be related to sustainable development goals) and how significant the positive impact should be.

7. A National Contact Point investigates cases reported by various parties.

8. Externalities are the positive or negative impacts of financial activity on third parties that are not directly related to the financial activity.

9. The Evli website provides access to ESG reports on funds. The reports include the sustainability ratings of funds, their distribution and the classification of funds in accordance with how well they comply with the Global Compact principles. More detailed information about the sustainability of fund investments, such as distribution by sector, as well as the ESG scores of individual investments and notes about minor sustainability issues, can only be accessed by Evli's sustainability team.

10. Factor funds exclude coal-mining companies from their investees, in addition to excluding 2% of the world's highest-emission companies and 25% of the most carbon-intensive companies in each sector.

6

Sustainability of Various Investment Products

Fund Selection

To assess the sustainability of funds, investors compare the funds' sustainability principles and practices with their own. In fund investments, the selection phase is particularly important, because opportunities to affect the practices of the fund are limited[1] after the investment has been made. A fund investor evaluates the way in which a fund implements sustainability through investment decisions and active ownership, as well as the competence of the asset manager of the fund, resourcing and reporting to investors.

The assessment of a fund's sustainability is affected by whether the fund is managed actively or passively. A fund that actively chooses its investments can be expected to consider sustainability analysis in investment decisions, while a passive fund invests in a selected index, such as a general index or an index focusing on sustainable companies.

Active ownership can be exercised by the asset managers of both active and passive funds. Index investments are managed by major financial companies, such as BlackRock, which often have significant holdings in many companies around the world and are among the largest shareholders in several companies. For this reason, at least some of the managers of index-based investments have become active as owners through general meetings and other engagement. Active ownership is emphasised, as (passive) asset managers making index-based investments are often almost eternal owners, and their operations have been referred to as 'marriage without the option of divorce'—you simply

© The Author(s), under exclusive license to Springer Nature
Switzerland AG 2021
H. Silvola and T. Landau, *Sustainable Investing*,
https://doi.org/10.1007/978-3-030-71489-5_6

have to get along. For this reason, asset management companies benefit from promoting the sustainability and good governance of investments.

Sustainability as Part of Funds' Investment Decisions and Sustainability Ratings for Funds

The principles of sustainable investments for funds usually describe the key guidelines applied by the funds, such as the consideration of sustainability aspects in investment decisions and the criteria for exclusion. Fund-specific sustainability ratings can be used in the assessment of their practical implementation.

The sustainability ratings of funds are based on company-specific sustainability ratings. The sustainability fund ratings of Morningstar, a company specialising in the assessment of funds, follow the company-specific ratings of Sustainalytics, while MSCI's fund ratings are summaries of the service provider's own company-specific sustainability ratings. Sustainability ratings are available for funds for which the service provider has sufficiently recent information about holdings and for which company-specific sustainability ratings are available for a sufficiently large proportion of the holdings.

Funds' sustainability ratings provide a relative estimate of the number of investments with a high sustainability rating in the fund in comparison with similar benchmark funds, such as funds investing in large European companies. In addition, more detailed sub-ratings are available that can be used to examine the fund's possible investments in sustainable development solutions or companies that have violated international norms. Comparisons of this type can help investors better understand how the fund applies its principles in practice.

The methodological choices behind fund ratings contribute to the ratings, which is why the ratings are only indicative. Their key strength is that they provide additional information to support fund selection, meaning that they indicate whether the sustainability analysis has had an impact on the investment decisions in practice. *In general, it can be assumed that companies with high ratings manage sustainability aspects better on average than companies with the poorest ratings. For this reason, fund ratings provide a relatively good, albeit slightly rough, overview of the level of sustainability of the companies selected for the funds.* Ratings can also be used as background information in discussions with the asset manager of the fund.

In other words, fund ratings do not reflect the whole truth about how sustainable the companies in which a fund has invested are in comparison with similar funds. Fund ratings prepared by various service providers may produce different results for the same fund because of differences in the underlying company-specific ratings. Investors may also justifiably interpret companies' sustainability differently from the service providers behind the fund rating.

Fund ratings describe the average sustainability profile of the investments in relation to other funds in the benchmark group. Discretion is used in determining the benchmarks, and a diverse range of funds can be included in the benchmark group. In addition, the results are scaled in fund ratings in such a way that differences are created between funds in the same benchmark group. In practice, however, the differences between the funds may be limited. This concerns, in particular, investments in small market areas where differences between companies' sustainability are minor (e.g. a fund investing in large Finnish companies).

Even a *thematic fund specialising in sustainability can have a poor rating*, because ratings are combinations of various aspects. A company offering products or services to solve sustainability challenges—for example, a company focusing on clean technology—can be included in a thematic fund because of the positive impacts of its main business operations. However, the same company may have shortcomings in the sustainability processes of its own operations or the related reporting, which is why its rating may not be particularly good. In other words, a poor overall rating does not directly indicate whether a fund has selected its investments in line with its theme.

Active Ownership—the Methods of Engagement Are Provided in Reports

Many investors seek to influence their investees to promote sustainability. If an investor only studies holdings in the fund, it may seem that investments are also made in companies that violate international norms, even though the asset manager says that they expect compliance from investees. In practice, however, the asset manager may primarily seek to engage to promote sustainability and remain as a shareholder even in companies that have experienced challenges. As fund sustainability ratings are in most cases based solely on information about holdings, the examination of fund ratings does not provide information about any engagement concerning the investments in question.

Information about active engagement by funds can be obtained directly from the companies managing the funds. In addition, comparisons can be made on the Principles for Responsible Investment (PRI) website using investor-specific reports[2] in which the signatories report on their sustainable investing practices annually. Investors report separately on their level of participation in votes at general meetings, as well as providing examples of engagement with companies to promote sustainability.

Assessment of Competence and Resourcing

Many funds state that they take sustainability, or ESG, into account in selecting investees. Investors would like to know who does this better than everyone else—in other words, who is particularly good at managing risks and identifying opportunities. The assessment of this based solely on materials available in writing is challenging, as the principles and reports related to different funds may resemble one another.

In assessing the level of sustainability, one of the indications is the number of personnel participating in sustainable investing and their experience and roles in the organisation, as well as the service providers used in the management of the fund. In addition, a good way to assess the level of ESG is access to examples of the fund's sustainability analysis concerning its investments—as far as possible, specifically analyses of companies selected by the investor customer that seem particularly challenging in terms of sustainability.

Reporting to Investors and Public Principles

Investors can use reports prepared by asset managers to monitor the implementation and development of sustainable investing. The most extensive reports provide information about topical sustainable themes and their processing, cases related to the fund, any engagement and the level of participation in general meetings. Some investors also send annual follow-up surveys to their fund managers.

Case: OP Monitors the Practices of External Funds Annually

The Finnish OP Financial Group (later OP) carefully evaluates the fund manager's approach to sustainability before making an investment. In addition to the funds under OP Asset Management, OP invests in funds managed by external international asset managers.

OP Uses Extensive Surveys to Assess Funds' Sustainable Investing

OP examines asset managers' sustainability practices both during the selection phase and through annual monitoring. The most important areas of the survey include ESG analysis and its integration into investment decisions, voting at general meetings and engagement. OP also asks external asset managers about their positions and principles in terms of sustainable investing, resources for sustainability analysis, ESG reporting, risk management and exclusions.

The most recent annual survey focused on the EU's sustainable finance regulations. One of its purposes was to check whether external managers had started to prepare for the upcoming changes. Emphasis was also placed on questions related to climate change to review fund managers' targets and metrics, as well as the fund's exposure to industries accelerating or mitigating climate change. The questions are selected in line with OP's priorities, but they are also checked for consistency against the section concerning funds in the PRI survey. Before making an investment decision, OP conducts an extensive study on the fund, including fund management companies' backgrounds, ownership structure and resourcing.

OP requires ESG practices from all the active equity and fixed-income funds that it brokers, and it determined minimum criteria for new fund investments for this purpose in 2017. The plan was to tighten the criteria by the end of 2020 to account for positive developments among managers and to include climate change. To set an appropriate level of requirements, OP reviewed responses to fund surveys from previous years to ensure that the criteria are sufficiently ambitious, but do not exclude a significant portion of potential external asset managers.

OP's ESG specialists determine the score for each question as follows, for example:

- The more extensively the asset manager votes at the general meetings of the companies included in the fund, the higher the score for *voting at general meetings*.
- *The use of service providers to support ESG practices* brings credibility to sustainable investment activities, which is why points are granted for using service providers.
- *Qualitative or numerical ESG reporting* is an integral part of sustainable investing, which is why more points are granted for extensive ESG reporting.

OP uses survey software to implement the fund survey more efficiently. The software automatically scores fund managers and compiles the results into a table (Fig. 6.1). These results are mainly compiled for internal use at OP, as the responses provided by external asset managers cannot be forwarded to customers.

The survey covers around 27 asset managers of equity funds. All in all, around 101 external asset managers participated, including asset managers in charge of real estate funds, among others. The scoring of the survey is adjusted based on asset class characteristics. For example, the maximum score for fixed income asset managers is lower compared with equity asset managers, because voting at general meetings, for example, is not possible concerning debt investments. Asset managers are assessed in relation to the maximum score for their respective asset classes. The maximum scores are determined based on the preconditions mentioned above for the various asset classes.

However, the survey is not comprehensive. OP's portfolio managers responsible for third-party fund selection meet with asset managers during the year, and ESG specialists have calls with some of the managers. Says Elina Rinta, Senior ESG Specialist, '*The survey alone does not fully capture the depth*

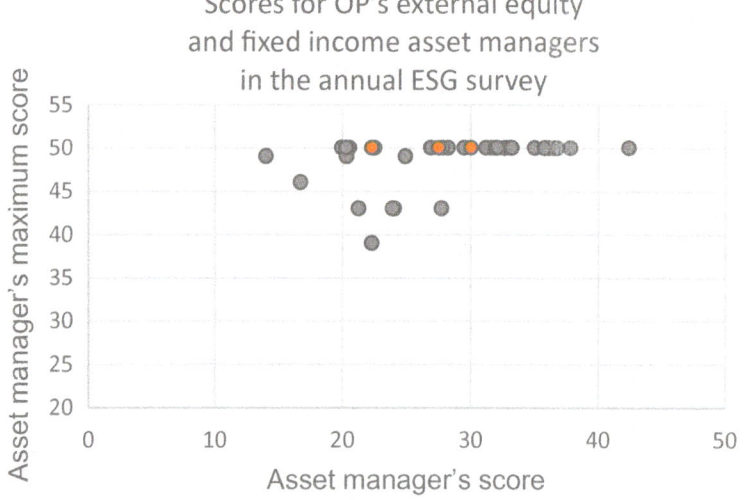

● Asset managers marked with an orange dot have provided the weakest answers with regard to the issues considered most critical by OP.

The dots describe the asset managers' overall performance in the survey. The asset managers who gave the weakest answers to critical questions have been highlighted, because OP seeks to have an impact by engaging at least with these external asset managers over the next 12 months.

Fig. 6.1 External asset managers' scores in the OP survey in 2018

of ESG analysis or engagement. There are many levels of analysis. Then again, some asset managers respond to our survey more boldly, while others are more cautious—which is why, based on the discussions, the asset manager's perceived competence may be better or worse in comparison with the impression provided by the survey. The scores of the survey are an indicative description of the level of sustainable investing. We do not look at ESG as being separate from the overall investment strategy of the fund. It is critical to understand what is relevant for a particular investment strategy.'

Examples of company analysis may be reviewed at the meetings; nevertheless, full clarity of the level of ESG analysis is not necessarily achieved. According to Rinta, some asset managers prepare better for the meetings than others and are therefore able to provide better examples of the analysis. ESG analysis is part of traditional investment analysis and involves a great deal of qualitative analysis in fundamental portfolio management. For this reason, it is not necessarily possible to fully identify the concrete impact of ESG analysis on investment decisions. OP also accepts various ways of conducting sustainability analysis and does not require the same format from everyone.

Meetings and Calls with Asset Managers Are Key Engagement Channels

OP encourages its asset managers to develop sustainable investment practices particularly in areas that OP deems critical. OP communicates directly about these development areas for funds, setting a clear target, which can be a requirement to put the principles of sustainable investing in writing, for example.

Rinta describes the discussions with external asset managers as follows: '*We seek to justify for the asset managers how they will benefit from the further integration of ESG into their investment processes. We are also interested in hearing what type of pressure they are experiencing from other investors. The EU's sustainable finance regulations stress the importance of the finance sector as a key enabler of sustainability in our economy. Engagement with external managers on ESG serves the very same goal.'*

Rinta stresses the importance of engagement in promoting sustainable investment: '*Through our engagement, one of our asset managers in an emerging market became one of the first signatories to the Principles for Responsible Investment in their country. When an asset manager begins to pose questions about sustainability to companies in their country, this can lead to a significant snowball effect on companies in that country over the long term.'*

OP updates the survey annually. Rinta describes the key principle of the survey as follows: '*External fund managers receive a large number of ESG surveys, so we want to keep our survey as concise as possible. This calls for an ability to focus on what is essential, even though it would be easy to just keep adding questions.*'

Passive Managers Are Expected to Promote Sustainability Among Investees

OP also uses external managers for certain passive investments, such as index funds and ETFs. Active ownership is critical for OP, as it uses general indices in addition to internally managed index funds, most of which favour or exclude investments based on ESG characteristics. Assuming all other criteria are indifferent, OP favours an ETF manager whose active ownership practices are more sustainable. With regard to index funds, OP also prioritises fund managers who promote sustainability among investees—and if gaps are identified in annual monitoring, OP engages with managers to help them become active owners.

Summary

The OP case shows that engaging in sustainable investment in Finland alone is not enough. OP's investment organisation is accountable to its customers for its sustainability promises, even for investments through international asset managers as its partners. To assess the operations of these partners, OP asks its asset managers annually about key methods of sustainable investing—that is, the implementation of ESG analysis and its integration into investment decisions, as well as voting at general meetings and engagement. In addition to providing an overview of the development of sustainable investing, the survey exerts positive pressure on asset managers particularly in countries where sustainable investing is not very advanced. In this way, the survey contributes to the spread of sustainable investment practices.

Background information

OP Asset Management, part of OP Financial Group, has around EUR 80 billion (gross) in assets under management. There are 66 OP funds—that is, funds managed by OP Fund Management Company. Of these, 10 are managed by

an external partner. OP Asset Management's exclusion and engagement principles also apply to externally managed OP funds. In addition, hundreds of funds
managed by external asset managers are brokered by OP in the customer portfolios. External asset managers provide customers with a comprehensive range
of global investments. The case description is based on an interview with Elina
Rinta, Senior ESG Specialist at OP.

Sustainability Indices

Stock market indices reflect the general price development in different areas
or segments of the markets. General indices are often formed on the basis of
financial criteria, such as market value or key investment indicators, whereas
sustainability indices include a limited portion of the investments in a general
index (only companies with a high sustainability rating, for example) or
re-adjust investment weights based on separately determined sustainability
criteria.

Common types of sustainability indices include thematic investments,
the most sustainable investments in a specific sector (Best-in-Class) and
exclusion, as well as combinations of these (Table 6.1).

Sustainability indices can be used in:

- **Active investing**: as a benchmark index for comparing the return impacts
  of active investment decisions with general market development.
- **Passive investing**: for building investment products (e.g. exchange-traded
  funds, or ETFs, and index funds).

More Systematic Consideration of ESG in the Selection
of Shares Through a Sustainable Benchmark Index

The value of funds is reported daily, and many long-term investors, such as
pension insurance companies, disclose their returns on investments quarterly
and annually. However, many sustainability aspects, such as climate change,
have an impact on returns over the medium and/or long term—and the
prediction of shorter-term impacts is also challenging. The performance of
individual portfolio managers, teams and entire investment units is often
assessed by comparing returns achieved through active choices with general,
short-term and medium-term market development.

Table 6.1 Key types and examples of sustainability indices

	Sustainability index type		
	Best-in-Class	Exclusion	Themes
Sub-categories	Sustainability ratings • MSCI ESG Leaders Indexes • STOXX ESG Leaders Indices	Violation of international norms and controversial weapons • MSCI ESG Universal Indexes	Carbon footprint and restrictions of fossil fuels • MSCI Low Carbon Target Indexes • MSCI Global Low Carbon Leaders Indexes • S&P Fossil Fuel Free Indices • S&P Fossil Fuel Free Carbon Efficient Indices
	ESG surveys and requests for material • Dow Jones Sustainability Index (DJSI) family	Unethical sectors • STOXX Sustainability ex Alcohol Gambling Tobacco Armaments & Firearms Indices	Climate ratings • STOXX Climate Change Leaders Index
	Special ESG focus • STOXX ESG Environmental/Social/Governance Leaders Indices		Sustainable development solutions • MSCI ACWI Sustainable Impact Index

Note Some of the examples in the table combine characteristics of several index types (e.g. best-in-class and exclusion). In addition to the sustainability index types provided here, there are other index types, such as factor indices combining financial and ESG criteria and indices emphasising companies' good sustainability ratings and positive trend (the level of ESG is improving)

The avoidance of longer-term risks can have a negative impact on short-term returns. Mere concern about short-term underperformance may lead to a situation where an investor lacks the courage to not invest at all in companies with high weightings in the benchmark index, even if they consider these companies challenging in terms of ESG. A company may seem risky based on ESG analyses, while appearing to be large and attractively priced from the perspective of the fund manager's return requirements. If key ESG risks are identified as part of an analysis, the avoidance of these risks can help the investor increase returns if they decide to not invest in such companies or invest less in relation to the index (underweight).

Sustainable benchmark indices can be used in the systematic consideration of sustainability aspects. Their benefits include that irresponsible companies are generally excluded from the index, meaning that investors are not encouraged to invest in such companies (if the rules of the investment organisation even allow for investments outside the benchmark index). On the other hand, from investment personnel's perspective, the use of sustainability indices in setting return requirements may also be fairer: if the company's principles prohibit investing in irresponsible companies in any case, their returns do not affect the assessment of performance when they are not included in the benchmark index.

A sustainability index based on a company-specific ESG study that is available to investors is particularly well-suited for active stock selection: sustainability aspects can be assessed in more detail as part of the analysis, and the views of the index on sustainability do not need to be followed as such. Such indices are available, for example, from MSCI, which uses its own sustainability ratings, as well as from STOXX, which applies the sustainability ratings of Sustainalytics to broad sustainability indices and the climate ratings of CDP to the Climate Change Leaders indices. S&P's indices, such as the Dow Jones Sustainability Index (DJSI), are based on surveys and requests for materials sent to companies, as well as on sustainability analyses based on these.

Sustainable ETF Index Funds Increase Market Shares

At the end of 2017, only around 1% of global exchange-traded funds, or ETFs, had a weighting related to ESG. This proportion continues to be low, but it has increased continuously since then. The marginal share of these investments is affected by the following factors:

- Through index investments, investors seek average market returns, and there is not enough research-based information available about whether sustainable ETFs generate higher or lower returns than investment products based on general indices.
- There is no single standard for sustainability indices. Instead, each service provider prepares their own—and the variation is wide.

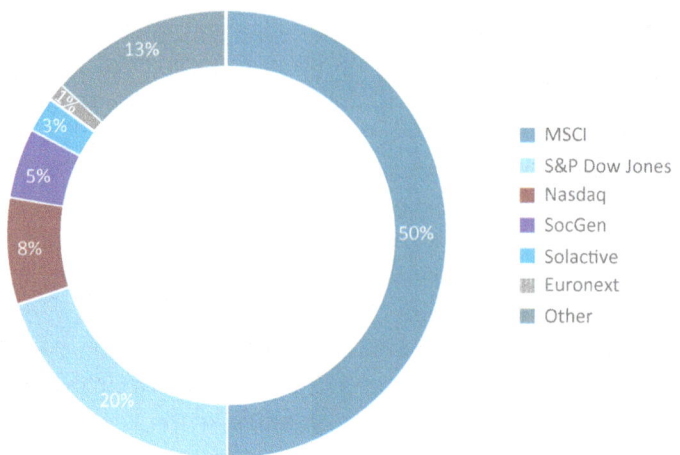

Fig. 6.2 Providers of sustainable exchange-traded funds (ETFs) >1% of assets under management (2017) (*Source* Deutsche Bank, Bloomberg Finance L.P. [Used with permission of Bloomberg Finance L.P.])

- From the perspective of large institutional investors, the challenges also include the lower liquidity of sustainable ETFs compared with conventional ETFs.

In 2017, 70% of the ETF market for broad and comprehensive sustainability indices was invested in products following the indices of the two largest service providers: MSCI and S&P Dow Jones (Fig. 6.2). The key types of sustainable ETFs are presented in Fig. 6.3.[3]

The Choices of the Service Provider Are Emphasised in the Preparation of Sustainability Indices

For investors using sustainability indices, it is key to understand that there is no single standard for preparing a sustainability index. Differences between indices arise not only from the criteria chosen for the index but also from the underlying analysis tools, such as sustainability ratings. For example, many of the tools emphasise the past, meaning that they do not necessarily reflect future sustainability, which is more essential for investors.

Inclusion in a sustainability index does not guarantee that the company is sustainable. For example, when the emissions scandal was exposed in September 2015, Volkswagen was still included in some sustainability indices, while it had been excluded from the MSCI ACWI ESG index, for example, in May 2015. The exclusion was based on issues exposed between 2013 and

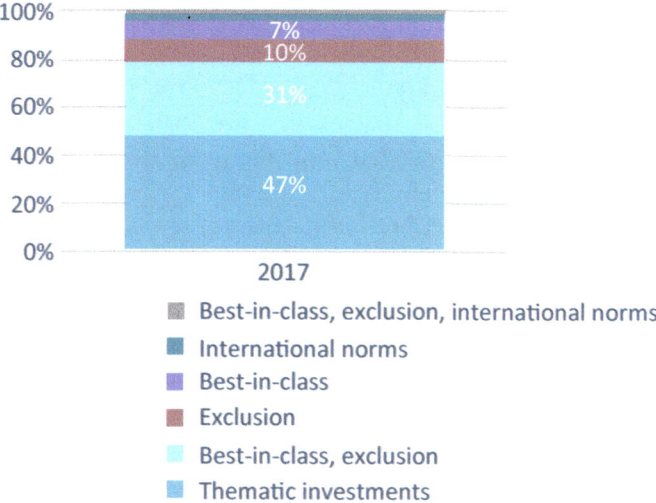

100% —

80% —

60% —

40% —

20% —

0% —

2017

- Best-in-class, exclusion, international norms
- International norms
- Best-in-class
- Exclusion
- Best-in-class, exclusion
- Thematic investments

Fig. 6.3 Types of sustainable exchange-traded funds (ETFs) (2017) (*Source* Deutsche Bank, Bloomberg Finance L.P. [Used with permission of Bloomberg Finance L.P.])

2015 concerning the quality of products and services, bribery, fraud and freedom of association, which had contributed to the downgrading of the governance rating since 2014. On the other hand, just one month before the exposure of the emissions scandal, MSCI upgraded VW's sustainability rating from BB to BBB because of a decrease in the company's reported carbon dioxide emissions from vehicles, as well as a reduction in recalls in previous years. Only after the fraud had been exposed was the company's rating downgraded to CCC, which is the lowest category.

Sustainability indices also differ from one another for reasons other than the underlying company analysis. Not all methodologies behind sustainability indices are equally multifaceted or intended to broadly describe the sustainability of investments. It is key for investors to understand on what grounds the companies included in the index have been selected. Some indices may focus on individual key figures or aspects, such as whether the company has signed the Global Compact initiative. There are also differences in methodologies between sustainability indices that broadly combine various aspects, and such differences are difficult to understand. Comparison is most feasible between indices that have also made the underlying company-specific analyses available to investors.

The content of a sustainability index may vary more from year to year than that of general indices, but their compositions may still become partly outdated. The compositions of indices are changed when something negative is discovered about a company's operations, for example, or when the companies' relative sustainability performances change in other ways. The composition of some sustainability indices (e.g. the DJSI) is based on company-specific surveys and requests for material, and if a company no longer responds, it will be excluded from the index. In addition, the criteria for determining the sustainability of companies change with the further development of the sustainability ratings behind the indices. It can be more difficult to be included in sustainability indices than to be excluded, which is why companies may be excluded despite being at least equally as sustainable as some of the companies included in the index. This is based on an intent to control the number of changes. Sustainability indices may also include companies whose level of sustainability has not decreased so much or whose issues are not so significant that the companies would need to be excluded in line with the rules of the index. For this reason, sustainability indices may include companies whose current rating is so poor that they would no longer be included in the index as new companies.

Different versions of sustainability indices using similar methodologies and initial data are offered to investors. There may be differences between indices using the same sustainability ratings in, for example, whether 25% or 50% of the most sustainable companies in the sector are included in the index (based on market value).

Investors Choose Between Standard and Customised Indices

Even if the investor's views are consistent with those of the chosen index provider in principle, differences may still arise concerning individual companies (the index may include a company that the investor has excluded). Investors also have different views on what products to exclude—for example, of all sin stocks, many investors exclude only tobacco, while sustainability indices do not necessarily have any exclusions, or all sin stocks are excluded at the same time. If an investor also makes exclusions based on a company's activities in line with international norms, for example, it is practically impossible to find an index that is consistent with the investor's views, unless they customise an index for their purposes.

Institutional investors can apply two different strategies in selecting a sustainable benchmark to minimise differences between the investor's views and the criteria of the sustainability index:

1. Selecting the benchmark index of the service provider whose analysis is most essential for the investment process. Inconsistencies may ensue if the investor uses analysis tools offered by different providers for different aspects of the sustainability analysis.
2. Selecting a customised sustainability index that meets the investor's criteria as closely as possible and/or lists of investments to be excluded.

Low-Carbon Indices for Climate Risk Management

As a way to manage climate-related investment risks, some investors have adopted what are known as low-carbon indices, which optimise the carbon footprint of the portfolio to be as small as possible (e.g. 50% smaller compared with the general index), while also keeping changes as minor as possible in relation to the returns of the general index (tracking error).

The rationale for using low-carbon indices has been that if the direct costs of climate change incurred by the company rise as a result of increases in the price of emission allowances or carbon taxes, investors who have made investments in the index will be less exposed to these costs. In addition, owners of underground fossil fuel reserves can be excluded from or underweighted in indices, with the idea being that if access to some of the reserves is prohibited, investors will not be affected by the reserves losing their value.

When choosing a climate index, it is good to understand that significant actual impacts cannot be achieved without changing the risk profile. Indices seek to emphasise the best companies in the sector, but the definitions of sectors are broad, and some low-carbon indices overlook life-cycle emissions in their emission calculations. In practice, such strategies have led to situations where oil companies have been excluded or underweighted, while investments in oilfield services companies have been increased—that is, companies that operate and maintain oilfields but do not own them. However, if oil drilling stops, the business opportunities of these service companies do not necessarily seem very promising.

The methodologies of climate-themed indices have diversified, and some indices place greater emphasis on the level of companies' climate risk management and their future plans, for example. As part of its sustainable finance legislation, the EU is working on a proposal for minimum standards for low-carbon and positive climate impact indices to increase consistency and comparability, as well as including a forward-looking aspect (future impacts will be taken into consideration).

Sustainability Assessment in Various Asset Classes

Sustainable investing is somewhat different for different asset classes. For example, in internally managed equity investments in listed or unlisted companies, the investor also has an opportunity to influence the company's operations even in ways that are not available to debt investors—such as voting at general meetings. In private equity investments, engaging with companies may be possible at a very early stage, as soon as ownership has been transferred.

The ESG analysis of fixed income investments often places more emphasis on risk management than on identifying opportunities for sustainability. The content and practices of hedge funds can vary widely, so comparable sustainability assessment is challenging, and practices are at an early stage of development compared with equity investments, for example. The UN Principles for Responsible Investment concern all asset classes. In practice, however, there are differences between asset classes in the development stages and practices of sustainability assessment.

Fixed Income Investments

Sustainability ratings and many other tools available for the analysis of listed investments can be used to support the analysis of both shares and corporate bonds, as the analysis tools concern the same companies. However, some of the new tools for the analysis of investment portfolios have been created only for shares, at least in the first stage.[4]

The risks of ESG are similar for equity and fixed income investments: if the probability of bankruptcy increases, the value of a fixed income investment decreases. However, the negative impacts of neglecting sustainability are reflected differently in different asset classes: while a fine imposed on a company, for example, may have a very negative impact on its ability to pay dividends, this does not necessarily have a direct impact from the perspective of a fixed-income investment, as companies must pay their creditors before paying their owners (creditors are higher in the order of priority). If the sanctions are very significant, the markets may deem the company insolvent and price it accordingly, and even if the company's solvency is not jeopardised, negative ESG news may have an impact on the value of fixed income investments if the financial markets deem the risks related to the company to be higher than before. When considering sustainability, the aim is to avoid investments that could become insolvent as a result of materialised ESG risks or whose credit risk would be repriced.

One of the most important purposes of a fixed income investor's company analysis is to form a truthful overview of the risks related to the company's capacity to service its debts. Pricing in the financial markets is based on probabilities, and all unforeseen costs related to a company's operations have a negative impact on its financial position while also increasing the probability of default. With low interest rates, the materialisation of even minor negative risks can have a significant impact on the market value of the portfolio.

When analysing the impacts of materialised sustainability risks, a case of suspected money laundering related to a bank can be examined as an example. When the suspicions came to light, the bank's share price decreased by more than 10%. Although analysts were convinced that the scandal or any ensuing fine would not affect the bank's ability to manage its senior debt, its market value decreased with the share price. For example, the market value of the bank's five-year unsecured senior bond fell by around 1.3%.

A decrease of more than 1% in value is significant, as the expected yield to maturity of the bond was around 1.2% before the news was released.

Riku Hyppänen, Portfolio Manager, Ilmarinen Mutual Pension Insurance Company

Various sustainability ratings and analyses have also been developed for government bonds. These examine bribery and climate impacts, for example, as well as a wide range of other sustainability aspects. In connection with determining the sustainability of government bonds, some investors refer to the exclusion of bonds issued by states that are subject to sanctions. From the perspective of government bonds, what makes sustainable investing even more challenging is the fact that investments in government bonds are used to hedge investments and as collateral in capital adequacy calculations, and the credit ratings and sustainability do not necessarily match.

Green Bonds

Green bonds have become one way to consider the positive sustainability impacts of fixed-income investments. Green bonds are bonds for which the issuer has determined a purpose of use, which is environmentally friendly projects, such as projects related to energy efficiency or renewable energy. Green bonds represent a small proportion of the global fixed income market, but their growth has been strong over the past years. In addition, there are even rarer sustainable bonds, such as social bonds and sustainability bonds, as well as blue bonds for the conservation of marine ecosystems and sustainable fishing.

With the growth of green bonds, investment products and indices focusing on green bonds have been introduced in the market to some extent, and some institutional investors are aiming to increase their investments in these bonds. The increasing popularity of green bonds is part of the trend of investors becoming more interested in climate impacts. However, it is good to understand that refinancing generally plays an important role in the debt markets, and this also applies to green bonds. Green bonds do not need to finance projects that would not otherwise be implemented, meaning that they do not involve what is known as the additionality requirement.

Issuers can themselves define their bonds as green and are not required to refer to a particular standard. Key standards for green bonds include the *Green Bond Principles (GBP)* and the *Climate Bonds Initiative*. In addition, the French government has introduced its own standard for green bonds, and the EU plans to introduce its own green bond standard. However, standards define criteria only for the portion of companies' operations for which green funding is sought. From a global sustainability perspective, it is good that, for example, companies with core business operations that depend on fossil fuels are also making green investments, at least to some degree—this can contribute to change in the real world. However, in terms of the management of investors' own (financial) climate risks, companies in which a larger portion of the core business operations is environmentally friendly may be more attractive investments.[5]

Many issuers obtain a **second opinion** (second-party statement) from an ESG service provider on the framework of the green bond and whether the projects to be financed are 'green' and therefore suitable. Some issuers also have their green bonds certified by an auditor (third-party verification) in accordance with the principles of the GBP or the Climate Bonds Initiative.

Some investors have set minimum requirements for the magnitude of positive impacts, but this can make it more difficult to find potential investments. The accuracy of the information provided in the bond prospectus and annual reporting varies. Nevertheless, studying the information can increase investors' understanding of the projects to be financed and the quality of the improvements. Information about green bonds by various issuers is also available from ESG service providers.

Green bonds are a relatively new phenomenon, and for the time being, the market is small. There is conflicting information about their impacts on financial expenses. Few institutional investors are willing to pay higher premiums for the 'greenness' of bonds, with the exception of green bond funds and similar. Some issuers are aiming to lower the cost of capital through green bonds, or at least attract new investors. **Green bonds have also been said to increase the CFO's awareness of sustainability aspects in many companies, and the significance of sustainable business operations has grown within the company as a result.**

Unlisted Investments

Similar aspects and questions can be used in the analysis of unlisted investments as for listed companies. In other words, the ESG themes that are material for the company are determined first. These are affected by the company's lines of business and countries of operation. The available sources of information are studied next (reporting and any third-party reports, and additional information is obtained through discussions with the company's representatives and site visits, for example), and sustainability aspects related to the business model are analysed (e.g. business viability in a changing operating environment). Based on various sources of information and the organisation's own views, some investors draw up *sector-specific question sets* that they use in assessing the sustainability of unlisted companies. In addition, some investors set sector-specific criteria for sustainability that are also applied to unlisted investments (e.g. the exclusion of coal companies).

The assessment of unlisted investments is affected by the fact that there is usually less information available about them than there is about listed companies. In general, unlisted companies often report less on their sustainability. On the other hand, large unlisted companies in particular can prepare sustainability reports, even comprehensive ones. Fewer ESG tools are available for the analysis of unlisted companies than for listed companies, as many operators do not cover companies that have not issued listed securities. *The analysis of unlisted companies can be supported by (sector-specific) sustainability analyses of listed companies.* Such analyses show which themes are relevant for companies in the sector and what developments in the operating environment have an impact, as well as indicating the ESG level of the benchmark companies.

There are ESG providers that also cover unlisted companies. For example, RepRisk monitors news about more than 100,000 companies and compiles claims made in public about sustainability issues. The 2 Degrees Investing Initiative think tank makes climate scenario assessments of listed and unlisted companies for loan portfolio analysis. In addition, some databases and service providers collect data on listed and unlisted companies about statements issued by the authorities and fines, for example, and the location, capacity and volumes of production plants.

Sector-specific databases can also be used in the analysis of unlisted companies. For example, Equasis indicates whether a shipping company has been reprimanded or prohibited from leaving a port because of serious infringements. The NGO Ship-breaking Platform collects data on scrapped ships. In addition, companies' key figures can be assessed in comparison with the benchmark group by using comparison data collected by Eurostat on sector-specific key figures, such as accident frequency. However, the accuracy and reliability of reporting vary between countries and companies. Furthermore, companies are never completely similar, and different operations lead to somewhat different results for sustainability indicators.

> *In-depth expertise is needed in the ESG analysis of unlisted companies, as ESG ratings reports by external service providers are not comprehensively available. We first evaluate public reports: the quality of reporting provides a rough overview of the company's ability to manage ESG risks. Extensive, transparent and assured ESG reporting indicates that the company has allocated resources to sustainability governance, while very limited reporting may suggest the opposite. Likewise, the publication of comprehensive ESG policies approved by the management indicate that the company has considered the sustainability aspects of its operations. Commitment to sector-specific responsibility initiatives and certified management systems (such as ISO 14 001) increases credibility and facilitates ESG analysis, as then it is often not necessary to do a detailed assessment of the company's own processes.*
>
> *In a more detailed assessment, the focus is on material sustainability aspects. For example, we examine ESG-related key performance indicators and the sustainability strategy, as well as involvement in any controversies. It is also important to assess the sustainability of the business model, such as whether a clothing company manufactures fast fashion and how changes in consumer behaviour may affect such a company.*
>
> Kari Pietilä, Senior ESG Analyst, Nordea

Table 6.2 illustrates the assessment of the sustainability of an unlisted company, using an imaginary healthcare company as an example. Investors are looking for long-term trends, such as population ageing, which increases the need for healthcare services and nursing homes. The SASB classification of sector-specific material aspects has been used in determining the themes and questions as far as applicable.

Private equity investors usually have extensive opportunities for the assessment and development of ESG. Private equity investment companies often provide their institutional investor clients with information about any sustainability-related concerns (*red flags*) detected concerning the investment. Institutional investors can examine the sustainability practices of a private equity investment company by using a survey prepared by the PRI (2015) and asking more specific questions about individual investments. Similar tools can be used to assess the sustainability of investments as for other unlisted companies (described above). When less public information is available, the person conducting a sustainability analysis is primarily responsible for focusing the examination on material aspects.

Table 6.2 Questions to determine the sustainability of a healthcare company

Theme	Key questions	Impacts
Clients' well-being/quality of service	• How does the company ensure that clients in nursing homes, for example, are treated safely and appropriately? • Does the company only meet the minimum statutory level (number of carers per resident) or are extra measures taken? • Does the company have a system in place for reporting suspected cases of neglect? How many cases have been reported? What measures have been taken based on the reports? • How does the company measure service quality (medical and client satisfaction) and impacts (e.g. patient injuries)? How have these figures developed? How does the company seek to improve quality? • Does the company have a certified quality system (e.g. ISO 9001) in place and what is the coverage of the system? How relevant is the system with regard to the organisation's operations?	• There are significant publicity risks related to clients' well-being in nursing homes in particular. An insufficient number of carers, for example, or the neglect of clients can damage the company's reputation and even an investor's reputation • Exceeding statutory requirements affects the clients' social well-being and employees' job satisfaction • Resourcing beyond the minimum requirement helps the company continue its normal operations in unexpected crisis situations
Information security and data protection	• How does the company ensure a good level of information security and data protection (certification, processes, training)? • Have there been any information leaks, fines or other failures?	• Failure to comply with the EU General Data Protection Regulation can lead to significant sanctions • Information leaks can lead to reputational losses and thereby affect the demand for the company's services
Transparency of invoicing	• How are the pricing principles and the coverage of the services described? To what extent is this information publicly available (considering competitive factors)? Is price information available to private clients on the website? • Have there been any disputes concerning this area? • Is contact information available if the invoicing is unclear?	• Transparent pricing principles on invoices and public price information for private clients help the company avoid disputes • Contact information increases customer satisfaction

(continued)

Table 6.2 (continued)

Theme	Key questions	Impacts
Recruitment and competence development	• How are consistent practices ensured between units, particularly in the treatment of clients, taking into account units acquired through public-sector outsourcing and corporate arrangements? • How does the company ensure well-being at work and competence? Does the company encourage its employees to participate in training provided by third parties? Does it maintain information about when training has been provided to employees? If changes have taken place in the field, will further training be ensured? • What kinds of incentive schemes are in place for employees?	• Highly competent employees and consistent HR practices affect the well-being of clients and the quality of the service • Incentive schemes and competitive salaries affect employees' work motivation
Business ethics	• What principles and processes does the company have in place to prevent conflicts of interest and address suspicions? • Have there been any legal cases or public allegations of misconduct? How have possible issues been processed and what has been learned in the process? • How have any other unethical situations been resolved (usually only the most serious cases become public)? What kind of process does the company have in place to avoid unethical situations?	• The appropriate implementation of competitive bidding processes related to the privatisation of the healthcare sector is key for future operating conditions and business continuity
Tax liability	• What information is available about the company's tax policy and tax footprint? • Are the company's practices consistent with the EU's and the OECD's projects to reduce tax avoidance and aggressive tax planning? Are changes to be expected and how will they affect the company's revenues?	• Allegations of irresponsible tax practices can lead to reputational losses and a loss of customers • Costs could increase if the company's tax arrangements were no longer acceptable in the future

In the preparation phase of private equity investments, it is often possible to obtain more information than when investing in a minority of the shares in a listed company, in which case companies must treat all shareholders equally. In connection with some acquisitions, an environmental risk assessment or a broader sustainability risk assessment (*Environmental Due Diligence* or *ESG Due Diligence*) is made, or at least these aspects are taken into consideration, as far as possible, as part of the assessment of legal risks (*Legal Due Diligence*).

Private equity investors also have a good opportunity to bring about significant changes when a private equity investment company becomes a major shareholder through the arrangement and is able to develop the company's operations even in terms of sustainability during the ownership. In practice, this can mean the implementation of energy efficiency projects, for example, or bringing sustainability to the core of the company's value creation strategy.

Hedge Funds

In the assessment of the sustainability of hedge funds, the focus has mainly been on good governance and compliance with the international SBAI standards (*Standards Board for Alternative Investments*). The standards include guidelines on the valuation of investments, the independent management of funds and the appointment of a ***compliance officer*** to monitor compliance with the rules and prevent misconduct, as well as the transparency of costs, for example. The PRI (2017) survey for hedge funds can be used in the assessment of ESG practices.

The mandate of hedge funds is broad, meaning that a single fund can include several asset classes. The same methods are suitable for some strategies as for equity and corporate bond investments, but they are not necessarily very suitable if the investment horizon is very short, just one day, for example. In-depth sustainability analysis takes time, so investment strategies with longer investment horizons generally have more resources for this purpose. There are also hedge funds that take sustainability factors (key figures) into account as part of seeking returns.

Identifying sustainability aspects becomes even more challenging with funds that do not invest in companies. There are conflicting views on whether investments in commodities, for example, have more positive or negative impacts: trading can be seen to increase the prices of commodities occasionally, as well as promoting the functioning of the market.

Opportunities for Private Investors

Private investors can also make sustainable investments. The implementation methods differ because of different resources for the investor's own ESG analysis and ESG analyses produced by service providers, for example. Private investors mainly have access to free public sources for the sustainability analysis of investments in shares and funds. A practical way to get started is to apply ESG ratings made public by service providers. A wealth of more detailed information is also available, although reviewing and interpreting the information requires effort and study. In addition, private investors do not have similar access to comprehensive discussions with the management of the investee company and fund managers.

> *Critical analysis and knowledge of the industry and competitors are necessary for an investor to identify a sustainable pioneer in a sector, as every company wants to emphasise its sustainability. Favouring sustainable investments is challenging, because the investor cannot rely on public market information. Instead, independent analysis and a critical approach are required in assessing which companies actually operate sustainably, and because there are different dimensions of sustainability, which dimensions are emphasised in various sectors and companies needs to be determined.*
>
> *In many companies, sustainability is connected to the technology in one way or another, in addition to being linked to thinking, the operating philosophy and values. In companies whose sustainability is based on their own unique technological expertise, that is difficult for competitors to copy quickly, easily or inexpensively, sustainability should be reflected in prices as a premium.*
>
> Jukka Oksaharju, Equity Strategist, Nordnet

Investments in Listed Shares

Private investors can apply their own sustainability criteria to the selection of investments, as well as participating as active owners in general meetings, where shareholders have the right to ask questions and—in some countries, such as Finland and Sweden—also make proposals concerning matters falling within the mandate of the general meeting. Although the opportunities to have an impact increase with the amount of money invested, a company usually reacts if numerous private investors ask the same questions concerning sustainability.

One or more sustainable investment methods can be applied in the selection of investments.

Favouring the most sustainable companies of a sector (known as the best-in-class method) enables investors to examine in more detail the companies that have been included in sustainability indices: the companies in some sustainability indices are public, while information about other companies is available only to the extent in which the investments of funds following sustainability indices (e.g. ETFs) have been listed. Company-specific sustainability ratings and summaries published by MSCI and Sustainalytics, among other service providers, can be used for rough assessments and comparisons of companies' sustainability. In addition, a wealth of information about many companies is available in sustainability reports and on websites. However, identifying the most sustainable companies based solely on reported information is challenging even for professionals.

To make thematic investments, investors can use theme-specific studies by non-profit organisations, such as the public summaries of climate-focused sector reports by *CDP*. One possible way to get started in finding front-runner companies is to examine the public Science-Based Targets list of companies that have set ambitious climatology-based targets for emission reductions over the next 5–15 years in line with the Paris Agreement.[6]

To identify investees that offer *sustainable development solutions*, investors can use the content of ETFs that invest in sustainable development companies, for example, as well as reports comparing the sustainability of companies in the sector (e.g. reports by CDP). In addition, many companies report on their sustainability solutions.

To exclude investments, private investors may choose to use institutional investors' public lists of exclusions. Some institutional investors publish a list of companies that they exclude based on operations in violation of their principles. In addition, for example, the NBIM (Norges Bank Investment Management), which manages the international investments of the Government Pension Fund Global of Norway, also publishes the grounds for each exclusion decision.

Interest in the sustainability of investments increases the desire to invest directly in companies. Finnish (local) companies are favoured because of better availability of information. The number of local investment events has risen significantly in recent years. More and more private investors have a realistic opportunity to meet members of the senior management of listed companies. Interest in matters related to governance is increasing, and investors want to personally assess the reliability of the management.

The assessment of sustainability is gradually being integrated into the investment selection criteria, alongside financial figures. Investment in sustainability is also a way to manage the risks related to investing activities: the market value of a company operating in a grey area may collapse if its suspicious operating methods become public. Private investors have traditionally made an impact by voting with their feet. This is likely to change in the near future. The Shareholder Rights Directive increases the power of the annual general meeting. At the same time, digitalisation is likely to lead to a situation where small shareholders find one another and can also have an impact on listed companies as a group of active owners. The combined holding of private investors is significant: Finnish private individuals own more than 10% of the market value of almost all companies on the Nasdaq Helsinki.

Sari Lounasmeri, CEO, Finnish Foundation for Share Promotion

Investments in Funds

In fund investing, the fund manager decides on individual investments and operating methods, meaning that a private investor must find a fund that is aligned with their own concept of sustainability. A private investor must prioritise between various sustainable investment strategies and other criteria for investments, such as the following: Is it more important to favour opportunities for sustainability, avoid the worst misconduct and exclude sectors that the investor considers unethical, or to favour a specific theme or a fund manager who actively influences investments?

Various investors' sustainability principles may seem similar on the surface, and based on these principles, it may be possible to find funds that appear to meet the private investor's own criteria. For ***actively managed funds***, it is important to assess the quality of sustainable investing—that is, how well sustainability analysis is conducted and considered in investment decisions. In terms of ***passive funds***, attention is paid to the selection of the index: the criteria used to compile the index and the quality of the underlying sustainability analysis. Both active and passive funds can involve active and successful engagement. Private investors can use partly the same means for assessment as institutional investors.

Sustainability ratings by Morningstar and MSCI are publicly available for ***comparing the sustainability of funds***. These ratings describe the sustainability of the investees in relation to benchmark funds (illustrated in Fig. 6.4). MSCI also publishes fund overviews, which provide further insight regarding the involvement of investee companies in various activities, such as exposure to green (e.g. alternative energy) and brown (e.g. thermal coal) revenue, violations of international norms and corporate governance performance in terms of board independence and board diversity.

When using fund ratings and overviews, it is good to consider the strengths and limitations of company-specific sustainability ratings. For example, a

Morningstar Sustainability

Morningstar Sustainability Rating

High

Ranking in the category: top 4%

Sustainability score: 45

Based on 79% of holdings

Fig. 6.4 Morningstar sustainability rating for the Aberdeen Global—Eastern European Equity Fund (2018). *Note* The five-globe sustainability rating means that in relation to its category (Emerging Europe equities), the fund was among the top 10% of sustainable funds. More detailed information reveals that its relative ranking was as high as the top 4%. The average score (45/100) for the fund's investees illustrates how sustainable the portfolio companies are in relation to the benchmark group in their sector. In other words, the portfolio companies were slightly less sustainable than average. Of the fund's holdings, 79% are in companies that have a company-specific sustainability rating by Sustainalytics (*Source* Nordnet and Morningstar)

fund with a low sustainability rating that invests in Nordic companies can in practice invest in companies in which ESG aspects are better managed than in a fund with the highest rating in an emerging market.

Another interesting publicly available fund assessment is *Climetrics*, which focuses on climate risks and climate-related opportunities. Its information is based, in particular, on the databases of CDP and ISS ESG, which is a commercial service provider. Its methodology combines data on the fund's holdings, the fund manager's practices and the investment principles. Therefore, Climetrics differs from Morningstar and MSCI sustainability ratings particularly in the sense that the rating is also based on aspects other than the fund's holdings alone. On the other hand, Climetrics has a narrower approach to sustainability aspects, as Morningstar and MSCI also cover other sustainability themes extensively, and climate risks are only one part of the whole. In addition, in the Climetrics rating system, a fund is compared with all assessed funds, while Morningstar and MSCI compare funds within the benchmark group (for example, funds investing in Finnish companies are compared with one another).

To support their investment decisions, investors can also study a fund manager's comparison concerning the management of climate impacts. The non-profit *Asset Owner Disclosure Project (AODP)* compares the world's 50 largest asset managers annually based on how well they have taken into account the financial risks related to climate change in their investing activities. However, the results are affected by the fact that the study is partly based on a survey, and not all asset managers respond to surveys. For this reason, some asset managers receive lower scores based solely on public reporting. In addition, the comparison is not fund-specific. Instead, it reflects the asset manager's general level of considering climate aspects.

When considering the sustainability of investment products, a rougher method can also be applied to examine *in which countries companies are more sustainable on average* than in others. For example, Morningstar's compilation[7] (Fig. 6.5) can be used for this purpose. According to the compilation, companies listed in the Netherlands are the most sustainable in the world, followed by Finnish listed companies, based on Sustainalytics' company-specific ESG ratings and detected sustainability issues.

Sustainable Investing Requires Study

In sustainable investing, as well as in investing in general, investments must not be made in anything that the investor does not understand. Investors

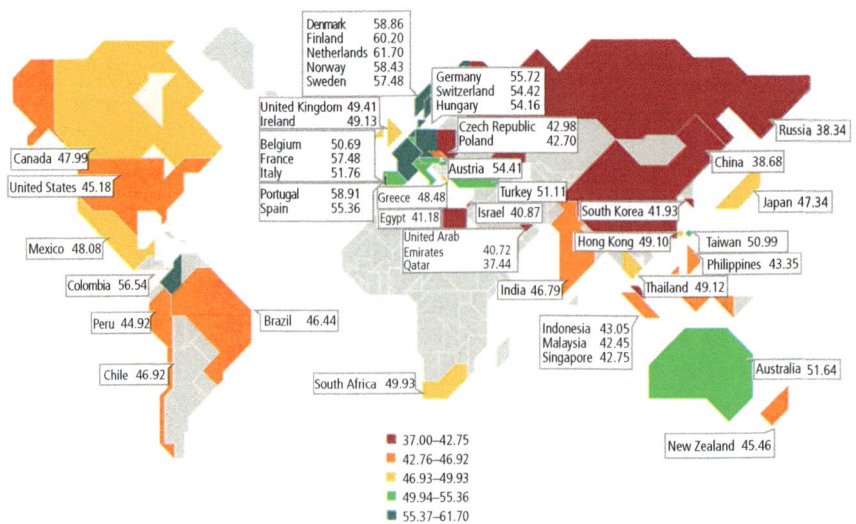

Fig. 6.5 Map of the sustainability ratings of country indices (2018) (*Source* Morningstar)

should familiarise themselves with ESG concepts and terminology. Using common sense and requesting more information from the fund provider is always a good idea if matters are unclear.

Notes

1. Exceptions to this are mandates given to asset managers by individual investors, where the opportunities to have an impact on asset management are significant, even during the investment period.
2. Investor-specific annual reports on sustainable investing can be searched for on the public PRI website. The 'Direct Listed Equity – Active Ownership' module reports the votes given at annual general meetings (percentage of [proxy] votes cast) and the number of engagement processes (number of companies engaged with, intensity of engagement and effort) during the reporting period.
3. Deutsche Bank's study takes into account more than 50 equity ETFs that: meet the criteria set for liquidity and low tracking errors; are based on established ESG ratings, rather than being based on individual themes; comply with the best-in-class method and possibly also use exclusions; have a sufficient number of investees (at least 100); and have low trading costs.
4. Connecting equity investments to sustainability information is more straight-forward: there are fewer identifiers for shares, just one per series of shares, for example. In corporate bonds, the issuer is not necessarily the parent company; instead, it can be another company of the same group. On the other hand, a new identifier is assigned in connection with each new issue. In addition, a fixed income investor does not have a holding in the company; instead, they have only invested in debt, which may also be one of the reasons why shares have been examined first in terms of sustainable investment.
5. In general, the credit risk related to green bonds is determined based on the comprehensive credit rating of the investee, with the exception of loans secured by physical assets, such as solar panels. In other words, the 'greenness' of a loan does not usually help investors to better manage the climate risks related to investees if it only reflects a small part of the company's operations.
6. The organisations behind the Science Based Targets (SBT) initiative include CDP, the World Wide Fund for Nature (WWF), the World Resources Institute and Global Compact. Their joint committee approves companies' targets as being compliant with science. The SBT website provides information about the companies that have set targets and are committed to setting targets by sector.
7. The Morningstar report covers all its global equity indices (Morningstar Global Markets Index members). Sustainability ratings can only be calculated for indices where company-specific ESG ratings are available for more than 67% of the market value. In the report, the coverage of all the 46 country-specific indices was sufficient in relation to the set limit.

References

Asset Owners Disclosure Project. (2018). *AODP global climate index 2017 / asset managers*. https://aodproject.net/managers/. Referenced 25 November 2020.

Climetrics. *What makes Climetrics unique?* https://www.climetrics-rating.org/methodology. Referenced 25 November 2020.

Morningstar. (2016). *Morningstar sustainability rating*. www.morningstar.fi/fi/news/148106/morningstarin-vastuullisuusrating.aspx.

PRI. (2015). *LP responsible investment DDQ: and how to use it*. https://www.unpri.org/private-equity/lp-responsible-investment-ddq-andhow-to-use-it/113.article.

PRI. (2017). *Responsible investment DDQ for hedge funds*. https://www.unpri.org/hedge-funds/responsible-investment-ddq-for-hedgefunds/125.article.

The *Wall Street Journal*. (2018). *Is Tesla or Exxon more sustainable? It depends whom you ask*. https://www.wsj.com/articles/is-tesla-or-exxon-more-sustainable-it-depends-whom-you-ask-1537199931.

Other Sources

Aldridge, C. (2016). *You, too, can master value chain emissions*. Greenhouse Gas Protocol blog. https://ghgprotocol.org/blog/you-too-can-master-value-chain-emissions.

Bloomberg. (2018). *How to build a sustainable bond portfolio*. https://www.bloomberg.com/news/articles/2018-08-29/how-to-build-a-sustainable-bond-portfolio.

Carbon Tracker Initiative. (2018). *Mind the gap: The $1.6 trillion energy transition risk*. https://www.carbontracker.org/reports/mind-the-gap/.

CDP. (2018). *Building pressure: Which cement companies will be left behind in the low-carbon transition?* https://6fefcbb86e61af1b2fc4-c70d8ead6ced550b4d987d7c03fcdd1d.ssl.cf3.rackcdn.com/cms/reports/documents/000/003/277/original/Cement_Report_Ex_Summary.pdf?1523261813.

CDP. *Sector research*. https://www.cdp.net/en/investor/sector-research. Read 25 November 2020.

Climate Bonds Initiative. *External Review*. https://www.climatebonds.net/market/second-opinion. Read 25 November 2020.

European Commission. *Emissions Trading System (EU ETS)*. https://ec.europa.eu/clima/policies/ets_en. Read 25 November 2020.

European Commission. *Paris Agreement*. https://ec.europa.eu/clima/policies/international/negotiations/paris_en. Read 25 November 2020.

Finnish Association of Authorised Public Accountants. (2017). Euroopan Unionin PIE-asetuksen soveltaminen Suomessa [*Application of the PIE Regulation of the EU in Finland*]. https://www.suomentilintarkastajat.fi/tilintarkastus/kysymyksia-ja-vastauksia/euroopan-unionin-pie-asetuksen-soveltaminen-suomessa.

Investopedia. *Externality.* https://www.investopedia.com/terms/e/externality.asp. Read 25 November 2020.

Lefkovitz, D. (2018). Morningstar sustainability atlas. *Morningstar.* https://www. morningstar.com/content/dam/marketing/shared/pdfs/Research/Sustainability_ Atlas_2018October.pdf?cid=EMQ.

MSCI. *MSCI ACWI sustainable impact index.* https://www.msci.com/msci-acwi-sus tainable-impact-index. Read 25 November 2020.

MSCI. *MSCI ESG Universal Indexes.* https://www.msci.com/msci-esg-universal-ind exes. Read 25 November 2020.

MSCI. *MSCI World OSRI 5% Issuer Capped Index (USD).* https://www.msci. com/documents/10199/14191646-df54-4004-8e15-71fcf1664436. Read 25 November 2020.

MSCI. *Volkswagen scandal underlines need for ESG analysis.* https://www.msci.com/ volkswagen-scandal. Read 25 November 2020.

Nordnet. *Aberdeen Global - Eastern European Equity Fund A Acc EUR.* https:// www.nordnet.fi/mux/web/fonder/fondfakta.html?classid=F00000J84Z. Read 25 November 2020.

Paris Agreement Capital Transition Assessment. General Questions. http://www.tra nsitionmonitor.com/en/faq/. Read 25 November 2020.

PRI. https://www.unpri.org/climate-change/directory-of-climatescenario-tools/ 3606.article. Read 25 November 2020.

Rabe, J., & Feldmann, O. (2018). *ESG Research: Integrating ESG in company research: Tackling the industry's alpha dilemma.* Deutsche Bank.

Responsible Investor. (2018). *Analysis: Investors and providers critical of proposed EU green index rules.* https://www.responsible-investor.com/home/article/analysis_ eu_green_index_rules/.

Responsible Minerals Initiative. http://www.responsiblemineralsinitiative.org/. Read 25 November 2020.

RobecoSAM. *Index family overview.* https://www.sustainability-indices.com/index-family-overview/. Read 25 September 2020.

SASB. (2018). *Materiality map.* https://materiality.sasb.org/. Read November 2020.

Standards Board for Alternative Investments. (2017). *The alternative investment standards.* https://www.sbai.org/wp-content/uploads/2016/04/SBAI-Standards-2017. pdf.

STOXX. *ESG & sustainability indices.* https://www.stoxx.com/discovery-search? category=theme&superType=esg%20%26%20sustainability&indexFamily=sta ndard. Read 25 November 2020.

STOXX. *Global ESG leaders.* https://www.stoxx.com/index-details?symbol=SXW ESGP. Read 25 November 2020.

Science Based Targets. *Companies taking action.* https://sciencebasedtargets.org/com panies-taking-action/. Read 25 November 2020.

Sullivan, R. (2011). *Valuing corporate responsibility: How do investors really use corporate responsibility information.* Greenleaf Publishing.

Sustainable Development Goals Knowledge Platform. *Division for Sustainable Development Goals*. https://sustainabledevelopment.un.org/about. Read 25 November 2020.

Task Force on Climate-related Financial Disclosures. (2017). *Implementing the recommendations of the task force on climate-related financial disclosures.* https://www.fsb-tcfd.org/wp-content/uploads/2017/06/FINAL-TCFD-Annex-062817.pdf.

Task Force on Climate-Related Financial Disclosures. (2017). *TCFD final report FAQs*. https://www.fsb-tcfd.org/wp-content/uploads/2017/06/TCFD-Public-FAQs-062817.pdf.

Transition Pathway Initiative. *TPI tool*. https://www.transitionpathwayinitiative.org/sectors/. Read 25 November 2020.

UN Association of Finland. Kestävän kehityksen tavoitteet (Agenda2030) [*Sustainable Development Goals (2030 Agenda)*]. https://www.ykliitto.fi/julkaisut/kestavan-kehityksen-tavoitteet-agenda2030.

UN Association of Finland. Kestävän kehityksen tavoitteet (Agenda2030) [*Sustainable Development Goals (2030 Agenda)*]. https://www.ykliitto.fi/yk70v/yk/kehitys/post-2015. Read 25 November 2020.

WRI, UNEP-FI and 2 Degrees Investing Initiative. (2015). *Climate strategies and metrics: Exploring options for institutional investors*. http://www.unepfi.org/fileadmin/documents/climate_strategies_metrics.pdf.

Part IV

The Link Between Sustainability and Returns

7

The Nordic Perspective on Integrating ESG

For our research project,[1] we interviewed representatives of 18 investment organisations that are publicly committed to sustainable investing. In practice, the material covers the views of Finland's largest institutional investors on the state of sustainable investing in Finland.

Goal and Status of Sustainable Investing

Motivation for Sustainable Investing

Of the Finnish investors we interviewed, the clear majority consider it important to take sustainability into account in investment decisions. Sustainability motivates institutional investors for three different reasons, which are well in line with the results of international studies. Most of the interviewees see sustainability as a risk management method, with its most important purpose being to avoid unfavourable impacts, such as loss of reputation. Institutional investors also examined the phenomenon through ***effectiveness*** and goals related to sustainability, with the purpose of promoting impacts that they regarded as positive. The majority of the investors we interviewed want to invest sustainably to improve ***financial returns*** as well. They seek to analyse aspects that are not part of typical economic analysis. However, creating a competitive edge through sustainable investing was initially seen as challenging, as there was a lack of expertise and experience: '*It felt like going* *through, again and again, the same financial statement information and other financial data that was already available to everyone. It began to feel like it was impossible to find additional returns, because all companies have been analysed so thoroughly. That was one of the reasons why we became interested in sustainable investing: it was a new source of information that could increase the return potential of the investment if we learned to understand and used the related data.'* (Anonymous interviewee.)

The Level of Implementation Varies

The level of implementation of sustainable investing varies between investment organisations, and major pension companies were regarded as the engines of sustainable investing in Finland. All of the interviewees deemed it important for sustainable investing to be understood in practice at different organisational levels. Sustainability should not be reflected only in the company's official principles of sustainable investing on its website or manifested only as a group of 'sustainability people' separate from the investment team. After its mainstreaming, sustainable investing was perceived to have become a more integral part of all investment activities, rather than consisting of individual sustainability products. Internationally, it is quite exceptional that, in Finland, ESG analysts often belong to the same teams as analysts and portfolio managers.

Investment organisations feel that the implementation of official principles of sustainable investing in practice is hindered by portfolio managers' individual ways of analysing investments, for example, and particularly by the fact that, in some cases, the portfolio managers did not want to explain the details of their analysis. For this reason, several organisations have come to a solution where the portfolio manager is responsible for the implementation of the organisation's principles of sustainable investing and is allowed to do this in their own way within the framework of the organisation's investment strategy.

According to the interviewees, differences in views between generations are reflected in the fact that younger professionals are more open-minded about ESG analysis. Some of the interviewees felt that it is difficult to make experienced analysts expand their analysis, as in their experience, the value of a share can be deduced directly from the company's financial statements and balance sheet. Major challenges related to the consideration of ESG aspects were seen to include not only issues related to the quality and availability of data but also the slow pace of changes in attitudes and culture.

Impacts Within Investment Organisations

What Do the Principles of Responsible Investment Indicate?

On their websites, many Finnish investment organisations announce that they have signed the Principles for Responsible Investment (PRI). Although the signatories report annually on their sustainable investment practices to the PRI, interviewees felt that the PRI does very little to monitor operations in practice and that the rules are loose. For this reason, the mere signing of the principles can hardly be considered to reflect the level of sustainability. The PRI has been monitoring the signatories more closely since 2018, but this was not yet visible to the investment organisations at the time of the interviews in 2017.

The interviewees see the signing of the PRI as a good start for the sustainability debate. It was also considered to signal that at least thought has been given to sustainability, that matters related to sustainability have been processed by the management team and that a process has been developed for sustainable investing. Membership of the PRI was also seen as permission to present challenging questions to the asset manager, as well as requests for additional information.

In addition, the interviewees pointed out that membership of Finland's Sustainable Investment Forum (Finsif) indicates an interest in matters related to sustainability and a willingness to learn more. Finsif was described as a forum for cooperation where people come together and invite experts as guests, and where new insights arise from events for everyone to apply to their organisation's investing activities in the way and to the extent that they see best.

Growing Competence Requirements

Expertise in sustainable investing was reported to have improved significantly in recent years, and the quality of the products offered to customers, such as thematic funds, was also reported to have improved. In addition, the number of public exclusion lists was mentioned as having increased. The idea of sustainability throughout the value chain has become established, attitudes towards aggressive tax planning within the law have become stricter, and requirements for transparency have become stronger over the past few years.

Information travels much faster than before because of social media and non-governmental organisations' increased levels of activity. This was considered to be reflected in the fact that image is increasingly important. As well as being lawful, operations must be acceptable in the eyes of the wider community. With the development of sustainable investing, the interviewees felt that investment teams need more resources for ESG analysis. The implementation of sustainable investing was perceived to be more laborious and difficult than conventional financial analysis. On the other hand, the easy accessibility of corporate management was considered to be one of the benefits of operating in Finland:

> In Finland, we meet with the company management quarterly. We can address anything we want at these meetings. By interviewing and asking questions, even a little craftily at times, we can find out how and why the company makes decisions and on what value base. And this is highly demanding work, because it calls for a great deal of knowledge, understanding, broad-based expertise and psychological abilities, for example, even from the person asking the questions. But this is the problem [with sustainable investing]: it is much easier to make a valuation of the company based on numbers in Excel. (Anonymous interviewee)

The interviewees felt that successful sustainable investing calls for cooperation between ESG experts and portfolio managers, where both parties' special expertise supports the analysis of the investment. The interviewees pointed out that it takes time to master ESG aspects, and it cannot be expected that the portfolio manager suddenly becomes an expert in sustainability only because they are showing more interest in sustainability, or that the portfolio manager is alone responsible for the preparation and interpretation of sustainability analysis. The portfolio manager's expertise in the assessment of financial impacts related to investments, for example, can complement analysis conducted by an ESG expert. On the other hand, the interviewees felt that ESG analysis involves many details that require in-depth special expertise. The interviewees also felt that effective cooperation between the ESG team and the portfolio manager is key for a successful investment process.

Critical Perspective

Greenwashing or Real?

Sustainable investing was also viewed critically, and the word 'greenwashing' was mentioned several times during the interviews. Generally, the interviewees considered their own organisation's investing activities to be sustainable, although differences of opinion within the organisation were brought up in many interviews. However, there were doubts about the genuineness of some operators' sustainable investing. For example, the sustainability scores of an investment portfolio can be improved quickly and easily by excluding emerging markets, where the coverage and scores of sustainability analysis are often weaker. This improves the sustainability scores, even if not much attention has been paid to sustainability in any other way. Generally, the interviewees felt that more is needed for sustainable investing than a superficial checklist approach.

Investors believe that greenwashing works only for so long, and stakeholders can differentiate between actual operations and sugar-coated communication. For institutional investors, ESG aspects were reported as being part of every competitive bidding process, and institutional investors require practical examples from their asset managers about how ESG aspects are considered in investing activities and investment decisions.

Views on Irresponsible Investing

Irresponsible investors were considered to include, for example, institutional investors who did not seriously think about the purpose of the investing activities and the values of the organisation, managed customers' assets indifferently or took too much risk, or whose investment horizon was too short term, or who managed the governance of their own investment organisation poorly or screened companies without thinking about their sustainability more comprehensively.

On the other hand, some of the interviewees saw more clearly that investors have different goals, starting points and operating methods, and therefore considered it natural that sustainable investing is implemented in different ways. Irresponsible investors were also considered to include an operator that focused on sustainable investing but managed their own organisation's sustainability matters poorly.

With Sustainable Investing Becoming Mainstream, Will Outperformance Become a Thing of the Past?

The analysis of ESG factors and their integration into investment decisions were considered a competitive advantage of the future. On the other hand, the interviewees were of the opinion that, with sustainable investing becoming more common, this competitive advantage may not last very long into the future. According to the interviewees, in ten years' time it may no longer be possible to generate better-than-usual returns through ESG analysis, because a large proportion of investors will be able to use ESG information equally well at that point.

> *In my view, the significance of ESG information will decrease in the future in this respect, and will become a basic precondition for operations, much like any other theme. Something new will always emerge and create hype for a while. Then the new thing changes, finds its level and becomes commonplace. (Anonymous interviewee)*

It seems that with the mainstreaming of sustainable investing, the capabilities of analysts and investors to analyse ESG data are expected to increase, and ESG information is expected to become an integral part of investee analysis.

With regard to ESG ratings, the interviewees mainly paid attention to companies with extremely poor ratings. ESG ratings were also used in situations where two investees were compared that were otherwise equally attractive. The ESG score was observed to have a strong impact on the selection of investments for funds focusing on sustainability themes in particular. With regard to Finnish companies, many interviewees mentioned meetings with the management as a significant part of the analysis.

The integration of ESG analysis into valuation models is still in progress. None of the interviewees used established models or calculation formulas in which a particular ESG rating, for example, would have a systematic impact on the company's valuation. Only one interviewee reported that they had seen individual examples abroad of valuation models that take ESG factors into consideration. However, some interviewees wondered how the ESG rating could be used in valuation in a more concrete manner. They were not yet certain about how ESG data could be used in quantitative models. The problems were also considered to include the fact that ESG data is not sufficiently consistent and comprehensive. However, ESG factors have an indirect impact on valuation, as ESG risks are taken into account in return requirements.

Some of the interviewees also considered the importance of financial responsibility, in which case uncompromised returns were often highlighted in investment decisions. According to the interviewees, the asset manager is not being responsible if they manage the customer's assets indifferently.

Of course, it must be kept in mind that for an asset manager, the primary responsibility commitment is to deliver the best possible returns at a controlled level of risk, and we cannot compromise on this. We cannot invest only in best-in-class ESG companies where all the good things are included in the prices. (Anonymous interviewee)

Note

1. The situation report on sustainable investment in Finland that is presented in the book is part of a more extensive academic research project by Silvola in 2017, the publication process of which was still in progress at the time of writing this book. For reasons related to research ethics, the interviewees are anonymous, and their identities are not known by anyone outside the research team.

8

Is Sustainable Investing Profitable?

Research-Based Information About the Financial Profitability of Sustainability

Several extensive summary analyses of published scientific articles have come to the conclusion that there is a statistically significant positive association between sustainability and financial profitability. Margolis, Elfenbein, and Walsh (2007) compiled 167 studies from 1972 to 2007 for their article. They noticed that these studies typically examined the association between the company's financial performance (e.g. Tobin's Q, ROA) and the sustainability aspects reported by the companies (e.g. Kinder, Lydenberg, Domini & Co., or the **KLD index**[1]). In conclusion, the researchers suggest that there is a small positive correlation between companies' financial performance and sustainability.

Friede, Busch, and Bassen (2015) later analysed a considerably larger sample that covered around 2,000 studies. According to their summary, the large majority of the studies reported positive results concerning the association between sustainability aspects and a company's financial performance. In their sample, sustainability covered a wide range of perspectives and measurement methods.

In this chapter, we present academic research findings that have been selected on the basis that they help explain the association between sustainability and returns. In addition, we illustrate the association through reports

© The Author(s), under exclusive license to Springer Nature Switzerland AG 2021
H. Silvola and T. Landau, *Sustainable Investing*,
https://doi.org/10.1007/978-3-030-71489-5_8

published by various investment organisations (Nordea, Schroders).[2] We also describe a critical perspective on research into sustainable investing.

Sustainability Ratings and Financial Profitability Are Interrelated

A study by Nordea (2018) analysed the ESG ratings of listed companies in the S&P 500 Index using MSCI's database. Figure 8.1 shows that between 2012 and 2018, financial profitability varied significantly between companies with a high ESG rating and companies with a low ESG rating. The financial performance of companies with the highest ESG rating (AAA) was around 35% better than the performance of companies with a poor ESG rating (B and CCC). The results show that a good ESG rating has a significant impact on a company's financial performance, while a poor ESG rating has a significant impact on financial underperformance. When measuring a company's financial profitability, both its operating result and the market value of its share were taken into account.

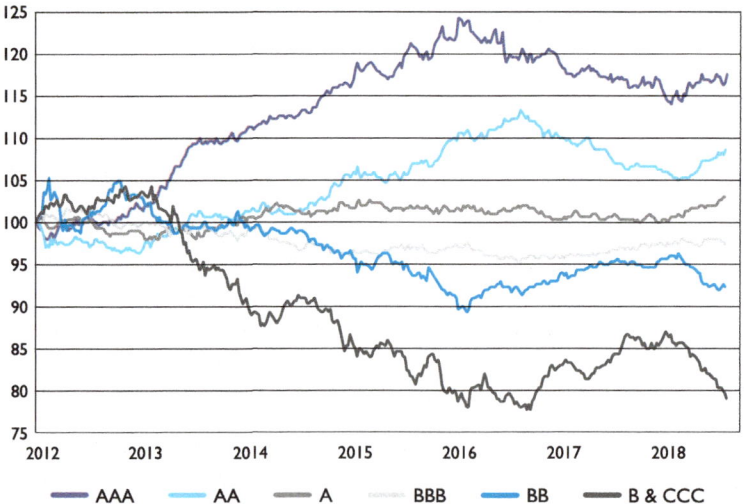

Fig. 8.1 Financial profitability according to MSCI ESG ratings (*Source* Nordea, MSCI ESG Research [Reproduced by permission of MSCI ESG Research LLC ©2021 MSCI ESG Research LLC All rights reserved])

Sustainability Improves Market Value

A study by Serafeim (2018) at Harvard University scientifically confirms the phenomenon mentioned above concerning the association between ESG level and financial profitability. According to Serafeim, the financial success of sustainable companies has increased over time and is affected by positive public information. In his model, Serafeim examines how changes in companies' sustainability levels (ESG level) affected the companies' market values measured using end-of-month values. Companies with a higher ESG level also have a higher market-to-book value and return on equity (ROE). An improvement in the ESG level had a twofold or threefold impact on the market-to-book value of companies whose sustainability had received positive publicity compared with companies whose sustainability aspects had been discussed in a negative light. From this it could be concluded that a company's reputation as a responsible company and its media image have a positive impact on its market-to-book value.

In his study, Serafeim combines MSCI's ESG rating with big data (all available data) from Truvalue Labs on the positive and negative publicity related to sustainability that the companies received between 2009 and 2018. The study is unique in the sense that it is the first study to combine MSCI's extensive database with big data on publicity concerning the companies' sustainability. Publicity was measured in terms of the number of articles. Truvalue Labs uses algorithms to find relevant ESG-related articles on a daily basis, which it then sorts in accordance with the Sustainability Accounting Standards Board's (SASB) materiality framework (SASB describes by sector which sustainability aspects are material in terms of financial returns).

Sustainability Ratings Have a Positive Association with the Return on Capital Employed

According to Nordea's study as well, the return on capital employed is associated with the ESG rating. Figure 8.2 illustrates that companies with the highest ESG rating (AAA) are more successful, generating up to a 50% higher return on capital employed (ROCE) than companies with a poor ESG rating (B and CCC) in 2017.

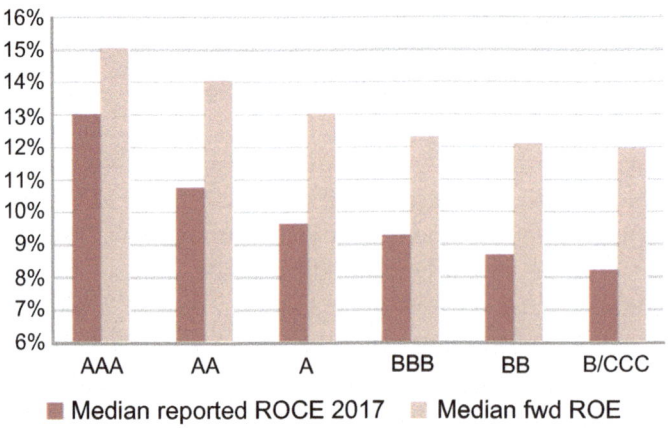

Material ESG Factors Generate Returns

According to research-based information, the materiality of ESG data has a significant impact on returns. Khan, Serafeim, and Yoon (2016) published an article in the prestigious academic journal *The Accounting Review* in which they analysed 2,000 US companies between 1993 and 2013. According to the results of their study, companies that outperformed the benchmark companies in their sector in terms of material ESG factors increased their profit margins more rapidly and generated better risk-adjusted returns. Correspondingly, high ESG ratings for immaterial factors did not produce the same reaction and sometimes even decreased returns. Materiality was determined in accordance with the SASB's sector-specific material ESG factors.

Researchers do not consider it likely that this phenomenon is driven by market demand caused by investors committed to sustainability, because it does not explain the better future returns in companies whose material ESG aspects are highly rated and because investors should have been able to distinguish between material and immaterial investments from publicly available information.

Rogers and Serafeim (2019) argue that the important question is not only *whether* an ESG theme is material, but *also to identify which ESG issues will become increasingly material in the future.* An ESG theme can become financially relevant when, for example, the norms of acceptable corporate behaviour change in society. NGOs, the media and other stake-holders respond by highlighting the misalignment between business and societal interests, and policymakers can react to that. The authors highlight that enough stakeholder pressure on an ESG issue can accumulate seemingly overnight, as was the case with the #MeToo movement.

Sustainable Companies Fare Well During Recession

Companies investing in sustainability are lower-risk investees regardless of the economic cycle (Albuquerque, Durnev, & Koskinen, 2012). The study shows that the customers of sustainable companies are more loyal to a sustainable brand and are willing to pay a higher (premium) price for products. The difference between sustainable and less sustainable companies was evident during the 2008 recession in particular. Stable net sales development and share price performance decrease the cost of capital, reduce the company's overall risk and make the share more attractive.

The study examined 3,005 companies in 34 countries between 2004 and 2010, meaning that the global impact of the financial crisis was taken into account. The researchers scored the companies based on their ESG data, considering good governance, for example, as well as risks related to employees, health and safety, recruitment and downsizing, workplace practices, and the environment and climate, among other factors.

Sustainable Companies During the Covid-19 Pandemic

Cheema-Fox, LaPerla, Serafeim, and Wang (2020) observed that sustainable companies have recovered rather well from the stock exchange slump caused by the Covid-19 pandemic in March 2020. They analysed more than 3,000 companies from around the world. According to the study, investees that actively communicated about their crisis response and showed credible commitment to their stakeholders were the least affected by the slump in terms of returns.

Corporate images were assessed using big data provided by Truvalue Labs. The resilience of the crisis response was measured in terms of action taken (or lack of action) by the companies with regard to human capital, the supply chain, and products and services. The companies' sustainability was measured based on ESG data provided by both MSCI and Sustainalytics, and the results showed a significant correlation between MSCI's data and crisis response activity.

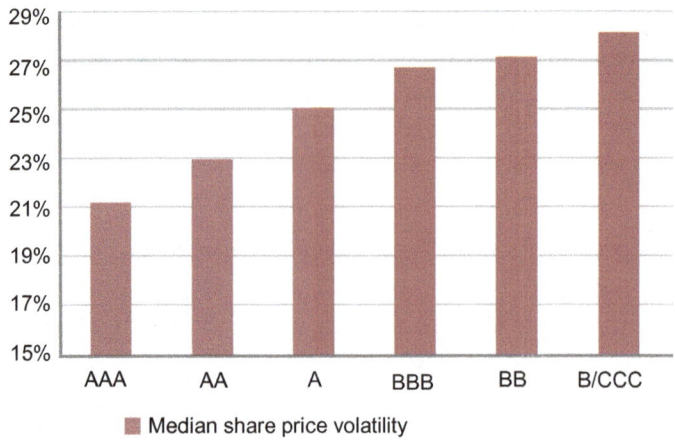

Fig. 8.3 Variation in the market value of shares according to an ESG rating (*Source* Nordea, MSCI ESG Research [Reproduced by permission of MSCI ESG Research LLC ©2021 MSCI ESG Research LLC All rights reserved])

The study concluded that companies' ability to respond flexibly and communicate to stakeholders was highlighted during a crisis, and their sustainability supported this goal. Despite the stock exchange crash, institutional investors continued to invest actively in these companies.

Lower Market Value Volatility

Academic research shows that a sustainable company has lower market value volatility than a company with a low ESG rating. According to Verheyden, Eccles, and Feiner (2016), the volatility and the loss risk of an investment portfolio are lower using the best-in-class method based on ESG levels than for unscreened portfolios. Nordea's study (2018) based on MSCI data also illustrates that share price volatility was eight percentage points lower for AAA-rated companies than for S&P 500 Index companies with the lowest ESG rating (B/CCC) between 2012 and 2018 (Fig. 8.3).

Additional Premium Based on Environmental Friendliness

Chan and Walter (2014) studied a total of 748 initial public offerings (IPO) and seasoned equity offerings (SEO; the sale of existing shares in a limited liability company to new investors) in the US stock market between 1990 and

2012. According to the results, environmentally friendly companies (rated using indices) received an average premium of 7% compared with companies that did not manage their environmental issues impeccably. A positive effect was detected in both the short and long term. According to the researchers, the 'green premium' is explained by the fact that investments in environmentally friendly companies involve a lower risk than investments in companies in the comparison group.

Irresponsibility Destroys Returns and Capital

Over the long term, the irresponsibility of a company can destroy shareholders' returns because of loss of reputation, for example, and any litigation costs (e.g. Renneboog, Ter Horst, & Zhang, 2008). ESG aspects play an important role in the short-term investment decision process of asset managers and are seen as a significant means of short-term risk management. In the event of serious problems, the impact of a potential breach on the market value of the investee is often very significant and rapid. For example, the Volkswagen emission scandal was widely reported in the news in 2015 and had a negative impact on the market values of shares across the automotive industry. In 2010, the Gulf of Mexico oil spill—also known as the BP oil disaster—caused the company's market value to decrease by around 50% over a period of three months. The nuclear accident at TEPCO's Fukushima 1 power plant caused the company's market value to decline, along with the market value of many other companies that use nuclear power.

Return Impacts of Various Methods of Sustainable Investing

Active Ownership Matters

Active ownership is an effective method of sustainable investing to create added value. Dimson, Karakas, and Li (2015) examined listed companies in the United States between 1999 and 2009, and identified 382 successful and 1,770 failed engagement processes where an institutional investor had warned the company of its key ESG-related problems or demanded changes to them. Successful engagement was found to have a positive impact on ESG factors and the company's finances. According to the study, the financial impacts of taking ESG factors into account are evident in the fact that successful (failed) active ownership leads to positive (zero) risk-adjusted excess returns—that is, returns outperforming risk-free investments that are +7.1% during the first year of engagement and +2.3% thereafter. The positive return impact is particularly significant in cases where the themes of engagement are related to governance (G) and climate change.

Studies support the idea that governance (G) plays a decisive role in ESG: if the governance is in order, then it is assumed that the other aspects are also managed well. In ESG analysis, both European and American investors give the strongest weight to factors related to governance (G) compared with factors related to the environment (E) and social (S) aspects (Duuren, Plantinga, & Scholtens, 2016).

According to a study by Dimson et al. (2015), active ownership is usually practised by all institutional investors committed to sustainability when the investee has shortcomings in governance (G) practices in particular. Active ownership is more likely to be successful when the investee has reputation issues related to sustainability but also has the ability to implement changes. Active ownership also increases the ownership share of institutional investors in the ownership structure. Cooperation among active owners increases the probability of success in the improvement of environmental (E) and social (S) aspects in particular. Successful engagement concerning E or S factors has a positive association with the return on assets (ROA).

Not All Exclusion Reduces Returns

According to an empirical study by Hong and Kacperczyk (2009), sin stocks generated 3–4% higher returns compared with shares in other industries in the US market between 1980 and 2003, and were 15–20% more undervalued on average because of avoidance by major institutional investors. However, more recent empirical material shows that, for example, the Vice Fund (now known as the Vitium Global Fund), which invests specifically in sin stocks, has underperformed compared with the S&P 500 Index in terms of returns since 2014, and that it has generated around 20% lower returns than the market over the past year in particular (Morningstar, 2019).

In addition, a recent academic study analysed the portfolios of the Swedish pension fund AP7 and the Government Pension Fund Global of Norway, as well as testing whether strict exclusions have affected their investment returns. The Government Pension Fund Global of Norway has previously reported that the exclusion of tobacco has not been financially profitable. Hoepner and Schopohl (2018) examined the impact of exclusion based on the sector and violations of international norms on the returns of these two investment funds. The time series for 2001–2015 shows that, taken as a whole, the exclusion[3] has not been detrimental to the profitability of the investments, as it has not reduced the average long-term return on investments. Of the excluded investments, only tobacco would have generated risk-adjusted excess returns. The risks related to the excluded investments have been higher on average than those related to the investments remaining in the portfolio. It should also be noted that exclusions have been a small part of the overall portfolio. In conclusion, the ethical goals of investors can be achieved without sacrificing financial returns. Then again, ethical exclusions do not generate additional returns.

ESG Integration and Positive Screening Generate the Best Returns

In their study, Kempf and Osthoff (2007) came to the conclusion that there is a very simple formula for generating returns: buying shares in companies with a high ESG rating[4] and seeking to divest shares in companies that perform poorly in this respect. According to the researchers, *the best returns can be achieved through positive screening by favouring the best-in-class companies*. Negative screening did not produce the same result. Favouring companies with the highest ESG ratings in their respective sectors resulted in the best outcome, generating excess returns of up to 8.7% per year, with the excess returns remaining significant even after reasonable trading costs had been taken into account. The sample is based on companies listed in the United States between 1992 and 2004.

Derwall, Koedijk, and Horst (2011) reported that maximum-return investing without consideration of ESG factors generated better returns in the short term, while consideration of ESG factors generated better returns over the longer term, from 1992 to 2008. With regard to geographical differences, it is known that European portfolio managers believe more strongly in the positive result impacts of ESG investing, while American investors expect lower risk from a sustainable investment portfolio. The result is based on a study by Duuren et al. (2016) of 126 international portfolio managers, the majority of whom use ESG information in investment decisions.

Best-in-class screening has been found to have a positive impact on the return on investment and loss risk in Europe and North America, where the availability and quality of ESG data are high (Verheyden et al., 2016). The study examined portfolios that included investments in the most sustainable 10 or 25% of companies in various sectors. The portfolios that included the best 10% and the best 25% were compared with an investment portfolio including all investees between 2010 and 2015. In the portfolios that favoured the most sustainable companies in their respective sectors, the shares generated stronger daily returns compared with the average distributions of the daily returns of the investees. Similarly, the other shares were more likely to generate negative daily returns than the screened shares. According to the researchers, the loss risk was slightly higher for the unscreened portfolios compared with the investment portfolios created using the screening method when differences in risk levels were examined in terms of the monthly returns of the portfolios. When comparing sectors, the highest positive impacts of the best-in-class method on the return on investment were detected in the consumer non-durables and health technology industries. The researchers found that ESG screening had the weakest impact on returns in the energy sector. According to the researchers, the differences in the best-in-class method are explained by differences in legislation, ESG levels and the availability of ESG data between sectors.

Challenges in Research and Criticism of Research into Sustainable Investing

Views have been expressed in the past that sustainable investments increase companies' costs and reduce their competitiveness in efficient markets (Friedman, 1970). *However, global changes in the business environment have created a situation where competitiveness in particular is being achieved by an increasing number of companies through sustainability.* Some previous studies show that sustainable investing does not have an impact on investors' returns or risks (see e.g. Auer & Schuhmacher, 2016; Halbritter & Dorfleitner, 2015). Auer and Schuhmacher (2016) used Sustainalytics' ESG data to investigate monthly returns, and report that active selection of high- or low-ESG-rated stocks did not provide superior risk-adjusted performance in comparison with passive stock market investments between 2004 and 2012.

On the other hand, some studies show that sustainable investing increases the diversification risk while also reducing diversification opportunities (see e.g. Hong & Kacperczyk, 2009; Renneboog et al., 2008; Statman & Glushkov, 2009). With sustainable investing having become more common, researchers have challenged the traditional portfolio theory, according to which investments should be diversified broadly across various investees to manage the risks related to investees. Studies have shown that although sustainable investing (e.g. ESG screening) limits diversification opportunities, the high ESG level of an investee significantly reduces the risk related to an individual investee, which is why the overall diversification risk of an ESG-screened investment portfolio is small (Hoepner, 2010; Verheyden et al., 2016). In a study by Verheyden et al. (2016), three out of four ESG-screened investment portfolios invalidate the diversification problem, as the risk-adjusted returns of ESG-screened portfolios exceed the performance of unscreened investment portfolios.

Because of the conflicting research results, investors must examine how, when and where the studies have been conducted. For example, sustainability has been measured in around 50 different ways, including the following:

1. Using an index of companies' reported sustainability indicators (e.g. the KLD index)
2. Using a single ESG rating.
3. Measuring E, S and G in numerous ways for each
4. Examining only the impact of positive screening compared with the impact of negative screening.

Differences between ESG levels may also arise from differences between the sources of ESG data, such as ESG ratings providers and ratings databases. Studies have shown significant differences between material provided by Bloomberg, ASSET4 and KLD, for example, in terms of scope and the consideration of risk factors (e.g. Dorfleitner, Halbritter, & Nguyen, 2015).

A recent academic study on five ESG rating providers (Asset4, KLD, RobecoSAM, Sustainalytics and Vigeo-Eiris) shows that the correlations between their ratings are 0.61 on average, ranging from 0.42 to 0.73, while the credit ratings from Moody's and Standard & Poor's are correlated at 0.99 (Berg, Kölbel, & Rigobon, 2020).

In addition, Barclays and Schroders, for example, have noted differences between sustainability ratings (MSCI, Sustainalytics, Thomson Reuters) in their reports. A comparison of different ESG rating providers by Schroders (2018) describes the percentages for the probability that the same company receives the same sustainability score from ESG agencies. According to the study, only slightly more than 20% of the companies with the best ratings were the same in accordance with the ESG ratings of MSCI and Sustainalytics. With regard to the poorest ESG ratings, the correlation between the ratings of MSCI and Sustainalytics is even smaller, less than 10%. In other words, not all studies are directly comparable. Instead, investors should always compare studies that are based on the same ESG ratings, for example.

Although sustainable investing has been generally found to be profitable, investors must always examine what method is meant by sustainable investing and how sustainability has been measured.

According to current knowledge, a large proportion of studies show a positive association between sustainability and financial returns. However, the limitations of research results must also be considered in their interpretation. *Time span between the completion of a study and its time of publication is usually measured in years.* For this reason, academic studies do not cover empirical data from recent years. For example, the exchange-traded funds (ETFs) that are currently available did not, for the most part, become available on the market until 2016 or later, meaning that not much scientifically published research data is available on them. Similarly, some of the indicators used in the early studies are no longer commonly used.

The results depend on the time horizon used in the study—in other words, whether the phenomenon (e.g. returns) has been studied over the long term or the short term—as well as what point of time is used in the examination. It is also worth noting that to measure ESG factors, older studies have used material from a time when the measurement of ESG was much more rudimentary than today. The age of the material and the measurement methods available at the time must be taken into account in interpreting studies. For example, the general limitations of sustainability reporting (Chapter 4) must be understood when the ESG data used in the study is based on sustainability information reported by companies. When interpreting research results, it is good to keep in mind the development of the phenomenon and its impacts on the conclusions:

- ESG data has been measured in studies using a total of around 50 different indicators.
- The number of companies producing ESG data has increased at an incredible rate. Early studies are from a time when the relative number of companies producing ESG data was small.
- The research results concerning the correlation between ESG data and financial returns are quite consistent. The correlation between ESG data and financial returns mean that there is an association, but the order of events cannot be determined based solely on this association.
- Explaining the cause-and-effect relationship is considerably more difficult than showing the correlation, and it requires consideration of the

time dimension and several control variables (e.g. sector, size, county, legislation).

- Most of the research is based on statistical methods. Interpretive interview studies conducted using social science research methods continue to be rare, but could help investors better understand complicated cause-and-effect relationships.

Notes

1. The KLD is an indicator often used in academic studies. The method was developed by researcher Amy Domini for measuring the sustainability of companies in the early 1990s. The KLD Social Index is based on this method.
2. With regard to reports provided by investment organisations, it must be kept in mind that they have not undergone scientific peer reviews.
3. According to the study, the number of exclusions by AP7 and the Government Pension Fund of Norway (NBIM) increased by around 500% between 2001 and 2015. By 2015, they had excluded a total of 129 investees on the following grounds: controversial weapons (50 exclusions), human rights issues (30), environmental issues (24), tobacco (21) and labour rights (7). Geographically, the number of exclusions was highest in North America (56), Asia (29) and Europe (22).
4. The ESG ratings are based on the KLD indicator. The indicator was originally developed under the supervision of sustainability researcher Amy Domini in the early 1990s and later laid the foundation for KLD Research & Analytics. Today, the KLD Index is part of the MSCI selection and is based on company-specific sustainability ratings. The KLD indicator is commonly used in research to describe sustainability, as it includes an extensive range of ESG dimensions. The KLD 400 Index, which describes the sustainability of the 400 largest companies listed in the United States, is also based on this indicator.

9

What Is the Profitability of Sustainability Based on?

The Impact of Sustainability on a Company's Profitability

A company's sustainability has a significant association with financial profitability. Investors must be able to identify the financial impacts of aspects related to sustainability, so they can comprehensively assess the risk-to-return ratio of the investment.

Net Sales

Sustainable companies are better able to shape their business operations as the world and operating conditions change. Sustainability affects net sales through sales volumes and sales prices. The global challenges of sustainability offer *new business opportunities*: companies can offer products and services related to renewable energy or clean water, for example. In addition, *some companies require sustainability* from their suppliers: this makes sustainability a prerequisite for sales, as well as enabling higher sales volumes for sustainable companies. Some consumers are also willing to pay a *higher price for a product or service* if it is produced responsibly. Ecolabels, domestic origin, ecological and renewable raw materials—as well as favouring products and services produced in the home country of the consumers—are typical ways of appealing to consumers to increase sales. According to some studies,

© The Author(s), under exclusive license to Springer Nature
Switzerland AG 2021
H. Silvola and T. Landau, *Sustainable Investing*,
https://doi.org/10.1007/978-3-030-71489-5_9

during recession, consumers remain most loyal to products that they consider sustainable.

> *The energy industry is a good example of how traditional business operations can face global sustainability challenges in a constructive and solution-focused manner. New business operations have been created by facing difficult issues boldly, relying on long-term expertise in the industry. These operations are not dependent on fossil fuel resources. What was previously seen as a threat to the future of the entire industry is now becoming a new growth path.*
>
> *Solar and wind energy have paved the way for the energy transition, which will continue with hydrogen solutions. Simultaneously, fossil molecules are replaced by renewable ones in fuels and plastics. Climate change is fundamentally shaping the whole energy industry, its earnings logic and cross-sectoral business models.*
>
> Kaisa Hietala, Board Professional and Entrepreneur

For investors, it is essential to assess the opportunities and risks related to net sales. The following questions, for example, can be used for this purpose:

- Does the company have business operations related to solutions to global sustainability challenges? What is the share of these products and services of the company's total sales and revenues? What kind of development can be expected in the future?
- What types of investments has the company made to promote sustainability and how are these investments expected to affect future cash flows?
- What are the risks associated with the development of net sales in terms of customers' increasing sustainability requirements or changes to legislation?
- How does the company take into account the expectations of the key stakeholders who evaluate the company? How do stakeholders affect the corporate image and business operations?

Operating Costs

Many companies seek to reduce costs through sustainable operations. Typical means include reducing the consumption of energy and water, as well as reducing waste or pollution. It is easier to motivate employees to save costs when reducing consumption is justified on environmental grounds.

Similarly, poor sustainability management or indifference can unnecessarily increase costs while also reducing the return on investment. Typical negative impacts include an unnecessarily high level of energy consumption and emissions, high employee turnover and environmental protection taxes.

The materialisation of even a single sustainability risk can cause the company to incur significant costs and loss of income. Naturally, costs also arise from the company's sustainability efforts. However, through these efforts, the company seeks to increase its net sales beyond the cost of sustainability work.

In an optimal situation, sustainable business operations increase companies' net sales more than they cost. If sustainable operations reduced expenses immediately, companies would have committed to sustainability long ago. Sustainable operations do not necessarily create a competitive advantage if the end customers are not willing to pay higher prices for sustainable products and services. As a rule, however, companies seek to respond to demand from consumers, as well as to statutory requirements for sustainable operations.

For example, the avoidance of plastic in packaging continues to increase production costs, at least for the time being, and if consumers are not willing to pay for the increase in costs through higher sales prices, the company's net sales will decrease because of lost customers. In these cases, sustainability must create such significant value for the customer that they are willing to pay a higher price for the product in order for the company's profitability to remain unchanged. This is why the end customers' consumption choices play a key role. Investors can also make an impact through their activities. For example, as a result of the EU Plastics Directive, investors have started to avoid companies connected to the use of plastic, which has been reflected in share prices and valuation factors. In other words, to create added value for shareholders, companies must consider the message sent by investors, as well as taking consumers into account.

Pasi Väisänen, Senior Analyst, Nordea Equity Research

Here are examples of questions that investors can use to assess the cost impacts related to sustainability:

- Does the company have significant past liabilities that may cause costs in the future? Such liabilities may include, for example, contaminated soil or past liabilities related to negative costs concerning people's health.
- How will political pressure and future legislation affect costs in the sector? Does the company operate in a sector where direct penalty costs, or indirect costs arising from higher taxes on raw materials, can be expected? Or does the company's sustainability strategy aim for a lighter cost structure in the future?

Financial Costs

The assessment of sustainability aspects is part of investment risk management. If a company fails to report material sustainability issues, this increases investors' risks through increased uncertainty. The terms of loan financing are weaker for a company that is assessed to be highly risk, meaning that its financial costs are higher.

In recent years, banks have increasingly granted sustainability-linked loans to their customers. In these loans, the interest margin is tied to the achievement of the company's sustainability targets, which is measured using separately negotiated key performance indicators, such as GHG emissions, accident frequency rates and human rights audits.

Investors also set higher return requirement for risky investees. The materialisation of ESG risks may reduce net sales and increase costs, in which case the company is no longer able to meet its loan repayments or other financial obligations. Consequently, the investee may end up in a situation where the return on the capital invested in the company is lower than the weighted average cost of capital (WACC) and creates no value for its owners.

In addition to avoiding company-specific risks, investors may also begin to avoid certain types of investees more broadly based on sustainability aspects. Examples of this include companies with business operations that depend on the production or use of coal—many investors have excluded such companies in recent years. As other developments in society also support the reduction of coal use, this investor behaviour, as it becomes more common, may also have a growing impact on companies' equity and debt financing costs.

Here are examples of questions investors can use when assessing sustainability aspects that affect financial costs:

- Are there significant sustainability risks related to the investee that should be considered in the return requirement? Can these risks drive the company into bankruptcy or significantly reduce future returns?
- Does the company have business operations that could lead to exclusions by investors and thereby affect financial costs as part of a broader trend?

Taxes

Taxes can have a significant impact on a company's net profit. Increasing attention is paid to taxes as an area of sustainability, but taxes are also a very challenging topic. Different stakeholders may have different views on the company's tax responsibility.

It is a somewhat complex issue, but also very interesting. Does sustainability mean paying more taxes? In that case, it reduces returns for the investor. Or does sustainability mean paying the appropriate and fair amount of taxes? Or does it mean transparency concerning tax payments? These considerations provide us with plenty to study and think about.

Reijo Knuutinen, Professor of Business Law, University of Turku.

As a rule, a company is required to pay taxes where its business operations take place and where its financial result is generated. International taxation became an increasingly material theme of the public sustainability debate when the Panama Papers—that is, documents leaked from a Panamanian law firm called Mossack Fonseca in 2016—brought attention to detailed information about assets invested in tax havens. This provoked heated discussion about aggressive tax planning, tax planning and tax avoidance.[1] The OECD (2015) estimates that the tax deficit caused by aggressive tax planning, or loss of tax revenue, is EUR 75–180 billion globally, and EUR 50–70 billion in Europe, according to an estimate by the European Parliamentary Research Service (2015). It is noteworthy, however, that tax deficits are also generated in the emerging markets (around EUR 50–93 billion, UNCTAD, 2015).

The international tax environment is undergoing a transformation, with the OECD and the EU developing new rules for international taxation and the automatic exchange of tax information between countries (e.g. the OECD's BEPS project to prevent Base Erosion and Profit Shifting and the EU's Anti-Tax Avoidance Directive). Mandatory statutory country-specific reporting related to tax payments has been increased for large companies in recent years, but the information is mainly submitted only to the tax authorities. However, there is pressure for the wider publication of country-specific tax information.

The same materiality principle that concerns sustainability reporting also applies to voluntary tax reporting, meaning that companies are allowed to report on their tax principles, as well as on the tax payments they deem material, to their chosen extent. However, the companies that would be expected to provide tax information often exclude tax matters from the scope of their voluntary sustainability reporting. In addition, through their reporting, companies can direct attention to the taxes that they want to highlight, in which case the reader will have to try to create an overview and identify the deficiencies in the reporting. To create an overview, it is a good idea to examine both direct and indirect taxes in various areas of business.

For a sustainable investor, the tax perspective is particularly challenging, as the return on investment can be increased, at least in the short term, through (aggressive) tax planning and tax avoidance. However, this may conflict with the investor's own sustainability principles or lead to increased risks through changes in legislation, for example.

Here are examples of questions that can be used in the assessment of aspects related to tax liability:

- How has the company defined its tax responsibility and tax principles?
- Does the sustainability information reported by the company include taxes at all? Why does the company not report on its taxes in more detail than what is provided in its financial statements?
- How openly does the company report on its tax footprint? Is the reported information material (financially relevant) tax information for the company?
- Does the group of companies include tax haven companies? For what reasons does the company operate in these countries?
- What is the effective tax rate of the company and does it differ from the normal effective tax rate for similar companies or the sector? What causes the difference?
- Can public data be used to assess risks related to taxation?
- Are there any tax considerations associated with the investee that may prove problematic because of changes in consumer behaviour, for example, or legislative changes?
- How will revenues be affected if the tax structures used are no longer acceptable and more taxes have to be paid?

Sustainable Investing and Economic Theory

There is no single universal theory for sustainable investing. The definitions and international frameworks discussed earlier in this book guide the notion of sustainable investment. Based on them, each investor determines their own sustainability strategy. However, sustainable investment can be better understood by examining widely known economic theories and comparing the principles of responsible investing with these theories.

Neoclassical economic theory, which today is considered mainstream economics, is largely based on the views of Milton Friedman, who won the Nobel Memorial Prize in Economic Sciences in 1976. Neoclassical economic theory is based on the idea that the most important task of a company is to create value for its shareholders.

Stakeholder theory, which was published by Edward Freeman in 1983, can be considered an alternative view to neoclassical economic theory. According to stakeholder theory, while the purpose of business is to generate profits for the company, stakeholders' expectations must be taken into consideration. While neoclassical economic theory directs all benefits to the shareholder, stakeholder theory takes other stakeholders—such as employees, customers, suppliers and non-governmental organisations—into account as well, seeking to benefit them in some way. In other words, value is created together with the stakeholders, considering their needs and expectations, but financial profits are eventually directed to the owner. Stakeholder theory is often seen as a theoretical framework for corporate social responsibility. It takes more broadly into account the company's environmental impacts and social dimensions, which materialise as impacts on the stakeholders. Michael Porter from Harvard Business School has elaborated on the idea behind Freeman's stakeholder theory by highlighting the idea of *creating shared value*. According to his idea, a company must not only generate profits for its owners but also satisfy the needs of society and solve problems in society by sustainable means (Porter & Kramer, 2011).

Within which theory does sustainable investing fall ideologically? Figure 9.1 illustrates the differences between the two theoretical frameworks. Neoclassical economic theory emphasises investors as stakeholders. However, it does not exclude sustainable business operations. It has been argued that the interpretation and application of Friedman's thoughts have been taken too far in the world of business, meaning that profits for investors can be generated 'at any cost.' The theory in itself, of course, does not encourage anyone to act irresponsibly. The image of irresponsibility may be reinforced by the fact

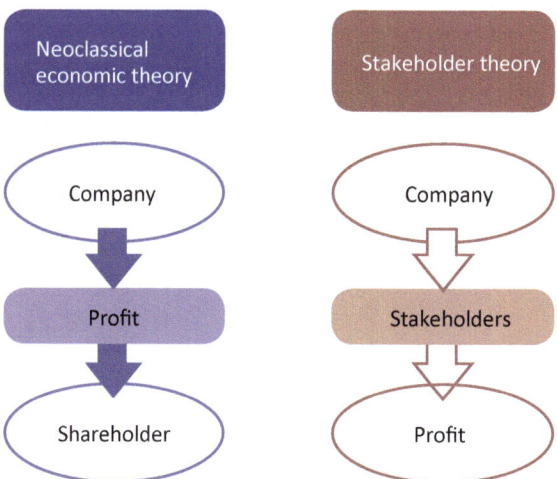

Fig. 9.1 Neoclassical and stakeholder theory

that for a long time, sustainability was manifested as a highly visible donation culture in the American business tradition.

Stakeholder theory, on the other hand, seeks sustainability through the consideration of stakeholders. In stakeholder theory, a company generates returns ideologically by taking its stakeholders into account. However, this does not guarantee the company's sustainability in its business operations in practice. Just as in neoclassical economic theory, the company does not automatically operate irresponsibly—instead, it can create value for stakeholders through products and services that provide solutions to global problems. According to both theories, a company must create value to shareholders, but this is achieved through different focuses: neoclassical economic theory emphasises owners as stakeholders, whereas according to stakeholder theory, returns to owners are generated by taking the expectations of key stakeholders into account.

From the perspective of sustainable investing, it is not necessary to put the theories in an order of priority. By understanding that there are special features, investors can analyse their own understanding of sustainable business operations and sustainable investing. Sustainable investing is not based solely and perfectly on a specific theory. Investors must determine their own principles of sustainability and assess the purposes of their investees in society.

People used to say that "the business of business is business," as Milton Friedman put it. This meant that moral statements are for individuals and politicians to make, not for companies. This position would be justified if compliance with laws and regulations were morally sufficient. But this is not the case, as not everything can be governed by law. For this reason, it is in the interest of society at large that moral issues are considered in business life and that people and companies act accordingly. The problem may be that it can sometimes be difficult to tell what is morally right. Effective non-governmental organisations can help here.

Image, reputation and brand are invaluable for companies. Therefore, ethical considerations are important for companies in terms of profitability, whether or not the owners or management have adopted the principles of sustainability. Market pressure, consumers and investors will at best drive companies towards more appropriate behaviour if sustainability is defined reasonably and can be measured well.

Sixten Korkman, Economist

The Association Between Sustainability and Strategy in Value Creation

Expectations concerning the significance of sustainable business operations and sustainable investing have become subject to wider debate. Expectations towards companies solving sustainability challenges in line with the *sustainable development goals*, in particular, have increased among institutional investors. Creating shared value has been highlighted in both research and business management literature, particularly by Michael Porter, the Bishop William Lawrence University Professor at Harvard Business School.

A sustainable company satisfies the needs of the surrounding society and provides solutions to problems in society, and thereby generates profits for its owners. A sustainable company is able to position itself in such a way that it creates positive added value to society, as well as generating profits to its owners. Examples of companies with clear positive added value include companies that help recycle raw materials, decrease pollution or reduce health problems. Sustainability should be included in the company's strategy and its mission – that is, the purpose of its business operations. Investors can also test whether the company has this type of "shared value" thinking or whether the company is just a machine to make money.

Pertti Korhonen, Board Professional

Porter defines strategy as activity through which a company seeks a competitive advantage. According to Porter, it is essential that these strategic functions are compatible with each other. The management must find a toolkit of compatible functions that enables the company to progress from the present to its future goals. Sustainability must be an integral part of the company's strategy, as well as being compatible with its other operations and being related to its special expertise. Then it is credible and benefits the company.

According to studies, pioneers of sustainability and strategic leaders benefit from an early start in implementing sustainability. According to extensive international material, the first companies to implement sustainability practices in a sector achieve wider market shares than companies that implement sustainability practices later (Albuquerque, Durnev, & Koskinen, 2012). The pioneering companies in a sector create a competitive advantage for themselves (Bhimani, Silvola, & Sivabalan, 2016). In light of research results, it seems that a strategy without a sustainability perspective is not an optimal choice (Porter & Kramer, 2006).

Based on their sustainability strategy, investees can be roughly divided into three categories: pioneers, leaders and beginners.

Pioneers have sustainability at the core of their strategy. Their business idea is created to support sustainable development. At its best, innovation helps other operators to engage in more sustainable business operations or customers to make more sustainable choices. This group includes clean tech and circular economy companies, for example. For an existing large company, it may not be realistic to change its business strategy completely in the short run. Therefore, its research-based technology incubators (spin-offs) can implement this strategy and seek new competitive advantage through sustainable development.

Leaders modify their business strategy by integrating sustainability into their existing strategy. This is not a superficial effort, as strategy work of this type often requires a significant change to the old strategy. For the change to be credible, the company must communicate its practical development needs and investments in more sustainable business operations to investors.

Beginners modify their strategy by adding some sustainability elements or creating a separate sustainability strategy. Sustainability is used in marketing, image creation and minor measures that do not cost too much or that bring cost benefits. These companies often imitate others rather than developing new solutions. Sustainability does not offer a competitive advantage, but the company does not gain a reputation for being completely irresponsible either. A large portion of companies are still at this stage, as it is also the introductory stage for beginners.

> *A sustainable corporate strategy is a basic prerequisite for successful business operations over the long term. A sustainable corporate strategy can also be a competitive advantage, but its absence or inadequacy significantly increases the company's risk premium for investors, making the company highly vulnerable to the growing sustainability requirements of consumers, customers and legislation.*
> Rami Vehmas, Senior Portfolio Manager, Ilmarinen Mutual Pension Insurance Company

A company that is a beginner in sustainability may publish a separate sustainability strategy, but not a sustainable corporate strategy. In such a case, sustainability has not yet been deeply integrated into other operations, and the synergies are limited. Highly advanced companies bring sustainability to the core of their strategy. Such companies are aware that sustainability has become a requirement of the stakeholders, and that there is normative pressure to comply. It is essential for investors to assess what kind of competitive advantage the company's strategy offers and how the sustainability strategy has been implemented at the operational level, all the way to investments and future returns.

The Role of Management

Management capability is often mentioned as one of the most important criteria for investment decisions. If a company's strategy strongly emphasises sustainability, it is also important to assess the state and practices of sustainability management. According to research results, companies do not achieve most of their sustainability goals, because their sustainability strategy remains separate from practical actions and remuneration, as well as from the management team's work (Bhimani et al., 2016). The existence of a sustainability manager correlates with the achievement of sustainability goals compared with companies where no one is responsible for sustainability aspects. In addition, the appointment of a sustainability manager signals to stakeholders that sustainability aspects are taken seriously.

Sustainability is a top-down approach that permeates through the whole organisation. Rather than being a separate function in a company, it is included in all business processes. Compliance with laws and international norms is only the beginning – the foundation on which the company's sustainable operations are built. From this foundation, the company can develop products and services that create a competitive edge, as well as offering solutions to global sustainable development problems.

For the board of directors to endorse the company's strategy, the board must be able to see sustainability as a competitive advantage. The board must be able to identify which sustainability aspects are material for the company, as well as setting relevant goals and indicators and monitoring their implementation. Excellent results will be achieved when sustainability goals are taken into account in the ERP system, remuneration and the bonus systems. This requires expertise and experience in sustainability, even from the board. It is also a good idea to provide the board members with training on sustainability issues. Today, sustainability is increasingly a hygiene factor for many investors – something that the company simply needs to get right.

Anne Brunila, Board Professional

The board of directors must be responsible for what the management is not necessarily responsible for in practice, particularly in terms of the company's long-term and short-term interests. Managing directors may listen too intently to analysts' expectations and make short-sighted decisions at the expense of the owner's long-term interests. The focus is too much on the current quarter, and the management may no longer be with the company to enjoy the success that materialises as a result of sustainable business decisions. I feel that the board of directors must protect the managing director and the company strategy from investors whose perspectives are too short-term. The world needs game-changers who understand the universal

ownership principle and consider the good health of the overall economy in the long term. A universal owner better understands the comprehensive impacts of business operations – that is, the long-term connection between ESG and generating returns.
                      Hiromichi Mizuno, Chief Investment Officer, Government Pension Investment Fund (GPIF), Japan 2015–2020, Board Professional (Tesla, Danone)

Measuring a company's performance is a prerequisite for strategic monitoring and management. Balanced scorecards have established their position as strategy monitoring tools in many companies. The management traditionally uses them to monitor not only financial performance but also customers and internal processes, as well as organisational learning and growth. The pioneers have now reached a stage where sustainability is being integrated into scorecards and remuneration. Remuneration can be based on an increase in the share of net sales from sustainable products out of total sales, improvement in employees' well-being (social responsibility), increase in the amount of recyclable or renewable materials or change in the carbon footprint, for example. In the literature, scorecards with a sustainability dimension are called *sustainability scorecards*. The setting and measurement of sustainability goals offers the management an opportunity to monitor changes in business operations along the way, as well as to detect potential warning signals and implement the necessary corrective measures in good time.

A growing number of companies provide ESG information on their websites and in sustainability reports. However, the pioneer in a sector usually determines the reporting standards, with the followers imitating the experienced producer of reports. Typically, a company that is new to reporting begins its reporting by means of a competitor comparison. Pioneers can also seek to influence legislators and interest groups, as well as the development of the sector more broadly, creating better opportunities for their business operations.

Ethical Corporate Culture as Part of Good Governance

Corporate scandals—such as Enron-style accounting fraud and the emissions scams of Volkswagen and other automotive industry companies—have almost invariably arisen from identifiable corporate ethics issues.

Typically, *the results of employee surveys are poor at problematic companies*. For example, the respondents are afraid that they will be punished if they report unethical behaviour, and they feel insecure when seeking advice on an ethical problem. Their colleagues engage in unethical behaviour and appreciate results more than integrity. According to the employees, the management can be bribed, and its members regard people as irresponsible and do not respect their employees. The supervisors are also prone to accepting bribes and do not take appropriate measures when they detect unethical or inappropriate behaviour. A problematic company does not indicate its ethical expectations and disciplinary guidelines clearly, leaving the employees unaware of the consequences of misconduct. Employee surveys at problematic companies have also often revealed that the employees are not encouraged to share their opinions, nor are they considered equal to the management. A problematic company approves unethical behaviour and does not address confirmed cases of misconduct quickly.

ESG ratings score companies' governance. However, the assessment and quantitative measurement of corporate culture and the legality of business operations as part of good governance are challenging, as corporate ethics is the sum of the ethical practices of many individuals. Internal audit and controls reveal many issues, but they are not always able to delve into the behaviour and ethical choices of individuals. Investors can, however, look at the following signs:

- Has the company determined any ethical guidelines or codes of conduct?
- Does the company have a whistle-blowing channel? Does the company disclose the number of reports filed through the channel and does it openly describe how the reports are processed?
- Does the company report on employee surveys that measure their perceptions of the legality of the workplace?
- How openly does the company report its discussions on the ethicality of work? Workshops and discussion events related to the topic, as well as elaboration on the results of employee surveys, indicate whether issues can be discussed at all.
- Is the company involved in legal proceedings with employees, customers or the supply chain concerning governance issues?
- How does the company fare in job satisfaction competitions? What is said about the company's corporate culture and workplace satisfaction on social media?

A company's successes are often highlighted in its sustainability reporting, and companies may feel reluctant to report on problems openly. However, it would be better for investors if companies also communicated about the development needs, as the complete lack of information causes suspicion and increases risks.

> *Even in sustainable companies, reports should normally be filed continuously, with the reported issues becoming smaller and more detailed over time. Alarm bells should ring if no reports are filed at all. Previously, the number of employees who had completed an online course on the code of conduct would typically be reported in a GRI-compliant sustainability report. Today, the focus is increasingly on impacts, such as the results of employee surveys that are used to measure the employees' perceptions of the ethicality of the workplace. The most essential aspect is to show how openly ethical issues can be discussed at different organisational levels, how easy it is for employees to address issues without fear of retaliation and how eagerly issues are addressed to resolve them.*
>
> Niina Ratsula, Ethics & Compliance Adviser, Code of Conduct Company

According to studies (McMurrian & Matulich, 2016; Svensson & Wood, 2008), companies with strong business ethics keep their stakeholders most satisfied. Correspondingly, poor corporate ethics can weaken financial results and eventually lead to the loss of all invested capital, as has been the case in many widely known corporate scandals. Many investors avoid companies with ethical problems because of risk management, as negative news has a negative impact on business operations and share prices. Ethical misconduct can also cause legal expenses and other costs that reduce the return on invested capital.

Note

1. These terms are often confused in public debate, and in everyday language, tax avoidance has become a general term for a range of tax problems. Tax planning refers to companies seeking to predict their tax consequences in various circumstances and minimise their taxes within the scope of tax legislation. There is no legal definition for aggressive tax planning, but it means exploiting the weaknesses of the tax system of a single country or the interfaces between different tax systems in accordance with current laws. Tax avoidance refers to companies actively seeking gaps and ambiguities, or legal loopholes, in tax laws to minimise their taxes. Tax avoidance complies with the rules of the tax system, but deviates from the purpose of the laws or the overall purpose in an effort to reduce or avoid taxes. In drawing the line between tax avoidance and tax planning, a key criterion is the fact that tax avoidance measures are somehow artificial. In other words, tax avoidance is not illegal, but it is questionable and disapproved of in terms of sustainability. Tax fraud and tax evasion are deliberate criminal

acts where the tax authorities are provided with false information in an effort to avoid taxes (Knuutinen, 2017, 125–139).

References

Albuquerque, R., Durnev, A., & Koskinen, Y. (2012). *Corporate social responsibility and asset pricing in industry equilibrium.*

Amel-Zadeh, A., & Serafeim, G. (2018). Why and how investors use ESG information: Evidence from a global survey. *Financial Analysts Journal, 74*(3), 87–103.

Auer, B. R., & Schuhmacher, F. (2016). Do socially (ir)responsible investments pay? New evidence from international ESG data. *The Quarterly Review of Economics and Finance, 59,* 51–62.

Berg, F., Kölbel, J., & Rigobon, R. (2020). *Aggregate confusion: The divergence of ESG ratings.* Available at SSRN: https://ssrn.com/abstract=3438533.

Bhimani, A., Silvola, H., & Sivabalan, P. (2016). Voluntary corporate social responsibility reporting: A study of early and late reporter motivations and outcomes. *Journal of Management Accounting Research, 28*(2), 77–101.

Chan, P. T., & Walter, T. (2014). Investment performance of 'environmentally-friendly' firms and their initial public offers and seasoned equity offers. *Journal of Banking & Finance, 44,* 177–188.

Cheema-Fox, A., LaPerla, B., Serafeim, G., & Wang, H. S. (2020, October). *Corporate resilience and response during COVID-19* (Harvard Business School Working Paper, No. 20-108).

Derwall, J., Koedijk, K., & Horst, J. T. (2011). A tale of values-driven and profit-seeking social investors. *Journal of Banking & Finance, 35,* 2137–2147.

Dimson, E., Karakas, O., & Li, X. (2015). Active ownership. *The Review of Financial Studies, 28*(12), 3225–3268.

Dorfleitner, G., Halbritter, G., & Nguyen, M. (2015). Measuring the level and risk of corporate responsibility—An empirical comparison of different ESG rating approaches. *Journal of Asset Management, 16*(7), 450–466.

Duuren, E., Plantinga, A., & Scholtens, B. (2016). ESG integration and the investment management process: Fundamental investing reinvented. *Journal of Business Ethics, 138*(3), 525–533.

European Parliamentary Research Service. (2015). *Bringing transparency, coordination and convergence to corporate tax policies in the European Union.* http://www.europarl.europa.eu/RegData/etudes/STUD/2015/558773/EPRS_STU(2015)558773_EN.pdf.

Friede, G., Busch, T., & Bassen, A. (2015). ESG and financial performance: Aggregated evidence from more than 2000 empirical studies. *Journal of Sustainable Finance & Investment, 5*(4), 210–233.

Friedman, M. (1970, September 13). The social responsibility of business is to increase its profits. *The New York Times Magazine*.

Halbritter, G., & Dorfleitner, G. (2015). The wages of social responsibility—Where are they? A critical review of ESG investing. *Review of Financial Economics, 26*, 25–35.

Hoepner, A., & Schopohl, L. (2018). On the price of morals in markets: An empirical study of the Swedish AP-Funds and the Norwegian Government Pension Fund. *Journal of Business Ethics, 151*, 665–692.

Hong, H., & Kacperczyk, M. (2009). The price of sin: The effects of social norms on markets. *Journal of Financial Economics, 93*(1), 15–36.

Kempf, A., & Osthoff, P. (2007). The effect of socially responsible investing on portfolio performance. *European Financial Management, 13*(5), 908–922.

Khan, M., Serafeim, G., & Yoon, A. (2016). Corporate sustainability: First evidence on materiality. *The Accounting Review, 91*(6), 1697–1724.

Knuutinen, R. (2017). Hyvät pahat verot [*Love and hate for taxes*]. Docendo Oy. ISBN 978-952291-347-0.

Margolis, J. D., Elfenbein, H. A., & Walsh, J. P. (2007). *Does it pay to be good? A meta-analysis and redirection of research on the relationship between corporate social and financial performance* (Harvard Business School Working Paper).

Morningstar. (2019). *Vice Fund*. https://www.morningstar.com/funds/xnas/vicex/betaquote.html. Referenced 25 November 2020.

McMurrian, R. C., & Matulich, E. (2016). Building customer value and profitability with business ethics. *Journal of Business & Economics Research, 14*(3), 83–90.

Nordea. (2018). *Research insights*. https://nordeamarkets.com/wp-content/uploads/2018/09/ESG_140918.pdf.

OECD. (2015). *Measuring and monitoring BEPS*. http://www.oecd.org/tax/measuring-and-monitoring-beps-action-11-2015-final-report-9789264241343-en.htm.

Porter, M. E., & Kramer, M. R. (2006). Strategy & society: The link between competitive advantage and corporate social responsibility. *Harvard Business Review, 84*(12), 78–92.

Porter, M. E., & Kramer, M. R. (2011). Creating shared value. *Harvard Business Review, 89*(1/2), 62–77.

Renneboog, L., Ter Horst, J., & Zhang, C. (2008). Socially responsible investments: Institutional aspects, performance, and investor behavior. *Journal of Banking & Finance, 32*(9), 1723–1742.

Rogers, J., & Serafeim, G. (2019). *Pathways to materiality: How sustainability issues become financially material to corporations and their investors* (Harvard Business Review. Working Paper 20-056).

Schroders. (2018). *Index-based ESG strategies: Key things to watch for*. https://www.schroders.com/pl/sysglobalassets/digital/insights/2018/thought-leadership/e.s.g.-in-passive-final.pdf.

Serafeim, G. (2018). *Public sentiment and the price of corporate sustainability* (Harvard Business School Working Paper, 19–044).

Statman, M., & Glushkov, D. (2009). The wages of social responsibility. *Financial Analysts Journal, 65*(4), 33–46.

Svensson, G., & Wood, G. (2008). A model of business ethics. *Journal of Business Ethics, 77*(3), 303–322.

UNCTAD. (2015). *World investment report 2015.* http://unctad.org/en/Publications Library/wir2015_en.pdf.

Verheyden, T., Eccles, R. G., & Feiner, A. (2016). ESG for all? The impact of ESG screening on return, risk, and diversification. *Journal of Applied Corporate Finance, 28*(2), 47–55.

Part V

Sustainability Trends and the Future of ESG

10

Changes in International Politics and Legislation

Sustainability of the Financial System

The short-term perspective of the financial system is increasingly considered problematic. At the same time, the transition to a low-carbon society is posing an immense challenge that requires the assessment of the impacts of climate risks on the financial system. The goal of financial system sustainability, as well as the legislation that is being prepared, is to change financial market incentives in such a way that they support sustainable investing and the consideration of long-term climate and environmental risks.

Cash flows should be aligned to support this direction. According to the European Commission, to achieve the targets of the Paris Agreement, for example, annual investments of EUR 260 billion in low-carbon and energy-efficient technology are needed in Europe alone. The public sector cannot manage this change on its own, and so the EU is seeking help from the private sector by creating legislation for the financial markets that would make such investments more profitable. Legislative changes should have an impact on the return on investment, which creates a steering effect and causes the investment market to correct the market, redirecting capital towards sustainable investments.

The purpose of the Sustainable Finance Action Plan is to stop motivating bad investments and support investments in line with sustainable development. This is the way to resolve climate change and support sustainable development. The size of the international financial market is USD 85 trillion, of which around

© The Author(s), under exclusive license to Springer Nature Switzerland AG 2021
H. Silvola and T. Landau, *Sustainable Investing*,
https://doi.org/10.1007/978-3-030-71489-5_10

USD 30 trillion needs to be reinvested because of the climate risk. The Economist Intelligence Unit[1] has estimated based on current developments that more than USD 4 trillion in capital will be lost globally because of climate change by 2100, with assets becoming stranded. A rise of six degrees in global average temperatures would have even more dramatic consequences.

Sustainable finance is becoming the largest financial market reform of our time since the introduction of double-entry bookkeeping. It is just a matter of how this change can be implemented in a controlled manner, without causing too much market disruption. The European Parliament seeks to avoid uncontrolled divestment of coal investments.

Sirpa Pietikäinen, Member of the European Parliament, EPP lead negotiator for the European Parliament's report on sustainable finance

The materialisation of the transition risk has been estimated to have significant impacts on the business opportunities, risks and value development of investees. In addition, new products and technologies that replace previous ones also gradually destroy the value of older products and technologies. Investors can seek to determine in advance how much capital is tied to such investments. This may concern, for example, cars with internal combustion engines, which are being replaced by evolving technologies, such as electric cars.

According to the European Parliament's report (2017), the OECD estimates that public subsidies for fossil energy amount to USD 160–200 billion annually. According to the IEA, this is 5% of the gross domestic product of the OECD and BRIICS countries[2] and more than double the amount of subsidies for renewable energy. Publicly subsidised fossil energy generates 13% of global greenhouse gas emissions. In light of these figures, it should be clear that there is political pressure to reduce public support for fossil fuels. Potential cuts in public subsidies, as well as potential reallocations of capital to renewable energy forms, are estimated to have a significant impact on the return on investment over the long term.

In some countries, amendments have already been made to the legislation concerning the financial sector in recent years. For example, France already has binding legislation in place that requires institutional investors to report extensively on the climate risks related to investments. The EU is taking the lead in reforming the financial system through proposed legislation on sustainable finance.

The EU Sustainable Finance Strategy

The EU Commission published an action plan on financing sustainable growth in March 2018 and the related legislative proposals in May 2018. Some of the items (listed below) of the action plan are still being developed further, which is why they involve uncertainties, and there were no guarantees at the time of writing this book that they will be implemented as such. Nevertheless, it is good for investors to be aware of what kind of legislation is being prepared and how the legislation will affect investing if it is implemented. The goal of the action plan is to direct assets to investments in line with the principles of sustainable development and make sustainable investing a key part of investment risk management, as well as increasing transparency and a long-term perspective on investing activities.

To build a sustainable finance system, the EU plans to make legislative amendments in areas that are key from investors' perspectives. *A classification system for sustainable economic activities (green taxonomy) and the related EU standards is being prepared.* The EU aims to list which activities are sustainable in terms of climate change, the environment and social aspects. The taxonomy is intended to be used in EU legislation[3] on sustainable finance, including standards (e.g. green bonds), sustainable benchmark indices and any future EU ecolabels for investment products (e.g. green bond standard). The goal is also to update the classification regularly.

The aim is to prevent the risk of greenwashing and thereby facilitate the collection of funding for environmentally friendly operations across borders within the EU. The definition is based on the EU's political goals, such as compliance with the Paris Agreement and the UN Sustainable Development Goals.

The proposed legislation aim to suggest obligations for institutional investors and asset managers to include ESG aspects in investment decisions and reporting. Therefore, in the future, sustainable investing would be a clearly defined part of investors' fiduciary duty towards beneficiaries.

The proposed legislation would create a new category of benchmarks: the 'EU climate transition benchmark' (aiming for emission reductions) and the 'EU Paris-aligned benchmark' (consisting of investments aligned with the 1.5-degree or the 2-degree target of the Paris Agreement). The purpose is to increase the transparency and consistency of the benchmark methodologies and elements for investors to be better able to assess their quality. The data underlying such benchmarks depends in turn on sufficient, standardised reporting from the constituent issuers.

The EU is exploring the ***more effective inclusion of the sustainability perspective in credit ratings*** and market reviews in an effort to make the consideration of ESG an obligation for credit rating agencies. According to studies, a company's sustainability has a positive association with financial costs and the availability of financing, as a high level of sustainability and the related transparency reduces risks. This measure would have an impact on the financial costs of all investees, but it should be taken into account when investing in debt (fixed income investments) and the financial sector in particular.

The EU legislation includes a specific goal to ***include sustainability in the capital adequacy requirements of banks and insurance companies***. This would mean the separation of capital adequacy requirements from financial risk and would therefore be a key change. The proposal states that banks, insurance companies and pension funds may be exposed to risks related to the neglect of environmental aspects (including the climate risk). There may also be risks related to customer companies' solvency and capital adequacy, as well as to the systemic risk possibly caused by the climate risk.

Identifying customers' sustainability expectations is becoming part of the requirements for investment advice. In future, companies providing investment products and insurance policies should take ESG aspects into account when advising customers. Providers of investment advice already have an obligation to assess the customer's investment targets and risk tolerance in order to be able to recommend financial instruments or insurance policies that are suitable for them. The EU is also looking into opportunities to take sustainability aspects into account in investor suitability assessments. In practice, this would mean that the customer's sustainability goals or sustainability profile should be integrated into investment advice.

The EU's Sustainable Finance Legislation Would Change Companies' Reporting Requirements

Despite the mainstreaming of sustainable investing, one of the key questions continues to be how extensively sustainability aspects are actually taken into account in investment decisions. Investors report problems related to the harmonisation, transparency and comparability of companies' sustainability information as the most common reasons for the limited use of ESG data (e.g. Amel-Zadeh & Serafeim, 2018). The EU's sustainable finance legislation seeks to address these issues by increasing companies' reporting requirements.

An investor who cannot interpret ESG data will be in trouble in the future. Not understanding ESG data can be compared to investing in a company without reviewing its financial statements, balance sheet and key figures, or only looking at the pictures of factories in its annual report. In the EU Sustainable Finance Action Plan, the starting point is that sustainability reporting will be standardised and that company-specific ESG data will be made transparent and comparable for investors. A similar reporting framework is needed for ESG as is already applied to financial information (International Financial Reporting Standards, IFRS). The company's disclosure obligation and due diligence play a key role in this.'

Sirpa Pietikäinen, Member of the European Parliament

The EU Non-Financial Reporting Directive (2014/95/EU) requires large public-interest entities to disclose material information about their key environmental impacts, social impacts and good governance aspects. The directive concerns more than 6000 companies in Europe. The lack of comparability of information between different companies remains a challenge, as companies use their chosen indicators to report on aspects that they consider material.

A group of technical experts established by the European Commission also examined the previous EU directive concerning the disclosure of non-financial information in light of whether guidelines could be added to report detailed information related to climate impacts. The EU plans to combine the **Task Force on Climate-related Financial Disclosures**[4] **(TCFD) framework**, which was published in 2017, and possibly other new recommendations with the forthcoming reporting guidelines. From an investor's perspective, the aim of the EU sustainable finance legislation for more consistent reporting may improve the comparison of the sustainability of companies.

The EU Is Preparing a Taxonomy of Sustainable Investments

In the summer of 2018, the European Commission set up a technical expert group on sustainable finance (TEG) to prepare technical details related to the EU's sustainable finance legislative proposals. The TEG has published a proposal for a classification system focusing on climate impacts in particular. However, further work on the technical details is required before the adoption of the classification system as part of EU legislation.

A key measure of the success of the EU's sustainable finance legislation is whether it will guide financing in the future and whether it will have an impact on companies' operations.

Providers of green financial products will be required to explain how their products relate to the EU taxonomy as a common standard for green economic activities. I can see the benefit of having more clarity around what is green and what is not – this could help catalyse market growth for sustainable products. On the other hand, I also see a risk that this is not going to touch the mainstream and will only apply to the niche of financial products that are labelled as green.

I'm hopeful that the Commission's initiative proves successful in the long term. Maybe it can be compared to the food market, where the EU introduced minimum standards for organic food products a few years ago. While the market is still small overall, it is the fastest growing, and by now even discounters have some organic products on the shelves.

Nico Fettes, Head of Product Development Capital Markets, CDP Europe, former member of the European Commission's Technical Expert Group on Sustainable Finance 2018–2020

Determining sustainable development is particularly challenging, and choices are made in the work. ***Sustainability is not black and white:*** for example, the same company can offer solutions to mitigate climate change and use forced labour to manufacture its products. Politics are also strongly involved in determining green investments, as the related definitions are guided by the goals and commitments set by the EU, which may change—thereby also changing the definition of green business. In addition, the same companies can have both positive and negative impacts, and sustainability ratings seem to focus on defining the 'greenness' of various activities, rather than determining what a green company is.

The EU's standardisation work also focuses on concepts and tools that are evolving rapidly, which is why the goal, in many respects, is to set minimum requirements. The standards may also be updated in the future: for example, with regard to the positive climate impact index, the definition of such investments is evolving rapidly. Some of the definitions being prepared are related to tools that divide opinions: for example, low-carbon benchmarks are one of the key areas of the EU's work, but they involve limitations that have also been discussed in this book (including the fact that the carbon footprint does not describe all climate risks comprehensively).

Investing that supports sustainable development, such as green investments and green bonds, is an evolving phenomenon and will lead to new and useful ***innovations***. Discussion has arisen concerning, for example, whether the incipient increase in green investment products should be standardised by means of minimum requirements that could be sufficient as such for some operators and could therefore, in the worst case, discourage the future development of standards.

Notes

1. https://eiuperspectives.economist.com/sustainability/cost-inaction/white-paper/cost-inaction.
2. The Organization for Economic Co-operation and Development (OECD) was originally established by European and North American countries. Today, the organisation also has members outside these regions, a total of 37 member countries at the time of writing this book. The OECD focuses on economic cooperation, and numerous internationally binding rules and recommendations have been prepared within its framework. BRIICS is short for Brazil, Russia, India, Indonesia, China and South Africa.
3. As part of its sustainable finance action plan, the EU will produce an extensive study on the quality of the sustainability ratings. The purpose is to evaluate methodologies and examine the structure of the markets and the coverage and depth of studies and ratings conducted by service providers, in addition to assessing the independence of operators.
4. The recommendations of the TCFD (Task Force on Climate-related Financial Disclosure) were prepared by the FSB (Financial Stability Board).

11

Sustainability Trends and International Frameworks

The responsibilities of institutional investors such as pension companies for returns on investment are long term, and therefore the **need to form views of the future and assess how successfully companies will manage and be able to adapt to future changes is emphasised** in investing activities. Development is driven by policy decisions, such as limiting negative environmental and climate impacts, as well as by rapid technological development that provides new solutions to sustainability challenges, such as the use of renewable energy. Changes that primarily appear as risks for one company may mean business opportunities for others.

The impacts of sustainability trends may materialise:

- as **long-term drivers of change gradually** when the price of emission allowances increases, for example, or the pricing of externalities improves
- **possibly also as sudden shocks and changes** if complex developments that materialise across the globe are triggered by a breakthrough in a single technology, for example, or by a natural disaster.

Sustainability trends, such as climate change and the availability of fresh water, involve risks that can affect many industries or a number of companies in a specific geographical area at once. Risks may also materialise at some point in the supply chain, meaning that the indirect effects can also be very significant and extensive. Risks related to respecting human rights, for example, are more company-specific and can therefore be managed by

© The Author(s), under exclusive license to Springer Nature
Switzerland AG 2021
H. Silvola and T. Landau, *Sustainable Investing*,
https://doi.org/10.1007/978-3-030-71489-5_11

spreading investments across various companies, for it is unlikely that all the companies included in a broad investment portfolio will face a human rights scandal or similar at the same time.

Sustainability trends also involve business opportunities concerning solutions to global sustainability challenges through new products, services and business models, for example.

Combating Climate Change and Adapting to Its Impacts

Climate change is a key risk to the future of human communities and thereby also to the economic system and companies. According to a special report by the Intergovernmental Panel on Climate Change (2018), limiting global warming to 1.5 degrees compared with pre-industrial levels would be advisable to limit the negative effects. In previous reports, the risk limit was considered to be 2 degrees.

Significant changes are required for global warming to stay within the risk limits. To limit warming to 1.5 degrees, carbon dioxide emissions would need to be reduced by 45% by 2030 compared with 2010, and net zero emissions should be reached by 2050. This would mean remarkably rapid changes in terms of energy production, land use, infrastructure (including transport and construction) and industrial production systems in particular. Correspondingly, if global warming exceeds the risk limits and the climate changes in many ways in different regions, this will have an impact on societies and the operating environments of companies.

The climate aspects of investments are divided into three categories in the *TCFD recommendations* for climate-related reporting (2017): transition risks, physical risks and opportunities. The risks arising from the transition to a low-carbon society are referred to as *transition risks*, which are caused by political changes, stricter legislation, rapid technological development and changes in the markets, among other factors. For example, the next changes to the EU's emissions trading system are made in 2021, and fewer free allowances than before are allocated to companies. The prices of emission allowances have also been on an upward trend, although the starting level has been low. Increased awareness of the climate crisis may affect companies not only through legislation but also if customers increasingly take climate impacts into consideration in their consumption decisions.

The changing climate also has a direct impact on concrete business risks. *Physical risks* can be related, for example, to an increase in extreme weather events or the impacts of higher average temperatures.

There are also significant *business opportunities* related to mitigating and adapting to climate change. These opportunities are related to the following aspects in particular: more efficient use of resources (e.g. energy-efficient buildings and more efficient modes of transport), renewable energy sources, new products and services (e.g. indemnity insurance against the impacts of climate change), access to new markets (e.g. partnerships with public-sector organisations and the introduction of green financial products) and the development of alternative products and solutions that facilitate adaptation to the consequences of climate change (e.g. improvements related to infrastructure).

Risks and opportunities related to climate change can be identified in various industries. The risks are related to, for example, *the role of companies focusing on fossil fuels* in a carbon-free future: the mitigation of climate change requires reducing and ramping down the use of fossil fuels. From an investor's point of view, critical considerations include, for example, the following: What is the time frame for implementing changes to the energy system and what will happen to companies focusing on oil and gas extraction if some of their underground fossil fuel reserves lose their value? Can these companies have a role in a future free from fossil fuels through their energy expertise and engineers?

A few years ago, an oil company described to me the challenge they were facing: that mainstream investors saw investing in renewables as "value-destructive" compared with investments in new oil fields, which were traditionally perceived as comparatively low-risk. This type of thinking was driven by a lack of certainty around carbon pricing, gaps in their knowledge on renewable energy investments in general and the short time frames over which performance is usually measured. The situation has, of course, changed dramatically: the success of renewable energy companies and the cost advantage of solar power over fossil-based energy are now almost common knowledge, and such investments are no longer automatically seen as being value-destructive. In my view, we need to have more focus on the strategic long term than what worked yesterday, last year's carbon emissions or quarterly report cycles. Structural changes and new thinking are needed within finance so we can maximise the flow of funding towards climate solutions and energy transition companies.

Shane Chaplin, Sustainability Analyst, Swedbank Robur

The impacts of extreme weather events and higher temperatures are expected to increase in the future. The changing climate will cause short-term shocks that may lead to higher costs for companies, as well as increasing the risk of accidents, among other consequences. For example, investments in wastewater storage are critical for mining companies to be able to manage larger changes in rainwater volumes and thereby reduce the likelihood of accidents. It would be key for investors to identify how physical climate changes are affecting companies' operations around the world and whether companies have prepared for growing risks by, for example, investing in infrastructure that facilitates the management of the practical impacts of climate change.

The bioeconomy offers new business opportunities, but there are also question marks over its sustainability. Renewable wood-based and plant-based raw materials are used to replace fossil fuels and materials. On the other hand, even the use of renewable raw materials involves conflicting perspectives, as forests sequester carbon from the atmosphere (this is known as the carbon sink effect). The use of biomass reduces the carbon sinks, at least over the decades. A significant decrease in the carbon sinks is problematic in terms of the 1.5-degree target in particular, because the remaining carbon budget is so small. For example, the Land use, land-use change, and forestry regulation (LULUCF Directive) of the EU requires changes in land use and forests to also be taken into account in monitoring country-specific emissions targets from 2021. This legislation might set limits to the expansion of bioeconomy based on forestry and cultivated products, as the changes in carbon sinks are considered when calculating the total emissions of a country.

There are business opportunities related to biofuels, but it is good to note that their sustainability impacts vary in accordance with the sources of the raw materials in terms of, for example, whether rainforests have been cleared because of this and whether their cultivation and purposes of use compete with food production. The future of renewable diesel is also affected by future vehicle technologies: the popularity of diesel cars has decreased because of their negative impacts on air quality. Some major cities around the world have decided to ban old diesel cars and are aiming for even stricter regulations in the future. In addition, some countries have set a goal of banning the sale of new cars with internal combustion engines in the coming decades.

The bans are based on particulate emissions, especially from diesel cars, as well as their health effects and the negative climate impacts of fossil fuels. As well as affecting car manufacturers, such bans would also have an impact on the manufacturers of renewable diesel, as the legislation in question is based on technologies used in cars, rather than on the raw materials used in the production of fuels. Many car manufacturers have also presented plans to focus on the development of electric cars in the future. The production of electric cars, on the other hand, has its own sustainability aspects concerning the use of battery technology and the use of minerals, for example.

The future returns on investment will be affected not only by developments in the operating environment but also by companies' ability to adapt and prepare for changes. From an investor's perspective, it is critical to understand the answers to the following questions: What are the environmental and social impacts of the planned investments of the various companies? What are the impacts of the raw materials used and products manufactured by the companies? Have production side streams been used in any way? What are the probable impacts of legislative changes and developments in consumer demand on the future of the companies? What is the company's ability to adapt and how has the company prepared for changes in the operating environment?

The transformation of the food industry can affect companies involved in the manufacture of food products. The production of animal-based agricultural products (red meat and dairy in particular) leads to deforestation, as well as causing direct greenhouse gas emissions from animal husbandry. The development of vegetable-based sources of protein and new products can also affect the future market positions of meat sector companies. At the same time, alternative animal protein production technologies are being developed in which animals are not needed for meat production. These can also have an impact on companies in the sector over time if the innovations can be commercialised. Predicting people's consumption habits and lifestyle changes is key in assessing the financial impacts of new food production methods.

For this reason, it would be important for investors to identify how companies have positioned themselves to benefit from the new opportunities arising from changes in food production (sources of vegetable-based protein in particular) and what climate risks and negative impacts are related to the operations, as well as identifying what potential technologies could be future winners in the longer term.

The TCFD Framework and Analysis Tools in Assessing the Climate Impacts of Investments

Climate change has been described as one of the key risks to the stability of the financial markets. This is why the TCFD working group established by the Financial Stability Board issued recommendations for reporting on climate risks related to financing in 2017. The working group recommended that the financial impacts of climate change should be included in the annual reporting of companies in the financial sector, as well as other companies. Since the beginning of 2020, TCFD-compliant reporting has been partly mandatory for institutional investors who have signed the PRI. The requirement concerns governance and strategy in the initial stage. The TCFD is also the basis for the reform of the EU's laws concerning sustainability reporting.

According to the TCFD guidelines, the boards of directors and management teams of companies should be responsible for the business impacts of climate change. The guidelines also describe how the impacts of climate change should be examined applying different time horizons and global warming scenarios, and that climate aspects should be integrated into risk assessment. The TCFD also lists individual indicators for reporting.

Case: The Government Pension Fund Norway Assesses the Future Impacts of Climate Change

The Government Pension Fund Norway (*Folketrygdfondet*, FTF) aims to better understand the climate risks of its investments. FTF uses the TCFD climate reporting framework to broaden the perspective on climate risks: the TCFD shifts the discussion from how portfolio companies impact climate change to how climate change impacts the companies.

Says Annie Bersagel, Portfolio manager ESG at FTF, '*We have a financial approach to responsible investment, meaning that we view sustainability issues in terms of long-term value creation, and the TCFD framework aligns with our approach. We also find that it leads to a more meaningful dialogue with companies about risks related to their business model over the short, medium and long terms, rather than a conversation about what they "ought to do" to minimise their climate impacts.*'

FTF started by updating their governing documents on responsible investment in line with the TCFD. For example, their principles for responsible investment and their ownership policy now state that identifying and addressing risks related to sustainability is the responsibility of top management. In other words, FTF did not limit the responsibility of management just to climate risks specifically, but also to sustainability more broadly.

Engaging with Companies to Deepen the Understanding of Climate Risks

We looked into quantitative scenario analysis frameworks, but we soon realised existing tools were not sufficiently mature, as we didn't find anything that would be useful for our investment process. The high level of uncertainty makes scenario analysis really complicated, and the analysis also requires a great deal of resources. As a result, we realised that we first needed to start by looking at our ownership in companies in sectors most exposed to climate risk, Bersagel explains.

FTF used the list of sectors exposed to climate risks provided as part of the TCFD supplemental guidance. These sectors include energy, transportation, materials, consumer staples and finance. However, FTF did not initially include finance in their scope, reasoning that the impact of climate risks on banking was too indirect, and that the finance sector is primarily exposed to climate risks through other sectors.

Within the sectors with the highest climate risk exposure, the FTF identified their largest holdings in Norway and decided to team up with three other Norwegian investors (KLP, DNB Asset Management and Storebrand Asset Management) to engage with the companies. The 15 targeted companies represent 45% of the FTF's equity portfolio and around 30% of its total assets. In the FTF's view, these companies cover the highest climate risks of their portfolio—and this is also where the FTF can have the most influence. At these meetings, investors ask questions, such as how the companies are addressing the transition risks related to climate change.

These TCFD meetings proved valuable, particularly in highlighting different levels of preparedness among the companies. Leading companies have done a great deal with regard to scenario analysis and assessing physical risks—and are developing plans to manage the related risks around their global operations with the help of consultants, such as securing their plants to be resilient against massive rainfall.

Says Bersagel about the relation of company dialogue to the FTF's investment strategy, 'In line with our *investment strategy, we are looking at quality companies that are managed well and that are adaptable to changes in their operating environment. As our portfolio managers have also participated in these meetings, we have noticed that the new information obtained has reinforced the perception they have already had of different companies.'*

The meetings also enabled learning and provided an awareness of risks that had not been previously recognised. For example, a seismic company explained that as the sea is already warming, cables are getting covered with marine growth—which means these companies now need to stop their work more often to clean the cables, which is costly and time-consuming.

The investors observed that several companies have identified their risk exposure as being low over the short term, and do not necessarily understand why they should report that. '*Our feedback has been that, nevertheless, it is helpful for the companies to explain why they don't perceive a risk arising from climate change over the short term, as this may not be obvious to investors:*

for example, expectations in 2018 of a positive outlook for the oil market due to supply shortages overriding any expected financial impacts of climate change,' Bersagel explains.

The Next Step Was to Produce a Set of Recommendations to Companies and Adjust Investment Risk Assessments

Based in part on feedback from the initial TCFD meetings, Folketrygd-fondet updated its expectations to companies on climate to incorporate the TCFD recommendations. The goal is to provide feedback to the companies for assessing climate risk and communicating with investors.[1] Companies are often interested in what type of information investors want and how they are going to use it—especially as they often receive multiple reporting requirements from different parties.

Bersagel also emphasises the following:

> *For us, one of the key aspects is to make sure that companies are very transparent in terms of the assumptions they use when they conduct their own scenario analysis. There is a great deal of uncertainty involved when modelling changes for the next decades, and we need to know what the underlying assumptions are.*

Beginning in 2019, FTF drew upon the insights from the meetings with companies to present sector-based qualitative scenario analyses of climate risk in the portfolio for the FTF investment committee. This work requires input from the FTF's internal risk team.

Review of Progress Two Years Later and Expansion to New Sectors

Over 2019 and 2020, FTF and the three collaborating Norwegian investors expanded the TCFD meetings to include the real estate and construction sectors, as well as banking and insurance. In addition, the investors engaged in follow-up meetings with companies they met in 2018, beginning with the energy and oil service industries. Bersagel notes that several of the companies took a major leap in their approach to climate risk:

> *While for some of the companies, no discernible change was apparent, others made opportunities related to the low carbon economy a key pillar of their strategy – a*

major change from companies that initially reported on climate risk solely in terms of own emissions, whether material or not.

This was particularly evident in subsectors of the oil service industry, in which opportunities related to offshore wind installation and carbon capture and storage became increasingly attractive.

FTF continues to work internally to find a meaningful form of scenario analysis that it can include in its public ownership report: 'The biggest weaknesses we see in existing frameworks are twofold. First, they tend to assume that we turn off the lights and go home until 2050, whereas we know that the composition of our benchmark, and therefore, our portfolio, will likely change dramatically over the next 30 years. Second, they tend to ignore the question of whether and to what extent climate risk may be priced into a security already.'

Bersagel believes that for FTF as an active manager, the dialogue with companies will remain the most useful tool for understanding and managing climate risk:

For the companies, the TCFD meetings provide a venue to ask their largest owners about our expectations relating to climate change, and about reporting. They appreciate that we bring company-specific and sector knowledge to the table and are concerned with how the companies create value over the long term, given their risk profile.

Nevertheless, Bersagel notes that there may come a day when it no longer makes sense to conduct this dialogue through a separate engagement.

We note already that for the energy sector, climate has assumed such a major role in our regular dialogue with management that it may at some point be redundant to engage in "TCFD" meetings as well.

Summary

The TCFD is a relatively new tool for analysing climate risks, and its use is expected to increase in the near future. In their sustainability reports, companies often focus on their own impacts on the environment (climate), while the TCFD is based on examining the impacts of climate change on the company. The TCFD provides the management and investors with a more multifaceted picture of the impacts of climate risks on the company. When a company publishes a TCFD-based report on climate impacts, investors know that the company has at least analysed climate risks and that its management is aware of the risks. However, the mere existence of the report is not enough; it is also important for investors to evaluate the assumptions used in the calculations. In addition, discussions with the management offer good opportunities for more in-depth analysis.

Background Information

Established by the Norwegian Ministry of Finance, Folketrygdfondet (FTF) manages the investments of the Government Pension Fund Norway in Nordic companies. Folketrygdfondet has around EUR 24 billion in assets under management, with around 85% of the total in Norwegian companies and 15% in Finnish, Danish and Swedish companies. The FTF is among the three largest shareholders for 47 companies on the Oslo Stock Exchange. It invests in listed equity and bonds. This case description is based on an interview with Annie Bersagel, Portfolio manager ESG at FTF.

Water Risks

Water-related investment risks are increasing. There is growing demand for freshwater reserves in particular. Business operations and people are dependent on water, which is needed for agriculture and industrial processes alike. Climate change accelerates the water crisis: there may be too much water in one region as a result of heavy rainfall, while another region may suffer from a shortage of water because of drought. However, moving water from one place to another is expensive. The water risks related to business operations are affected not only by availability but also by poorer water quality and stricter legislation concerning the prevention of water pollution.

The following factors affect the increasing water risks: *Increasing competition* for water leads to the excess use of groundwater reserves in key economic areas, such as the United States, South Africa, Mexico and South Asia. *Combined with pharmaceutical residues, emissions from agriculture and industry* reduce water quality for society and business operations. *In many countries, the ineffective monitoring* of water reserves makes the aforementioned risks even worse: when there are no rules, companies are able to use water for their operations at the same time as there is a shortage of water in the area, which can lead to disagreements with the local residents and even to unrest and instability. In terms of water adequacy, *negligence can lead to boycotts of the company's products* in situations where, for example, the company manufactures water-intensive products in areas that suffer from drought. Consumers can easily start boycotting companies whose operations are considered to have negative impacts on the local community.

For me, it has been eye-opening to realise that in California, for example, it is not known how much groundwater is left, and that its use was not regulated by law until 2014, although California is suffering from an acute water crisis. Half of all vegetables in the United States come from California, where the land is so fertile that this pays off, even though the soil needs to be irrigated continuously.

Outi Helenius, Head of Sustainability, Evli Bank (investment assets around EUR 13 billion)

To assess the water risks affecting return on investment, the following aspects should be examined: companies' ***dependency on water use*** (process water and water discharged into natural waterways in the company's own operations and elsewhere in the value chain), the ***adequacy of the water resources*** available to the company (operations in water-sensitive areas) and ***water risk management*** (the company's measures to reduce water risks). For example, a company that has always relied on the availability of process water in its operations can suddenly face a situation where water is no longer available during some months of the year. This means that the company must make alternative arrangements to ensure water availability or discontinue the process for a certain part of the year. If climate change causes longer periods of drought or changes in water availability, these challenges may become more pronounced in the future.

The investor can start by analysing a specific sector with high water risks, for example (the Investor Water Toolkit provided by Ceres helps investors understand sector-specific water risks; see Table 11.1), or by assessing regional risks (e.g. the Aqueduct tool provided by the World Resources Institute). Company-specific information about the key aspects of water risks is fragmented across various sources. This makes it challenging and laborious to collect data and analyse water risks, because it may be necessary to examine each of the investee's factories and the adequacy of their water sources separately, for example.

A report by Ceres (2017) presents energy, food and beverage production as examples of industries with high water risks. Energy production often requires large volumes of water, including hydropower and the use of cooling water in coal-fired, gas-fired and nuclear power plants. In addition to being impacted by diminishing water resources, power plants are affected by the increase in water temperatures, which means that the available natural water can no longer necessarily be used as cooling water.

Table 11.1 Sector-specific material water risks

GICS Industry	Supply Chain Water Quantity	Supply Chain Water Quality	Operations Water Quantity	Operations Water Quality	Product use/End of life Water Quantity	Product use/End of life Water Quality
Food Products	High		Medium			
Beverages	High		High	High		
Household Durables		Medium	High	High	High	High
Construction Materials		Medium	High	High		
Paper & Forest Products		Medium	High	High		
Oil, Gas & Consumable Fuels	High		High	High		
Energy Equipments & Services			High	High		
Metals & Mining			High	High		
Water Utilities			High	High		
Electric Utilities			High	High		
Chemicals			High	High		Ceres Addition
Containers & Packaging		Medium	High	High		
Hotel, Restaurants & Leisure	High		High	High		
Real Estate Management & Development			High	High		
Internet Software & Services			High	High		
Semiconductors & Semiconductor Equipments	Medium		High	High		Medium

■ =High Risk   ■ =Medium Risk   ☐ =Unclear or Low Risk   ■ Indicates Ceres Addition

The table illustrates the materiality of water, impacts at different parts of the value chain by industry (medium to high risk industries listed only). The Ceres classification is based on SASB's Materiality Map combined with Ceres' Investor Water Hub analysis and risk ratings.

Sources Ceres and SASB©2021. Reprinted with permission from Ceres and The SASB Foundation (All rights reserved)

The discharge of warmer water into natural waterways has an impact on fish, for example, and may be in violation of environmental permits. Food and beverage manufacturers are exposed to water risks through agriculture in particular. According to estimates, around 70% of freshwater is used for cultivation, feeding farm animals and processing raw materials. However, the use of freshwater for these purposes varies considerably between countries and crop varieties (Hoekstra & Chapagain, 2006). Population growth is increasing pressure related to freshwater reserves in food production.

Engagement Is a Key Way to Reduce Water Risks

It may be challenging to reduce water risks through diversification, as the same risks may concern all companies in a specific sector in the same area. In addition, the operations of one company affect other companies that are dependent on the same water sources. In other words, if the factory of an investee pollutes the water, this may also increase the costs of all the other companies using the same source of water. By influencing investees to promote the better management of water risks, investors can bring about positive change that may have more extensive impacts than measures taken by individual companies.

Case: PGGM Analyses Water Risks and the Preparedness of Companies

If your investment horizon is long enough, water scarcity will affect investments financially as a result of pollution and increasing demand, for example. We assess water as a risk factor, but we also look at the positive impact through opportunities to invest in solutions related to water scarcity, says Piet Klop, Senior Advisor, Responsible Investment at PGGM.

PGGM decided to take a closer look at the sectors, regions and countries that are most at risk. PGGM has used various data sources to assess the water dependency and water security of investees—including company-specific data on water usage, combined with more general data on water risks in various sectors and localities. For example, applying the S&P Trucost Water Risk Monetizer, PGGM used **shadow water prices** to estimate the value-at-water risk for selected companies. This modelling effort considers water scarcity in the specific environments where companies are operating and not just the actual price that companies are currently paying for water.

The EBIT % calculated reflects intensifying competition, as well as tightening regulation, and can be up to 10% of EBIT for the most water-dependent companies. Says Klop, *'This is a very rough estimation of water risks, but a great starter for engagement. We have asked companies for their views on company-specific figures, and have also asked them about the measures they have put in place to reduce water dependency and improve water security. For example, a company in a highly water-stress area, such as Arizona in the United States, may have put in place a closed-loop system and is effectively reducing its cooling water withdrawals to zero. This more specific information is needed to better understand the company's real exposure to water risks.'*

With regard to the contextual part of this analysis, Klop explains the following:

*We rely on the Aqueduct database of the World Resources Institute to learn how secure water supplies are in specific localities. This enables us to combine company water use (dependency) data with geographical water security data. Some of this may not even require company-reported data: there is a comparative analysis of Indian utilities combining **big data and satellite images** for a measure of their exposure to water risk. You can observe their facilities from space (Google Earth) to see what type of cooling technology they have in place and where they are located— perhaps near a river in a water-stressed area or on the coast with the possibility of using sea water for cooling.*

You can easily compare this type of data, and there is no distortion—and it enables a rough peer-group comparison. As satellite images get better over time, this type of information will become a great addition to company-disclosed information in ESG analysis in the future.

Although PGGM makes a great effort to learn about water risks material to its investments, this is more for awareness-raising purposes at this point. Klop concludes:

Water risks are not yet having much of a material impact on our investment decisions, as the data is still poor. *The vast majority of our listed equities are invested passively, and it may be premature to tilt index investments based on water risk calculations at the moment. Meanwhile, we are working to improve the dataset with various data providers and engage with our portfolio companies that have high water risks in their operations, such as utilities in India, or in their supply chains, such as meat producers in the United States.*

Investors should prepare for water risks, especially in long-term investments, because freshwater availability is predicted to become a problem, particularly in areas of rapid population growth. Transferring freshwater from other regions to these areas is not ecologically sustainable or financially sensible. Responsible investors evaluate the dependency of their investments on water use and seek to minimise the negative impacts of their investees on the (future) availability of freshwater resources.

Summary

Based on the PGGM case, it can be stated that investors need to seek water-related data from extraordinary sources, because the quality of such data continues to be insufficient and its availability poor.

Background Information

PGGM manages approximately EUR 246 billion in assets for Dutch pension funds. The case description is based on an interview with Piet Klop, Senior Advisor, Responsible Investment at PGGM.

Respect for Human Rights

Human rights are defined in international law, and each country implements them through its own legislation, as well as enforcing them in its area of jurisdiction. Respect for human rights in international operations that exceeds the minimum requirements of local laws was long based on voluntary implementation and what is known as 'soft law,' such as voluntary international norms and the OECD Guidelines for Multinational Enterprises. In recent years, the responsibility of multinational companies for negative human rights impacts has expanded gradually and has become clearer because of developments in international human rights principles and local legislation.

The UN Guiding Principles on Business and Human Rights were endorsed in 2011, and the related reporting framework was issued in 2015. These principles define the business responsibility to respect human rights, prevent human rights abuses in company value chains (conducting *human rights due diligence*) and correct severe negative human rights impacts.

Binding national legislation has also been developed in recent years that obligates large companies to report on the steps they have taken to prevent negative human rights impacts and ensure human rights are respected. In 2010, California adopted the Transparency in Supply Chains Act, requiring large companies to disclose their efforts to eradicate modern slavery and human trafficking from their supply chains. Since then, mandatory human rights reporting has spread with similar Modern Slavery Acts adopted in the UK in 2015 and Australia in 2018, for example.

Some of the current and upcoming human rights legislation requires companies to address human rights proactively, moving beyond reporting requirements. France enacted a law in 2017 for large companies to prepare an action plan to avoid negative human rights and environmental impacts. In the Netherlands, a law has been passed that requires companies selling products in the country to take due care to ensure that child labour is not used in the manufacture of products. In addition, a law coming into force in 2021 obligates large companies operating in the EU to monitor the procurement of minerals from conflict areas. These 'conflict minerals' include tin, tantalum, tungsten and gold. In 2020, the EU also started preparing new legislation to set extensive requirements for companies to ensure respect for human rights—including legal consequences for companies that cause adverse human rights impacts.

Although human rights laws concerning international business operations are at a national level, their impacts are broader: in the United Kingdom, for example, the modern slavery legislation imposes obligations on all companies with a business presence in the UK whose annual net sales exceed a certain amount. The sphere of influence also expands when companies examine compliance and require that human rights are respected in the supply chain as part of fulfilling their obligations. However, to date, no significant penalties have been imposed for non-compliance with statutory reporting requirements.

In other words, the impact of laws concerning human rights currently arises more through reputational risks. Reputational risks related to human rights have increased with transparency and because the expectations of both legislators and stakeholders focus on respecting human rights. The Covid-19 pandemic has highlighted the need for a green and just recovery, accelerating legislative developments to promote business respect for human rights and bringing more attention to this topic among investors as well. Awareness is expected from companies and investors, and it is no longer enough to address issues only after they have been publicly exposed.

> *The importance of human rights has been growing in recent years, and we consider human rights to be a key focus of our ESG agenda. The concern is related not only to financial risks, but also to the intrinsic problems associated with negative human rights impacts. There is a growing consensus that companies are accountable to their stakeholders, and this responsibility also includes human rights. As a mostly US-centric investor, we approach human rights from two perspectives: what is happening globally in supply chains, and what is happening locally here in the US. So, we will engage companies on, for example, topics such as forced labour in a retailer's Asian supply chain, user privacy at a technology company, and diversity and inclusion in all company workforces. Another example is our shareholder proposal at Alphabet (Google's parent company) focused on protections for whistle-blowers when it comes to human rights matters. Our goal is to strengthen whistle blowing, as an effective tool for protecting human rights.*
>
> *A more advanced assessment of human rights is not easy, but we are learning more every day about how material impacts related to human rights may be measurable. This may be especially important in consumer companies where reputational risks may also have a financial cost.*
>
> Jonas Kron, Chief Advocacy Officer, Trillium (investment assets around EUR 2 billion)

Investors Can Be Criticised for Negative Impacts Caused by Companies

The owners of companies can also be blamed for the negative impacts of business operations. In accordance with the UN Guiding Principles on Business and Human Rights, investors should also be aware of the potential negative human rights impacts of their investees. Even in terms of reputation management, addressing issues only after they have become public is not optimal. Instead, risks should be assessed and managed proactively.

Violations of international standards, and of the OECD Guidelines for Multinational Enterprises in particular, can be reported to the *National Contact Points (NCP) of the OECD*. A new trend is that since 2015, the reported issues have most commonly concerned the financial sector (25% of reported issues in 2017), as well as loans for controversial projects and owners' responsibility.

A case from 2013 where non-governmental organisations filed a report on Posco, a South Korean steel company, and two of its minority shareholders is regarded as a precedent for minority investors' responsibility for human rights violations. The minority shareholders concerned were Norges Bank Investment Management (NBIM), which manages the Government Pension Fund Global of Norway, and the Dutch ABP pension fund and its asset manager, APG. Posco was planning to build a factory in India, and according to the non-governmental organisation that filed the report, the project would have led to the forced displacement of 20,000 local residents.

The Norwegian NCP issued a Final Statement on the case. The NCP concluded that the NBIM had violated the OECD Guidelines for Multinational Enterprises mainly on two accounts: by refusing to cooperate in any way and by '*not having any strategy on how to react if it becomes aware of human rights risks related to companies in which NBIM is invested, apart from child labour violations.*' The NCP also issued several recommendations to the NBIM concerning aspects such as dialogue, transparency and the identification of human rights risks (in accordance with a due diligence process).

What also made the Posco case interesting was that the Dutch NCP found APG to be in compliance with the OECD Guidelines. As a result of the reported issue, APG agreed to continue engagement with Posco (also on behalf of its customer ABP). Surprisingly enough, the Korean NCP stated that there was no need to further process the allegations against Posco, as they were associated with the actions of the Indian government, rather than being related to Posco. For this reason, their legitimacy should be assessed not by a National Contact Point of the OECD but by the Indian courts of law. According to media reports, Posco withdrew from the project in 2017.

Gaps in Reporting Affect the Assessment of Human Rights Risks

With regard to human rights, the company-specific ESG analysis tools available to investors often emphasise cases covered by the media and their assessment, as well as the comparison of public principles and processes, such as audits. However, the information commonly described in sustainability analyses does not cover everything: for example, the audits reported by companies generally concern direct (first-tier) suppliers in particular. On the other hand, audits also vary in terms of quality and coverage, and do not provide information about all human rights impacts.[2] Comprehensive assessments of the significance of human rights risks and the prevention of negative impacts are somewhat laborious. They also require the expansion of data sources into reporting by companies, meetings with the management and any other supplementary sources of data for analysis.

To address human right impacts proactively, investors can engage with investees that are more exposed to human rights risks based on their sector and countries of operation. For example, the UNEP Finance Corporate Impact Analysis Tool provides insights on human rights risks and their severity in various sectors. Combined with information about indices related to human rights risks (e.g. from Verisk Maplecroft), the tool helps investors focus detailed efforts on companies that are more likely to face human rights controversies in the future.

Data Protection and Information Security

Information security can be examined as part of sustainable investing from at least two perspectives. First, the investor can assess how vulnerable the company is to information security issues affecting the continuity of its core operations. For example, if the control systems of ships were sabotaged, would deliveries be delayed or would the ships' systems shut down completely? How long would it take to get the backup systems running? What alternative ways does the company have to ensure the continuation of its core operations? What type of business damage would an information security attack cause? Second, the investor can look at the company's business model in terms of how responsibly the company operates with regard to its customers' data privacy.

Failures in data protection and information security could potentially lead to financial losses and compensation, as well as affecting share performance. For example, the data privacy scandal related to Facebook and Cambridge Analytica resulted in both financial and reputational damage for the companies. In addition, the EU General Data Protection Regulation (GDPR), which came into effect in 2018, has prompted companies to further develop their practices. Sanctions can be imposed for violations of the GDPR, with the fine being up to 4% of the company's net sales or no more than EUR 20 million.

With a growing number of connected devices, information security risks increasingly also concern traditional industries, where information security expertise has not typically been at the core of business operations.

> *Information security will affect every organisation. All devices are gradually turning into computers, meaning that the operations of all companies are connected to digitalisation. Every company is becoming a software company. Losses caused by information security crises can also be significant, usually up to around EUR 300 million. The management may be replaced, but companies do not usually go bankrupt because of information security issues.*
>
> *For example, industrial automation systems have historically not been protected at all. Although factories and power plants are systems controlled by computers, they have been kept disconnected, thinking that no one can access them. Today, however, it is surprisingly difficult to keep devices disconnected from the public Internet. For example, when a network configuration is conducted or when an employee starts using a remote connection from home, the system is suddenly visible in the public Internet and is surprisingly open. As a result of these responsibility risks, major investments have been made in industrial automation to bring product security systems into the twenty-first century. Some industrial service companies also see this as a business opportunity and offer their customers better information security, in addition to automation, for example.*
>
> Mikko Hyppönen, Chief Research Officer, F-Secure

There are many types and levels of information security attacks. They can be divided into categories in accordance with the underlying operators. **Governmental entities** conduct information security attacks. Even if companies are not directly subject to governmental cyberattacks, they can be secondary victims if they use the same software as the government under attack. Governmental entities are looking for vulnerabilities that are not yet known to anyone else, which enables them to conduct complicated attacks that are very difficult to protect against.

Well-funded criminal organisations are also able to look for vulnerabilities and commit information security attacks. For example, they can use the information accessed for criminal purposes or encrypt companies' information and demand compensation for removing the encryption.

Industrial spies seek to break into competitors' information systems to access business secrets and use them in their own business operations.

Script kiddies download malware from the Internet and try their luck. Such attacks are relatively easy to protect against. The attacks are usually targeted at publicly known vulnerabilities for which security updates may already be available. Failure to install updates in a timely manner increases exposure to attacks.

Assessment of Risks Related to Information Security and Data Protection

In sustainability analyses available to investors, risks concerning information security and data protection are often assessed at a relatively general level. Such assessments focus on the principles and information disclosed by the companies concerning the provision of training to the employees, for example, and any previous information security breaches. Companies may also be wary of disclosing detailed information about their information security and data protection processes, as the disclosure rules require companies to report the same information to everyone—and companies are not likely to be willing to disclose anything critical in terms of information security.

The likelihood of the materialisation of information security and data protection risks and its potential consequences are affected by practical measures, such as whether companies have backup copies of their files and whether software is updated whenever updates are available. In addition, the level of preparedness to detect information security breaches varies between companies. Not all companies care about their information security vulnerabilities as much as others, and some may assume that nothing will happen. Corporate culture matters in this respect, but its evaluation from the outside is challenging.

Here are examples of questions that investors can use to examine companies' levels of preparedness in order to assess company-specific information security risks in more detail:

- ***Does the company have a chief information security officer*** and what is their place in the organisation—that is, to whom do they report? The appointment of a person in charge indicates that the company takes information security seriously and has allocated resources. Most companies do not itemise their investments in information security in their budgets. Therefore, to assess a company's level of investment in information security, investors can find out how many subordinates the chief information security officer has and what is the proportion (percentage) of the information security function of the IT department (the information about the number of employees can also be compared with that of other companies in the same sector).

- *Does the company report on the implementation of information security on its website?* For example, companies can report on how they process customer data and what kind of information security systems they have in place. Reporting on data security suggests that the theme has been identified as a risk and that something is probably being done to ensure and improve information security.
- *Does the company conduct information security audits?* Having audits conducted by a credible party, such as a major consulting firm, indicates that the company is investing in information security. Reporting on audit results would also provide interesting information; however, this involves challenges from the company's perspective, as reporting on any information security vulnerabilities could be detrimental.
- *Has the company insured its operations against information security risks?* Insurance companies do not issue insurance against security threats if certain technical issues have not been taken care of—in other words, insurance shows that the basic level has been met. In addition, cyber insurance covers any compensation the company has to pay to customers for any information security breaches.
- *Does the company have a bug bounty programme?* In other words, does the company pay a reward if someone reports to the company a problem they have detected in its systems? Independent experts look for such vulnerabilities in companies' information systems and typically give companies 90 days to respond before publishing information about the vulnerabilities they have discovered. Programmes that offer rewards for detecting information security issues mean that an increasing number of benevolent independent experts are looking for such vulnerabilities.[3] In addition, malicious individuals are less motivated to target information security attacks at such companies when there are also companies with information systems that are easier to break into. Bug bounty programmes are used by many major companies, such as Facebook and Google.

- *How often do the senior management or the board of directors of the company discuss information security at their meetings?* Even if discussing information security matters is not yet very common, questions about the topic can prompt the company to think about whether information security should be discussed more often.

Other Globally Significant Sustainability Challenges

In addition to the sustainability trends described above, other sustainability themes may have a significant impact on investees in the coming years (Mercer, 2018). Some of these themes involve considerable uncertainties, and the prediction of company-specific impacts is even more challenging than with regard to the topics described earlier. Practical tools to analyse their company-specific impacts are also not yet available; not widely at least.

Societies and business operations are dependent on ecosystem services, such as the functioning of biodiversity. The destruction of ecosystems, such as the mass extinction of pollinating insects, would have a considerable impact on agriculture, for example, if plants needed to be pollinated by hand extensively, one by one. The increase in pest insects can cause trees to be destroyed and thereby affect the availability and prices of wood raw material. To assess company-specific risks, investors can seek to examine companies' operations in high-risk areas. On the other hand, however, the definitions of high-risk areas may change. Companies' results may be dependent on the free availability of ecosystem services. Yet such services may not necessarily be identified, let alone reported to investors.

The excess use of natural resources erodes ecosystems and creates pressure to transition to an economic system that does not continuously produce new products from new materials. To reverse the growth trend in demand for metals and energy, it should be possible to separate economic growth and the consumption of natural resources from perceived well-being.

The circular economy, where materials are used more efficiently, has been presented as a solution to the sustainability challenge. This would mean using, repairing and modernising recycled materials. The circular economy is still largely voluntary, but the EU has drawn up a circular economy action plan that emphasises renewable sources and the reuse and recycling of materials. The problem of plastic accumulation in natural environments is also beginning to be addressed, and legislation banning certain disposable plastics, for example, is being planned in the EU. The use of plastic is a problem, especially when it is not recycled or when it is used, because of its low cost, in products where its use is not necessary. Legislation seeks to indirectly accelerate the development of renewable materials, because plastic continues to be an inexpensive material in food product use, for example, as well as being a highly usable material in many other respects, because it reduces spoilage and extends the shelf life of products.

To assess company-specific preparedness, investors can ask how companies take recycling into account in product design and what they are doing to ensure that materials from their products will not end up as landfill waste in the future. This is referred to as product life-cycle thinking, which often requires cooperation between various parties. To assess the future impacts of plastics bans, investors can also examine how dependent various companies are on plastic as a raw material. If the popularity of plastics decreases, this will also have an impact on energy companies that deliver oil-based products to be used as raw materials in the chemical industry, for the manufacture of plastics, for example. On the other hand, the development of alternative raw materials, such as bioplastics based on renewable sources, offers business opportunities.

Flows of refugees can be caused by global overpopulation and by large areas becoming unsuitable for living. Coastal areas, as well as equatorial regions, are particularly vulnerable to the risks of climate change. Climate change and natural disasters can lead to developments that may make large areas unsuitable for living, potentially also contributing to the escalation of any conflicts. Some examples of the impacts of climate change have already been witnessed when, for example, drought in the south-eastern Mediterranean caused a poor harvest and drove people to cities with inadequate living conditions, which increased unrest and was one of the factors behind the Arab Spring and the Syrian civil war.

Meeting the basic needs of a growing population at a reasonable price is a challenge. Basic needs include healthcare, water and energy, for example. Demand for the fulfilment of these needs is increasing with population growth and higher income levels, which puts more pressure on limited natural resources.

Geopolitical power relations are changing, and competition for natural resources is becoming more intense at the same time. The sources of growth are mainly concentrated in Asia, and are linked to urbanisation and other demographic changes. The population in Western economies is ageing, while the population in Southeast Asia and Africa in particular is growing rapidly.

Broader changes in society can have surprising impacts on companies' operating environments, and these impacts are challenging to assess and predict. The Finnish pension company Keva studied the risks and opportunities related to investing activities through a global survey in 2017. Around 70 managers of equity and fixed income portfolios in developed and emerging markets responded globally. According to the study, the globally most significant risks related to equity and fixed income investments are regarded to include the increasing polarisation of society and the growing disparities in income and wealth. This can be seen as an investment risk, because a more even distribution of income would shift cash flows towards consumption, as well as generating cash flows for companies, while the concentration of assets to the wealthy is more likely to shift assets towards investments and away from consumption. Companies can have an impact on the distribution of income in society by paying attention to employee relations and the terms of employment, as well as to remuneration for the management and the company's tax policy.

Brexit and the election of Donald Trump seem clear social reactions to problems that were created 10–20 years ago or more. Resistance to globalisation, as well as increased nationalism in response to increased inequality and the redistribution of spending power, are affecting economies and companies, but this massive social change was largely missed by the finance and sustainable investing communities. Societies are looking at reversing globalisation, which has led to politically unstable environments, with the ruling political parties changing more frequently.

In my view, financial and ESG research seem to focus too much on things that we think people should worry about and not on things that people actually worry about. We need to understand what the social trends are that drive the way in which people behave. This is why we here at Schroders have started to look at the issues that societies are most concerned about, as well as at the results of those challenges and their implications for investments, for example, through the reliance of economies on global trade flows.

Andrew Howard, Head of Sustainable Research,
Schroders

Identifying Future Winners and Losers

The impacts of companies on sustainability trends are complicated, and the same companies can have both positive and negative impacts, which is why investors need to think about the net effects. For example, societies seek to reduce the consumption of plastic, but on the other hand, plastic packaging can improve the shelf life of food products, meaning that food waste should also be optimised at the same time.

The impacts of all sustainability trends are not expected to materialise simultaneously in all sectors and geographical areas, and on the other hand, sustainability trends also change over time. Long-term investors must think not only about the development of sustainability trends but also about their impacts on operating environments and companies' future competitiveness and profitability.

A sustainable investor considers ESG factors when making investment decisions and assesses their impact on the returns in relation to the risks. It is possible that there are currently companies in the market that involve ESG risks so large that the companies are not worth investing in over the long term. Sustainable investors begin to avoid such investees. On the other hand, an ESG analysis may reveal that the investee holds great potential (positive risk) that has not been detected and priced yet. This leaves greater room for an increase in value. When the valuation is based on future cash flows, their forecasting is key in identifying future winners. Better ESG analysis skills help investors assess and predict the financial impacts of sustainability: risks, business opportunities and return potential. ESG factors often affect returns with a delay, meaning that predicting these factors is crucial.

Some of the companies providing solutions to sustainability challenges are still small; it may not be easy to invest in them yet, or it may not be possible to invest significant amounts of money in them. However, many large companies have separate spin-offs within their groups of companies that develop solutions to sustainability challenges using financing provided by the groups. The challenge for investors is to identify future winners through analysis, and this requires an understanding of not only sustainability but also of investment analysis.

A sustainable investor ultimately examines the impacts of ESG factors on the investee's chances of survival. Will the factors limit business opportunities or will they provide new opportunities to create a competitive edge? Is the company part of the global sustainability problem or does it provide solutions? ESG analysis helps investors choose sustainable investees that generate good returns in relation to the risk taken.

Most of the ESG practices have been associated with organisational efficiency. This is very important, but you shouldn't stop there. The link to strategy is what allows you to outcompete in this new business environment where ESG issues are becoming financially material. There are no magic tricks, but there are some principles which we can learn from. First, you must understand which ESG issues are financially material to your organisation considering your industry, business model and competitive position. You should not concentrate only on the current ESG issues that you can already see but also apply a forward-looking perspective. How are they going to influence your supply chain, changing customer expectations or employee requirements in the future? This introduces a dynamic perspective which is important when so many industries are being disrupted. Tesla, Oatly and Beyond Meat are all examples of this wave of innovation. One way to identify these winning companies is to check whether they have set clear, ambitious and transparent targets and have real organisational commitment starting with the board of directors in achieving these goals.'

Professor George Serafeim, Harvard Business School

Notes

1. Folketrygdfondet's expectations: https://www.folketrygdfondet.no/getfile.php/ 132672-1583755775/Download%20centre/Other%20documents/Folketrygdfo ndet%27s%20expectations.pdf.
2. The impacts of companies are also evident outside their factories, and a comprehensive overview of the situation of the factories cannot be achieved if audits are announced in advance – for example, the children who normally work in a factory may stay at home on the day of the audit.
3. Discovering vulnerabilities brings credibility to experts in online communities and also helps them secure consulting assignments later.

12

Global Investment Trends and Impacts on Sustainable Investing

The Increasing Popularity of Passive and Factor Investing

Passive (index) investing has become more common in recent years, along with factor investing, which is based on quantitative criteria. ESG ratings and data can also be taken into account in these investment strategies. However, unlike the market value of companies, for example, ESG ratings and individual figures are not objective or comparable. Instead, they also considerably reflect the weightings and views of their providers. In addition, the fact that investors would need to be able to identify individual indicators that are material across sectors makes the selection of individual factors even more challenging. Something essential may be overlooked when ESG analysis is directly based on individual figures and indicators.

A comprehensive analysis of ESG aspects is laborious, as well as including a qualitative assessment, which conflicts with increased cost pressures. There is pressure to reduce management fees, even in actively managed funds, in response to the popularity of low-cost passive investments. In factor funds, ownership is usually highly diversified, and company-level analysis is not part of the investment strategy.

Despite their limitations, investment products that take sustainable investing into account have also become more common in passive investments. Although sustainability ratings and individual indicators are not comprehensive, they can still be indicative and quite effective, bringing

© The Author(s), under exclusive license to Springer Nature Switzerland AG 2021
H. Silvola and T. Landau, *Sustainable Investing*,
https://doi.org/10.1007/978-3-030-71489-5_12

sustainable investing to a section of the investment market where ESG aspects have not traditionally been considered.

On the other hand, investors are increasingly interested in ESG analysis, and sustainable investing is an argument that can be used to justify higher costs. It seems that there are developments in two directions: while passive investing has become more common, growth has also been relatively rapid in investing that seeks positive impacts, especially investments related to sustainable development goals.

Opportunities for Broader Analysis

The data sources and tools used in sustainability analysis have become more diversified. Conventional sustainability ratings and analyses are most useful when investors are not profoundly familiar with the investees to begin with. They apply standardised approaches, and although methodologies are being further developed, these analyses remain consistent year after year.

Creativity and innovation can help investors identify other data sources in addition to traditional ESG analysis sources. Such other sources include, for example, satellite images and social media discussions (e.g. the information provided by Glassdoor[1] about employer reviews or product reviews on Amazon and other online stores). Alternative data sources may provide information about companies' ESG performance that is not necessarily disclosed in sustainability reports and the related analyses. However, social media can also provide distorted information, and not all user reviews are necessarily genuine.

Examples of analysis using alternative sources of information include a study by Exane BNP Paribas that assessed employee satisfaction in companies in sectors where attracting and retaining highly competent employees is key for success (the analysis focused on IT services, software, support services and medical technology development).

The first question we wanted to answer was what could be the best metrics to carry out the evaluation. After going through academic literature, discussing with sector analysts covering the stocks and checking data availabilities from companies' reporting, we have settled on a specific set of criteria for each sector.

We have used Glassdoor as one metric of employee attractiveness and satisfaction, as well as to explore momentum (it is increasingly used by candidates in their job searches and decision-making). In addition, we used LinkedIn to learn more about the experience and profile of HR directors, which can be helpful from a qualitative viewpoint. The results of our analysis tend to be more dynamic and time-sensitive compared with the typical ESG analyses carried out by ratings agencies, and may be able to better capture the momentum and turnaround stories, for example, looking at how the arrival of a new HR director can be correlated with changes in Glassdoor scores.

Carole Crozat, (former) Director, Head of Socially Responsible Investment, Exane BNP Paribas

As yet, the use of alternative sources of information is relatively manual and time-consuming in many research organisations, and often concerns a limited number of companies. Opportunities to automate data collection may be in sight, through the development of IT systems, for example.

Some investment organisations have started to take advantage of the opportunities provided by artificial intelligence, big data and machine learning. The purpose is to streamline data collection processes and enable the use of large amounts of data. There are already isolated examples of the use of advanced information technology in the analysis of sustainable investment.

To identify sustainable development investments, we wanted to screen the entire investable universe with the help of artificial intelligence. AI helped us meet two challenges: the high number of companies that needed to be screened, and the identification of companies providing products and services that support sustainable development. APG has had data scientists as part of its investment teams since 2016. In 2018, we took over Entis, a data analytics company, to accelerate our use of AI and big data for sustainable investing. However, this is a human-centric process that requires a great deal of cooperation and workshops between experts – the role of human beings is essential in teaching AI to determine screening rules. Of course, technology has its own challenges, such as data quality. It's crucial to use the right data sets. Clear and transparent audit trails are also very important, and they help us achieve more extensive acceptance of the use of AI within the organisation.

We are continuously developing our use of AI. Under the Sustainable Developments Investmets Asset Owner Platform (SDI AOP) we are currently developing forward-looking solutions to identify companies that are likely to contribute to the UN Sustainable Development Goals in the future. In addition to achieving the Sustainable Development Goals, we are aiming to assess the real life outcomes of our sustainable development investments.

Terhi Halme, Senior Sustainability Specialist, APG Asset Management (investment assets EUR 538 billion)

Knowledge of Sustainable Investing Has Become a Requirement

The mainstreaming of sustainable investing has been rapid, and a large number of experts have been recruited in the sector in recent years. For example, in an interview by the *Financial Times* (2018), the sustainability-focused recruiting company Acre reported that while it received two or three enquiries per month concerning sustainable investment experts until a few years ago, the number of such enquiries is now 12 times higher. Business schools are now rapidly including sustainability in the degree programmes of universities. However, the current challenge is that many graduates do not have a particularly broad understanding of *both* financing *and* sustainability.

Business managers and investment professionals also face increasing demands to better understand the rapidly developing field of sustainable business. Sustainable investing has been included in executive programmes, and many organisations provide training for these purposes. Prominent associations of financial analysts—the CFA UK and the European Federation of Financial Analysts Societies (EFFAS)—are also offering their own ESG certificates for investment professionals. The purpose of these programmes is for new and experienced professionals to update their skills and knowledge on how to integrate ESG into their day-to-day work.

> *Our purpose is to make sure that investment professionals are technically and ethically competent to serve their clients well. Clients understand that ESG factors are financially material and expect their managers to help them meet their fiduciary duties by integrating ESG into analysis, valuation and investment decision-making. The qualification equips investment professionals with the tools to integrate ESG into the investment decision-making process, build and refine their ESG strategies and signal their competence to clients. The skills learned will be equally applicable to all asset classes.*
>
> *The Certificate in ESG Investing has been designed for practitioners working in investment roles but is also suitable for anyone looking to improve their understanding of ESG issues working in sales & distribution, wealth management, product development, financial advice, consulting and risk, and it can now be taken anywhere in the world.*
>
> Christina Curtin, Director of Education at CFA UK

The themes of sustainable investing have expanded, as well as requiring more multifaceted expertise than before. Newer themes, such as decent wages to live on, information security and tax planning, have emerged alongside environmental impacts, health, safety, human rights and other aspects that have long been assessed as part of sustainable investing. The availability of usable ESG data and analyses has increased, as has the expertise required for their interpretation. On the other hand, sustainable investment teams do not need to have comprehensive expertise related to ESG aspects, as external sources such as service providers and analysts can be used for support.

This book provides the means to benefit from sustainability data in investment analysis. We also hope that the book encourages investors to approach new ESG tools with healthy curiosity and criticism. Every analyst and investor needs to determine the essential goals they want to achieve and the questions they want to be answered through the study of data and analysis and discussions with company management.

Investors no longer need to discuss whether sustainable investing is profitable. They are now discussing which forms of sustainable investing yield the highest returns—even beating the market.

Note

1. Glassdoor is a recruitment website that combines job advertisements with reviews, salary information and other information provided by employees about companies.

References

CERES. (2017). *Investor water toolkit*. https://www.ceres.org/sites/default/files/reports/Ceres_InvestWaterToolkit.pdf.

European Parliament. (2017). Fossil fuel subsidies. http://www.europarl.europa.eu/RegData/etudes/IDAN/2017/595372/IPOL_IDA(2017)595372_EN.pdf.

Financial Times. (2018). *Battle to recruit ESG specialists intensifies*. https://www.ft.com/content/9b6ef052-c0a3-11e8-84cd-9e601db069b8 (Referenced 25 November 2020).

Hoekstra, A., & Chapagain, A. (2006). Water footprints of nations: Water use by people as a function of their consumption pattern. *Water Resource Management*. https://waterfootprint.org/media/downloads/Hoekstra_and_Chapagain_2006.pdf.

IPCC. (2018). *Headline statements*. http://report.ipcc.ch/sr15/pdf/sr15_headline_statements.pdf.

Mercer. (2018). *Investing in a time of climate change*. https://www.mercer.com/content/dam/mercer/attachments/global/investments/mercer-climate-change-report-2015.pdf.

OECD. *Human rights breaches related to manufacturing of iron in India.* Korea, Republic of (South): https://mneguidelines.oecd.org/database/instances/kr0010.htm, Netherlands: https://mneguidelines.oecd.org/database/instances/nl0 023.htm, Norway: https://mneguidelines.oecd.org/database/instances/no0009. htm (Read 25 November 2020).

TCFD. (2017). *Final report: Recommendations of the task force on climate-related financial disclosures.* https://www.fsb-tcfd.org/wp-content/uploads/2017/06/FINAL-TCFD-Report-062817.pdf.

The Norwegian National Contact Point for the OECD Guidelines for Multinational Enterprises. (2013). Final statement. https://www.responsiblebusiness.no/files/2015/11/nbim_final-1.pdf.

Other Sources

BBC. (2017). *France set to ban sale of petrol and diesel vehicles by 2040.* https://www.bbc.com/news/world-europe-40518293 (Read 25 November 2020).

European Commission. *Conflict minerals the regulation explained.* http://ec.europa.eu/trade/policy/in-focus/conflict-minerals-regulation/regulation-explained/ (Read 25 November 2020).

European Commission. *Land use and forestry regulation for 2021–2030.* https://ec.europa.eu/clima/policies/forests/lulucf_en (Read 25 November 2020).

European Commission. (2018). *Proposal for a regulation of the European Parliament and the council on the establishment of a framework to facilitate sustainable investment.* https://eur-lex.europa.eu/legal-content/EN/TXT/?uri=CELEX%3A5 2018PC0353.

FAIRR. *The coller FAIRR protein producer index.* https://index.fairr.org/ (Read 25 November 2020).

Financial Times. (2018). *Investors ignore human rights at their peril.* https://www.ft.com/content/b37d8b76-49d6-350b-8d86-86ff586f9f41 (Read 25 November 2020).

ICS-CERT. *Cyber threat source descriptions.* https://ics-cert.us-cert.gov/content/cyber-threat-source-descriptions (Read 25 November 2020).

Kuvaja & Koipijärvi. (2017). *Yritysvastuu – Johtamisen uusi normaali* [Corporate responsibility—The new normal of management]. Finland Chamber of Commerce.

Ministry of Finance. *Kestävän kasvun rahoittamista koskeva toimintasuunnitelma, tiedonanto 17.4.2018* [Action plan on financing sustainable growth, communication 17 April 2018].

Ministry of the Environment. *Kiertotalous* [The circular economy]. http://www.ym.fi/fi-FI/Ymparisto/Kiertotalous (Read 25 November 2020).

OECD. (2018). *Annual report on the OECD guidelines for multinational enterprises 2017.* http://mneguidelines.oecd.org/2017-Annual-Report-MNE-Guidelines-EN.pdf.

OECD. *National contact points for the OECD guidelines for multinational enterprises.* https://www.oecd.org/investment/mne/ncps.htm.

PRI. (2018). *The European Commission Action Plan.* https://www.unpri.org/dow nload?ac=5173 (Read 25 November 2020).

PRI. (2019). *TCFD-based reporting to become mandatory for PRI signatories in 2020.* https://www.unpri.org/news-and-press/tcfd-based-reporting-to-become-mandatory-for-pri-signatories-in-2020/4116.article (Read 25 November 2020).

Rabe, J. & Feldmann, O. (2018). *ESG research: Integrating ESG in company research: Tackling the industry's alpha dilemma.* Deutsche Bank.

Reuters. (2018). *Greater Paris to ban old diesel cars from summer 2019.* https://www.reuters.com/article/us-france-paris-pollution/greaterparis-to-ban-old-diesel-cars-from-summer-2019-idUSKCN1NH2BC (Read 25 November 2020).

Triponel Consulting. (2018). *Human Rights Expectations of Companies in Recent Laws—Thomson Reuters Interviews Anna Triponel.* https://triponelconsulting.com/2018/08/08/human-rights-expectations-in-recent-laws-thomson-reuters-int erviews-anna-triponel/ (Read 25 November 2020).

UNEP Finance Initiative. *Human rights guidance tool for the financial sector.* http://www.unepfi.org/humanrightstoolkit/ (Read 25 November 2020).

United Nations. (2011). *Guiding principles on business and human rights.* https://www.ohchr.org/Documents/Publications/GuidingPrinciplesBusinessHR_EN.pdf.

World Bank Group. *High and dry: Climate change, water and the economy.* http://www.worldbank.org/en/topic/water/publication/high-and-dry-climate-change-water-and-the-economy (Read 25 November 2020).

Index

© The Editor(s) (if applicable) and The Author(s), under exclusive
license to Springer Nature Switzerland AG 2021
H. Silvola and T. Landau, *Sustainable Investing*,
https://doi.org/10.1007/978-3-030-71489-5

Printed by Printforce, the Netherlands